M000308503

POLITICAL JURISPRUDENCE

Political Jurisprudence

MARTIN LOUGHLIN

Professor of Public Law,
London School of Economics & Political Science

OXFORD
UNIVERSITY PRESS

OXFORD

UNIVERSITY PRESS

Great Clarendon Street, Oxford, OX2 6DP,
United Kingdom

Oxford University Press is a department of the University of Oxford.
It furthers the University's objective of excellence in research, scholarship,
and education by publishing worldwide. Oxford is a registered trade mark of
Oxford University Press in the UK and in certain other countries

Published in the United States of America by Oxford University Press
198 Madison Avenue, New York, NY 10016, United States of America

British Library Cataloguing in Publication Data
Data available

Library of Congress Control Number: 2017953069

ISBN 978–0–19–881022–3

Printed and bound by CPI Group (UK) Ltd,
Croydon, CR0 4YY

Preface

I have recently been writing about constitutions but the preliminaries keep getting in the way. By this I mean the most basic elements that establish the authority of the office of government. I provided an account of those elements in two earlier books: *The Idea of Public Law* presents the conceptual building blocks of the subject, and *Foundations of Public Law* outlines its conceptual history.[1] But there were aspects I was not able to consider in detail, some of which I later examined in various essays. This book brings together a selection of those essays with the aim of providing a fuller statement of the subject of political jurisprudence.

All but one of these have previously appeared in print. Since they have been written for different occasions, all have been revised either to eliminate overlap or to streamline presentation of the argument. I am most grateful to the editors and publishers for permission to reproduce from the following:

1. 'The Nature of Public Law' in C Mac Amlaigh, C Michelon, and N Walker (eds), *After Public Law* (Oxford: Oxford University Press, 2013), 11–24.

2. 'The Political Jurisprudence of Thomas Hobbes' in D Dyzenhaus and T Poole (eds), *Hobbes and the Law* (Cambridge: Cambridge University Press, 2012), 5–21.

3. 'The Constitutional Thought of the Levellers' 2007 *Current Legal Problems* 1–39.

4. 'Burke on Law, Revolution and Constitution' (2015) 29 *Giornale di Storia Costitutionale/J. of Constitutional History* 49–60.

5. 'Droit Politique' (2017) 17 *Jus Politicum: Revue de Droit Politique* 299–335.

6. 'Santi Romano and the Institutional Theory of Law' in S Romano, *The Legal Order*, M Croce trans. (London: Routledge, 2017), x–xxviii.

7. 'Politonomy' in J Meierhenrich and O Simons (eds), *The Oxford Handbook of Carl Schmitt* (New York: Oxford University Press, 2017), ch. 21.

In selecting these papers, the greatest challenge has been to show how particular jurists or particular themes contribute to a common strand of thought. Since the distinguishing features of political jurisprudence are outlined in the Introduction, I will say nothing further about that. But I should here emphasize the significance of constitutions in regulating political activity. My argument is that the role of constitutions cannot be explained without having regard to a series of historic transitions: from sovereign to state, from state to constitution, from law to legality, and from political right to constitutional legality. Political jurisprudence shows us how

---

[1] M Loughlin, *The Idea of Public Law* (Oxford: Oxford University Press, 2003); id., *Foundations of Public Law* (Oxford: Oxford University Press, 2010). Since I build on the analysis in these books in this work, I will refer to them throughout by the abbreviations IPL and FPL respectively.

conceptual change reflects political change, how concepts, as weapons in the cause of change, serve political as well as scholarly purposes.

I am beholden to many people for assistance on these various occasions; they are thanked in the originals and I trust I may be forgiven for not reproducing that list. But it would be remiss if I did not record certain general debts. Two papers were drafted when I was Crane Fellow in the Law and Public Affairs programme at Princeton in 2012–2013 and for that opportunity I thank the then Director, Kim Scheppele. I am most grateful to Denis Baranger and Olivier Beaud for inviting me to hold the Chaire Villey at the University of Paris, Panthéon-Assas in spring 2016 during which period Chapter 5 was written. Most recently, in 2016–2017 I was awarded a EURIAS Senior Fellowship at the Freiburg Institute of Advanced Studies. FRIAS has proved to be an ideal environment in which to complete the work and I would wish to record my appreciation to the Rector, Bernd Kortmann, his staff, and to the EURIAS/Marie Curie programme team. Finally, I owe a special debt of gratitude to Chris Foley and Samuel Tschorne whose editorial skills have helped me improve the final version and to the editorial team at OUP, on this occasion Jamie Berezin and Eve Ryle-Hodges, for a most fruitful collaboration that has now extended over many years.

Martin Loughlin
Freiburg-im-Breisgau

June 2017

Contents

Introduction

Every school of jurisprudence makes specific claims about the autonomy and rationality of law. Political jurisprudence is no exception. It claims that law is to be understood as an aspect of human experience called 'the political'. This is an idea that jurists commonly suppress. The claim may be controversial but should not be misunderstood.

Law as an aspect of the political does not mean it is simply an instrument of ruling power. Nor does it imply that legal questions are in reality political questions. Political jurisprudence takes its orientation from the fact that people are organized into territorially-bounded units within which authoritative governing arrangements have been established. This is a distinctive way of being and acting in the world, the world of the political. The political should not be confused with politics. Politics is a set of practices that has evolved to manage conflicts that arise between individuals or groups. The political, by contrast, refers to a decisive and more basic phenomenon, that the primary form of the political unit—the state—is embedded in structures of authority and obedience whose power is such that they shape their members' sense of justice and injustice, right and wrong, freedom and servitude, good and evil.

Political jurisprudence, then, asserts that law is an aspect of the political and that the political is an autonomous way of viewing the world. From these basic premises, a key insight into the relationship between law and the political is disclosed. Political jurists, those who cultivate this type of jurisprudence, are able to explain how law operates to strengthen the integrative forces of the political. The political might be founded on a rudimentary inclusionary-exclusionary distinction, and therefore on whatever is needed to preserve the unit's collective identity, but the authority of its worldview is strengthened through institutionalization. Viewed from this perspective, law is an aspect of the political. But to perform its authority-generating functions effectively, law must operate relatively autonomously. The political and the legal operate relationally, without one being reduced to the other.

Although rarely identified as a distinct school, political jurisprudence has generated a rich body of knowledge about the nature of that relationship. It has evolved as a common European discourse extending from the work of Bodin in the sixteenth century to Schmitt in the twentieth. Many of the innovative jurists, including Bodin, Grotius, Pufendorf, Montesquieu, Hauriou, Romano, Heller, and Schmitt, practised law. Some, such as Hamilton, Burke, and de Tocqueville, trained as lawyers but made their mark in other roles. Others, including Hobbes, Spinoza, Rousseau, and Hegel, are commonly regarded as political philosophers. All of them made

Political Jurisprudence. Martin Loughlin. © M Loughlin 2017.
Published 2017 by Oxford University Press.

significant contributions to political jurisprudence. They belong to this school by virtue of their analyses of the constitution of political authority in the language of rights, duties, powers, and liabilities.

The advances made by these jurists are examined in the chapters that follow. My objective in this introduction is to explain why their work belongs to this branch of jurisprudence. Political jurists neither possess a common political philosophy nor hold similar views on political questions. They are participants in a common conversation about the relationship between the legal and the political and of the way that political authority is constituted. And their methods are invariably anti-rationalist, historicist, nominalist, relativist, or pragmatic in character.

* * *

✓ Political jurisprudence maintains that the question of how political authority is constituted is the key to understanding the nature of legal order. This distinguishes it from other theories of law. Most theories begin by presupposing the authority of the legal order, a presupposition most explicit in legal positivism. Since the latter half of the nineteenth century, legal positivism has established itself as the dominant school, typically defining law not as a norm incorporating a value but either as an object to be explained empirically or as a logically self-authorizing set of norms. Once the authority of the legal order is presupposed and law treated as a matter of fact or logic, the province of jurisprudence narrows. It is limited to the task of explaining the structural form of positive law.[1]

The reason for this move is not difficult to understand. If jurisprudence includes questions about the rightness of the forms of government through which laws are enacted, then—or so it is assumed—there would be no end to controversy about the nature of law. But that is not all: if the broader method were adopted then no credible claim could be advanced that law is a branch of scientific knowledge.

One of the earliest proponents of such a limit to the province of jurisprudence was Friedrich Carl von Savigny. In his lectures on legal method in 1802–3, Savigny declared that 'in no way can public law—the systematic representation of the constitution of the state—be brought into the concept of jurisprudence'.[2] Although he was later to revise that view,[3] many jurists followed his lead and argued that constitutional

---

[1] This applies both to accounts such as Austin's (below n.4) that explains law as a set of commands (i.e. orders backed by threats) as well as to normative versions of legal positivism that define law as a scheme of interpretation of material events: H Kelsen, *Introduction to the Problems of Legal Theory*, BL Paulson and SL Paulson trans. of first edn. [1934] of *Reine Rechtslehre* (Oxford: Clarendon Press, 1992); HLA Hart, *The Concept of Law*, L Green, J Raz and PA Bulloch eds (Oxford: Oxford University Press, 3rd edn. 2012).

[2] FC von Savigny, *Vorlesungen über juristische Methodologie, 1802–1842*, A Mazzacone ed. (Frankfurt: Klostermann, 2004), 139: 'Auf keine Weise lässt sich aber das Staatsrecht—systematische Darstellung der Staatskonstitution—in den Begriff der Jurisprudenz bringen.'

[3] See FC von Savigny, *System des heutigen römischen Rechts* (Berlin: Veit, 8 vols 1840–1849). Savigny then argued that law is created neither by legislative will nor universal reason but through the customs of a people: see H Kantorowicz, 'Savigny and the Historical School of Law' (1937) 53 *Law Quarterly Rev.* 326–43.

law is not part of jurisprudence.[4] This is the basis of the orthodox modern jurisprudential view that assumes the existence of the state. Once adopted, the science of jurisprudence can devote itself to a series of technical questions concerning the structural form and methods of interpretation of the laws enacted by the state.

For political jurists, this is a mistake. It narrows the scope of juristic inquiry to such a degree that it distorts understanding of the modern form and function of law. It leads to the assumption that law is an autonomous system of rules independent of the cultural matrix that shapes its character as institutional order. The life of the law, say political jurists, is not logic but experience (see Ch.6).

Political jurists explicitly reject legal positivism. But they also reject the claim, prominent in the work of most contemporary anti-positivist jurists, that law has intrinsic moral authority. The differences here are more nuanced, not least because political jurists accept that the establishment of institutional order produces good consequences. Anti-positivist jurists argue that no precise distinction can be drawn between description (what the law is) and justification (what the law ought to be). But because they equate legal order and right order they also claim that law has an intrinsic moral quality. They maintain not just that law is an interpretative practice but that, in order to understand it, a 'theoretical ascent' must be made from the specific dispute at hand to a 'moral reading' of the constitutional order.[5] Anti-positivist jurists invariably promote a normativist jurisprudence founded on an abstract and morally-infused conception of 'legality'. Legality quickly comes to rest on the authority of reason itself.[6]

From the perspective of political jurisprudence, this anti-positivist stance is distorted. It skews legal analysis towards a model-guided reading of texts, whether libertarian, liberal, or republican, and this converts legal interpretation into a type of moral reasoning. The authority for this rests on an idealized version of legality generated by a set of universal moral axioms. Rather than explaining the often messy practices of actual regimes, normativist analysis constructs an idealized representation of constitutional order and then promotes that idealized model through a particular scheme of interpretation. Its starting point is not the political world and its form of government but a belief in 'the moral sovereignty of the community of rational beings'.[7]

Political jurists, by contrast, argue that reason can organize and clarify arrangements but cannot tell us what ought to be. They maintain that values are not self-evident, that values conflict, and that conflicts of values are resolved not through reason but by an exercise of will. Rejecting the existence of universal values in this domain, political jurisprudence is both anti-rationalist and relativist.

---

[4] See, e.g., J Austin, *The Province of Jurisprudence Determined*, WE Rumble ed. (Cambridge: Cambridge University Press, 1995), 216.

[5] See, e.g., R Dworkin, *Freedom's Law: The Moral Reading of the American Constitution* (Oxford: Oxford University Press, 1996); id., 'In Praise of Theory' in his *Justice in Robes* (Cambridge, MA: Belknap Press, 2006), ch.2; TRS Allan, *The Sovereignty of Law* (Oxford: Oxford University Press, 2013).

[6] See, e.g., Allan, ibid. 44, arguing if we accept, as we should, that the rule of law is the fundamental ideal 'our concept of law is closely linked to our ideas about justice and freedom'.

[7] I Hunter, *Rival Enlightenments: Civil and Metaphysical Philosophy in Early Modern Germany* (Cambridge: Cambridge University Press, 2001), 366.

Political jurisprudence therefore rejects both legal positivism and normativist anti-positivism, the former because it limits the province of jurisprudence by presupposing authority and the latter because it assumes the moral authority of an idealized legality. Both are features of Enlightenment thinking, with positivism asserting that scientific analysis requires the dissection of a phenomenon into its most basic units—in this case, rules—and normativism maintaining that universal moral standards can be rationally applied across all cultures and periods.

Political jurists, however, argue that the relationship between law and authority can neither be presupposed nor assumed to rest on a set of universal values. Authority is generated through a political process that draws people together in a common undertaking. In this process a special type of political power, *potestas*, is produced. *Potestas*, 'power-to', is the capacity of a collective singular, 'the people', who unite around a common political project and are willing to sacrifice immediate self-interest for the common good. That power is consolidated through institutionalization. Consequently, the power that established rulers deploy, *potentia* or 'power over', is the product of the power generated as *potestas*. Since *potentia* expresses the power of domination inscribed in legal rules and regulations, law's form, meaning, and force is in reality determined by the relationship which is created between *potestas* and *potentia*.[8] It is in this sense that the manner of constitution of political authority holds the key to understanding the nature of legal order.

* * *

Political jurists agree that how political authority is constituted is the central question, but they do not agree on the answer. Responding to the upheavals that led to the emergence of the modern state, they devised conflicting accounts of the nature of law, of the basis for political authority, and of the relationship between the legal and the political. What they shared was not the solution but rather an acceptance of the challenges presented by the transition from the medieval to the modern world. Political jurists recognized that this transition leads to the emergence of an autonomous domain of the political and that the challenge is to devise a conceptual language through which its constitution can be explained.

During this critical transitional period, conflicts were fought out not just in parliaments or on battlefields but also through learned tracts. Once the authority of the old order had been eroded, a series of intense disputes erupted in which contending claims to the authority of common law, sovereign prerogatives, and parliament's standing as the authorized representative of the sovereign people were thrashed out.[9] For political jurists these disputes are not just symptoms of crisis; they are intrinsic to modern political and legal practice.

The ways in which these tensions have been managed vary according to regime and context. Studies of the meaning and status of *droit politique* in French jurisprudence (Ch.5) and of constitutional legality in general (Ch.8) reveal that these tensions are now commonly expressed through the abstract discourse of

---

[8] See further Loughlin, FPL, 11–13, 104–6, 164–77, 218, 407–8, 415–16, 459–62.
[9] The respective claims are examined in the chapters that follow on Burke (Ch.4), Hobbes (Ch.2), and the Levellers (Ch.3).

constitutionalism. That these tensions are now being played out in courts and other official forums demonstrates the prescience of de Tocqueville's observation that in a constitutional democracy 'there is scarcely any political question that... is not re- solved, sooner or later, into a judicial question'.[10] But the fact that these issues are now put before a judge rather than being managed through less formal and more deliberative processes does not mean that they cease to be political.

The challenges presented by the constitutionalization of political questions are highlighted in the vexed subject of constitutional interpretation. Constitutional in- terpretation involves an interminable interplay between the relative authority of text, precedent, and principle. The problem is that however much constitutional scholars seek to finesse this, no authoritative method exists for weighing the different factors. Jurists have produced rigorous analyses of the canons of textual interpretation, of techniques for reasoning with precedents, and of methods of balancing general prin- ciples. But they have been unable to produce robust methods of weighing the relative importance of the different factors. This is because these factors express different conceptions of law. Schematically, these can be called law, legality, and superlegality.

By *law* is meant an artificial reason acquired through deep immersion in source- based legal materials. Law is local knowledge and it evolves incrementally in accordance with contemporary requirements. In the hands of its most experienced practitioners, this artificial reason of the law becomes both a dispositional habit and a virtue of character, qualities that sustain the autonomy of law. Once established, its traditions confer authority on the judiciary to declare that 'causes which concern the life, or inheritance, or goods, or fortunes of his [the sovereign's] subjects are not to be decided by natural reason, but by the artificial reason and judgment of law'.[11] This 'rule of law' restrains the ruler's powers but in recognizing that even the office of ruler depends on these same customary practices, it also strengthens ruling au- thority.[12] As skilled practitioners of this art, judges maintain their autonomy as 'lions under the throne' by recognizing a distinction between *jurisdictio* and *guber- naculum*, between matters legal and matters political.

Legality, by contrast, expresses a modern form of law that emerges once the insti- tution of the state is established. The cultural practices of the law are gradually over- laden with an instrumental idea of law as legislation, law as an expression of will of the sovereign authority. Once the idea of law as a formal system combining pri- mary and secondary rules is instituted,[13] a regime of legality is established. Legality, notes Max Weber, 'is a rational technical apparatus, which is continually transformable

---

[10] A de Tocqueville, *Democracy in America*, H Reeve trans., DJ Boorstin intro. (New York: Vintage Books, 1990), vol.1, 280.

[11] Sir E Coke, Twelfth Reports, *Prohibitions del Roy* (1607) 12 Co. Rep. 63.

[12] Although this idea of law as the *lex terrae* is deeply engrained in common law thought, it was most systematically elaborated by sixteenth-century French jurists who sought to overthrow the universal metaphysics of medieval scholasticism and to restore the idea of law as a system of practical knowledge (*juris prudentiae*) geared to the concerns of civil government. See WF Church, *Constitutional Thought in Sixteenth-Century France: A Study in the Evolution of Ideas* (Cambridge, MA: Harvard University Press, 1941); DR Kelley, *Foundations of Modern Historical Scholarship: Language, Law, and History in the French Renaissance* (New York: Columbia University Press, 1970).

[13] Hart, above n.1, Ch.5. Primary rules impose obligations (i.e. they impose duties and confer rights and privileges) and secondary rules confer powers (and, correlatively, immunities).

in the light of expediential considerations and devoid of all sacredness of content'.[14] The modern science of legality is advanced by jurists who conceive the state as a formal-rational regime that uses legislation as its normal working tool and who develop precise criteria for rule-governed action and consistent canons of rule interpretation.[15]

The third iteration, law as *superlegality*, is a relatively recent innovation that has gathered momentum from the so-called rights revolution of the last fifty years.[16] Superlegality is a conception of law as a set of fundamental norms that derive from general principles of liberty and equality. In place of law as an expression of artificial reason acquired through practical experience, or legality as an expression of will (whether the will of the people instituted in the constitution, or the will of the majority formalized in legislation), superlegality presents law as the elaboration of scholastic reason. It is neither a set of practices operating in a discrete sphere of government (law), nor an instrument of political power (legality). Superlegality is a set of abstract principles that limits the range of legitimate action of governing majorities.

Many disputes in law are over facts and many involve ambiguities in the interpretation of texts and precedents. Operating in these ordinary ways, law evolves as an autonomous practice. But the closer one gets to core matters concerning the constitution of political authority, the more disputes turn on the relative authority of conflicting conceptions of law, legality, and superlegality. Constitutional disputes invariably entail claims about the relative authority of case law versus legislation, of legislative will versus constitutional principles, of constitutional principles versus judicial precedents. These conflicts, political jurists maintain, cannot be resolved by legal method; they require the exercise of political judgment. In the process, the very idea of the constitution becomes the subject of intense dispute: is it a text whose meaning is discoverable through normal canons of legal interpretation, a product of the constituent power of the people that possesses a special status, or an expression of a society's fundamental political principles?

These conceptions work at different levels of abstraction and call for different types of institutional response. Their influence varies according to time and place, depending on prudential assessments of what is needed to maintain political authority. It is tempting to present them as temporal phenomena, with law representing traditional practice, legality legislative will, and superlegality universal reason. One effect of the 'social acceleration of time',[17] however, is that each conception vies with

[14] M Weber, *Economy and Society*, G Roth and C Wittich eds (Berkeley: University of California Press, 1978), 895.

[15] See, e.g., LL Fuller, *The Morality of Law* (New Haven: Yale University Press, 2nd edn. 1969), outlining criteria of rule-governed action. Fuller considers these criteria to establish the 'morality of law', though they can also be seen as criteria of functional efficacy.

[16] The term 'superlegality' comes from Hauriou, see below Ch.6, IV. It is developed further in C Schmitt, 'The Legal World Revolution' (1987) 72 *Telos* 72–89, at 75–6.

[17] WE Scheuerman, *Liberal Democracy and the Social Acceleration of Time* (Baltimore: Johns Hopkins University Press, 2004); H Rosa, *Social Acceleration: A New Theory of Modernity*, J Trejo-Mathys trans. (New York: Columbia University Press, 2013).

others contemporaneously in dissonant ways.[18] Their relative power is a consequence of a political judgment and it is this that determines the nature of a regime's legal order.

* * *

Political jurisprudence assumes that the constitution of political authority determines the nature of law and that the manner of its constitution is continually contested. It should also be emphasized that the constitutional schemes of political jurists are in a precise sense political. Political jurists are political thinkers in that they are neither utopians nor philosophers seeking universal knowledge. They work with the world as they find it.

Political jurists do not commonly espouse an optimistic philosophical anthropology. They are much more likely to view humans as being born helpless and dependent rather than free and equal in rights.[19] It was a characteristic exaggeration of Carl Schmitt to have claimed that 'all genuine political theories presuppose man to be evil'; after all, he then made it plain that by 'evil' he really meant that man is 'a dangerous and dynamic being'.[20] But his essential point stands: theories that presuppose man's goodness are not genuine political theories. They negate or neutralize the political by subordinating it to claims about universal morality. Without a relatively pessimistic conception of human capacity, the political is deprived of its specific meaning, and consequently of its existence as an autonomous perspective on the world.

Political jurisprudence is the jurisprudence of experience. There is, notes Stuart Hampshire, an 'unavoidable split in morality between the acclaimed virtues of innocence and the undeniable virtues of experience'.[21] In its search for rational coherence, moral theory 'has covered over the rift and the tidier picture has become a kind of orthodoxy, even though it contradicts experience'.[22] Consequently, most works of moral philosophy—including the moral reading of the constitution—'have a fairy-tale quality, because the realities of politics, both contemporary politics and past politics, are absent from them'.[23]

Suspicious of universal and abstract ways of thinking about law, political jurists focus on its local and concrete expressions. Their claims about the relationship between the legal and the political come from intense engagement with the pressing political issues of their times. It is not by chance that Bodin's *Six Books* were published shortly after the Saint Bartholomew's Day Massacre of 1572 or that Hobbes and the

---

[18] See, e.g., R Post, 'Theories of Constitutional Interpretation' (1990) 30 *Representations* 13–41, showing that, in reaching a 6–3 decision, the justices of the US Supreme Court in *Marsh v Chambers* 463 US 783 (1983) rested their various rulings on each of these conceptions.

[19] É Balibar, *Spinoza and Politics*, P Snowden trans. (London: Verso, 1998), 60: 'a formula such as "men are born and remain free and equal in their rights" would have no sense from [Spinoza's] perspective.... As for birth, it certainly does not mark the moment at which the individual is first able to affirm his right. On the contrary, it is the moment at which the individual is, in himself, most powerless.'

[20] C Schmitt, *The Concept of the Political*, G Schwab trans. (Chicago: University of Chicago Press, 1996), 61.

[21] S Hampshire, *Innocence and Experience* (Cambridge, MA: Harvard University Press, 1989), 12.

[22] Ibid.   [23] Ibid.

Levellers produced their conflicting accounts of political and legal authority during the course of the English civil war of the 1640s. It is no accident that Pufendorf's studies were published in the aftermath of the European wars of religion or that Burke was obsessed with the impact of imperialism on the British constitution and of the significance of the revolutions of his times. It is not coincidental that the works of Madison and Hamilton or Sieyes and Constant were written in the heat of revolutionary movements. Even Hegel's philosophy of right might be read as a response to the disintegration of the Holy Roman Empire. Tocqueville's study was inspired by the emergence of a novel type of government, Hauriou and Romano were responding to the emergence of the administrative state, and Schmitt was driven by the collapse of the Kaiserreich and the struggle to build social democracy in the turmoil of the Weimar republic.

Many leading political jurists were active participants in these momentous events, whether as 'Crown jurists' such as Bodin and Schmitt, political agitators like the Levellers, judges such as Romano, or parliamentarians and ministers like Burke, Madison, Hamilton, Sieyes, and Constant. This lends vitality to their work. Living through turbulent periods in which 'the ceremony of innocence is drowned',[24] they were acutely aware that getting it wrong could have dramatic consequences.[25] They invariably disagreed with one another on both method and substance. There is, after all, not a great deal that unites Hobbes and Montesquieu on the concept of law (Chs 2 and 5), or Rousseau and Burke on the concept of political right (Chs 5 and 4), or Saint-Just and Romano on the character of institutions (Chs 5 and 6), or Lilburne and Schmitt on sovereign power (Chs 3 and 7). What unites them is the abiding conviction that political action is the product of local conditions rather than general theories. However radical their schemes, they were not seminar-room thought experiments offering some blueprint for an idealized world. Their schemes were intended to be implemented in the world in which they lived.

*   *   *

I should now make explicit that political jurists are historicists. The world of the political is shaped by concrete historical forces. In this world, there are no universals and nothing has a fixed identity. All phenomena—institutions, practices, customs, concepts, values, and rationalities—are the products of history. They are given form within specific historical contexts to serve particular purposes and the meanings they acquire are determined by those same conditions.

This historical consciousness explains why political jurists reject the normativist appeal to universals, whether of morality or reason. Critical reasoning must remain conscious of its own historical situation. Theory entails reflection on specific conditions, 'the apprehension of the present and the actual, not the erection of a

---

[24] WB Yeats, 'The Second Coming' in P Larkin (ed.), *The Oxford Book of Twentieth-Century English Verse* (Oxford: Oxford University Press, 1972), 79: 'The blood-dimmed tide is loosed, and everywhere/ The ceremony of innocence is drowned'.
[25] On being asked what he did during the Terror, Sieyes is famously reported to have replied: '*J'ai vécu*' (I survived).

beyond, supposed to exist, God knows where, or rather which exists, and we can perfectly well say where, namely in the error of a one-sided, empty, ratiocination'.[26] To extrapolate from circumstances and give universal significance to the values and beliefs of a particular age is to peddle an ideology.

In place of normativism, political jurists advocate nominalism, the conviction that universals are merely constructs of the mind. 'All law', declaimed Schmitt, 'is situational law'.[27] But here he was claiming no more than did Blaise Pascal when the latter observed that our sense of justice cannot transcend time and place. 'Three degrees of latitude overthrow jurisprudence', notes Pascal. 'A meridian determines the truth. Law has its periods.'[28]

Political jurisprudence impels us towards a historical understanding of the constitution of authority. It is a lived experience, not the product of some virtual contract. Having made a people what they are, history continues to shape the present. Contrary to the separation postulated by legal positivism, fact and value unite in an experienced political reality. Practices blur any clear distinction between norms and facts, resulting in a 'normative power of the factual' that expresses a contestable form of political right.[29]

The historicist orientation of political jurisprudence reflects the insights of philosophers who, drawing a distinction between the natural and human worlds, sought a scientific understanding of the human world. The conclusion they drew was that 'the more we examine the causes of the reasons for human beliefs and practices, the more we discover that their purpose and meaning is conditioned by their specific historical cultural context, the less we should be inclined to universalize those beliefs and practices'.[30] For this reason, they preferred to talk of a worldview, an interpretation of meaning rather than science: *Weltanschauung statt Wissenschaft*.[31] A worldview connotes a general perspective on human life generated by historical experience and cultural practices rather than by scientific formulae. It suggests that, rather than making any claim to universal truth, political jurisprudence explains how a particular way of conceiving the political is established in a particular regime.

* * *

Many of the most pressing legal and political issues of our times arise from certain basic tensions in contemporary constitutional thought: between liberalism and democracy, between norm and exception, between identity and difference, or

---

[26] GWF Hegel, *Philosophy of Right* [1821], TM Knox trans. (Oxford: Oxford University Press, 1952), 10.

[27] C Schmitt, *Political Theology: Four Chapters on the Concept of Sovereignty* [1922], G Schwab trans. (Chicago: University of Chicago Press, 2005), 13. See further Ch.7, IV.

[28] B Pascal, *Pensées* in his *Pensées and other writings* [1670], H Levi trans. (Oxford: Oxford University Press, 1995), § 94.

[29] See Loughlin, FPL, 216–21.

[30] FC Beiser, *The German Historicist Tradition* (Oxford: Oxford University Press, 2011), 11.

[31] Cited in Beiser, ibid. 374.

between community and cosmopolis.[32] How might constitutional democracies reconcile the tension between liberty and democracy? Under what circumstances can the suspension of constitutional norms be justified to protect constitutional order? Can the basic principle of equality of rights be reconciled with the emergence of a right to difference? How do constitutional regimes respond to the fact that globalization leads to governmental legitimacy and governmental effectiveness pulling in opposing directions? Political jurists provide powerful tools for addressing these pressing issues in constructive ways but for misguided reasons they have been shunted to the margins of the discipline. The aim of *Political Jurisprudence* is to restore this tradition of thought to a position of central importance.

---

[32] See M Loughlin, 'Constitutional Theory: A 25th Anniversary Essay' (2005) 25 *Oxford J. of Legal Studies* 183–202.

1

Public Law as Political Jurisprudence

I. Introduction

Jurists commonly draw a distinction between public law and private law, between the law regulating relations between institutions of government or between government and its subjects on the one hand, and the law regulating relations between subjects on the other. In this conception, public law is a subset of positive law. This division has provided the basis for organizing the standard categories of law: public law is assumed to have a distinctive anatomy and can be sub-divided into constitutional law, administrative law, civil liberties law, criminal law, revenue law, EU law, and public international law. Working within this general framework, jurists investigate the way public law is constituted as a set of authoritative institutions, principles, rules, and methods. The more ambitious accounts also explain how these various rules and practices form a coherent whole.

Since the latter half of the nineteenth century, a great amount of scholarly effort has been expended in providing a comprehensive exposition of public law as a set of rules that establish and regulate the workings of the institutions of government.[1] This endeavour has culminated in the aim of promoting the harmonization across Europe of these rules and principles of public law.[2] But at this decisive moment the fundamentals of the subject are also being exposed to heightened levels of critical scrutiny. Many question whether the standard organizational categories (sovereignty, jurisdiction, ultra vires, etc.) are still authoritative, arguing that the basic framework needs to be re-conceptualized.[3] Presenting a direct challenge to the

---

[1] Some insight is revealed in the monumental survey of German public law scholarship undertaken by Michael Stolleis: see M Stolleis, *Public Law in Germany, 1800–1914* (New York: Berghahn Books, 2001); id., *A History of Public Law in Germany, 1914–1945* (Oxford: Oxford University Press, 2004). By comparison, the number of landmark texts in the development of British scholarship until, say, 1970 is remarkably small: we need not look much beyond the works of AV Dicey, WI Jennings, WA Robson, SA de Smith, JDB Mitchell, and the Wades (ECS and HWR).

[2] See, e.g., the work of Armin von Bogdandy and his colleagues to lay the foundations of a *ius publicum europaeum*: A von Bogdandy et al (eds), *Handbuch des Öffentlichen Rechts in Europa: Ius Publicum Europaeum*, (Heidelberg: CF Müller Verlag, 6 vols, 2007–16); A von Bogdandy and J Bast (eds), *Principles of European Constitutional Law* (Oxford: Hart/Beck, 2nd edn. 2009); A von Bogdandy, 'Deutsche Rechtswissenschaft im europäische Rechtsraum' (2011) 66 *Juristen Zeitung* 1–6.

[3] Exemplary of those seeking to bring about what has been referred to as a 'paradigm shift' at domestic, European, and global levels, respectively, are: TRS Allan, *Law, Liberty, and Justice: The Legal Foundations*

Political Jurisprudence. Martin Loughlin. © M Loughlin 2017.
Published 2017 by Oxford University Press.

philosophy of legal positivism which has been so influential over the last 150 years, these critics now claim that, rather than expressing a particular allocation of institutional competences, the architecture of public law is an edifice of abstract and value-laden principles of legality.[4] In these uncertain circumstances, when the push for harmonization coincides with the claim of transformation, any account of the subject is likely to remain contested.

My argument is that the nature of public law is unlikely to be revealed by focusing on contemporary controversies. Those debates have exposed many issues for consideration, but there is a danger that symptoms will be mistaken for causes. Any attempt to specify the basic characteristics of the subject must consider the conditions of its formation. It then becomes evident that the subject cannot be a subset of positive law. Scholars of the formative period of public law before the last 150 years of legal positivist influence were engaged in a more basic investigation. Not limiting themselves to the question of how public authority is conducted through the forms of law, they posed a more fundamental question: how can the constitution of public authority be justified in legal terms?

During the Middle Ages that question had been addressed in the language of natural law, a type of law regarded as 'higher' than and prior to ordinary (or positive) law. Ordinary law was made by the ruler and bound the subject whereas natural law, sometimes called 'fundamental law', bound the ruler. With the formation of the modern world, that hierarchically-ordered world was radically re-constituted. Natural law was secularized, rationalized, and (in part) positivized as understanding based on religion was overcome and scholarly thought differentiated through distinct modes of understanding human activity—economic, scientific, technical, historical, aesthetic, political. These profound changes resulted in the formation of new ways of conceiving collective ordering. The political was recognized as a distinct mode of existence, founding its autonomy on the concept of sovereignty and on the institution of the state. This led to a radical reworking of medieval ideas of natural law,[5] and this new anthropocentric 'science' of natural law provided the basis for the creation of the concept of public law. Public law was formed in the modern world as the jural coding of an autonomously-conceived political domain.

---

of British Constitutionalism (Oxford: Clarendon Press, 1993); N MacCormick, *Questioning Sovereignty: Law, State and Nation in the European Commonwealth* (Oxford: Oxford University Press, 1999); M Kumm, 'The Cosmopolitan Turn in Constitutionalism: On the Relationship between Constitutionalism in and beyond the State' in JL Dunoff and JP Trachtman (eds), *Ruling the World? Constitutionalism, International Law and Global Governance* (Cambridge: Cambridge University Press, 2009), 258–324.

    [4] This seems to be the essential point underpinning the otherwise rather convoluted debates in the UK over ultra vires v. common law (see, e.g., C Forsyth (ed.), *Judicial Review and the Constitution* (Oxford: Hart, 2000)) and over the broader issues debated by Allan and Craig: see TRS Allan, 'Constitutional Dialogue and the Justification of Judicial Review' (2003) 23 OJLS 563–84; P Craig, 'The Common Law, Shared Power and Judicial Review' (2004) 24 OJLS 237–57.

    [5] R Tuck, 'The "Modern" School of Natural Law' in A Pagden (ed.), *The Languages of Political Theory in Early-Modern Europe* (Cambridge: Cambridge University Press, 1987), 99–122.

II. Natural Law Transformed

In this more basic understanding of the subject, public law is concerned with the establishment and regulation of governing authority; it therefore addresses questions of 'right' (*droit*) relating to modern governmental ordering. Viewed in this light, the works of many leading political philosophers of the early-modern period are attempts to explicate the nature of public law. This undertaking flourished from the late-sixteenth to the mid-nineteenth centuries, extending from the earlier work of such jurists as Bodin, Althusius, Lipsius, Grotius, Hobbes, Spinoza, Locke, and Pufendorf to the later writings of Montesquieu, Rousseau, Kant, Fichte, Smith, and Hegel.

In the next chapter, the contribution made by Hobbes will be examined. But consider now, by way of illustration, the influential work of Samuel Pufendorf. In his magnum opus, *De jure naturae et gentium* (1672), Pufendorf eliminated all sense of a personal God from the workings of the world. Presenting an account of natural law not as the expression of the divine will of God but as 'the dictate of right reason', he set in place an anthropocentric conception of natural law. By reworking natural law in this way, he was able to lay the foundations of the authority of emerging nation-states. Following Grotius' views on man's natural sociability and Hobbes' on man's passion-directed nature, Pufendorf showed that although it is in man's rational interest to maintain the principle of sociability, his passions undermine this capacity for sociability. The only rational solution was to establish a sovereign power that could impose rules of sociability in the form of positive laws.

Pufendorf's analysis supplanted medieval natural law theories that government is a form of moral ordering with a modern account in which the principles and precepts of natural law are formed immanently within an evolving civil relationship. His account of the nature of 'modern' natural law provides the frame of the emerging idea of public law.

Pufendorf's jurisprudence held great sway across the continent of Europe. After the first university chair to profess natural law was established at Heidelberg in 1661, a chair that Pufendorf was first to occupy, the subject was quickly introduced throughout the German lands and thereafter across many other parts of Europe. This influential body of natural jurisprudence was placed at the service of specific political objectives, not least by opposing the Roman lawyers whose work bolstered the authority of the Holy Roman Empire with arguments that justified the sovereign authority of territorial nation-states.[6] Natural jurisprudence laid the foundations of the modern concept of public law: public law as political jurisprudence.

This political jurisprudence operated according to its own internal dynamics. In order to establish the absolute authority of the sovereign, and thereby realize the autonomy of public law, the monarchical image of the sovereign ruler had first to be

---

[6] See K Haakonssen, *Natural Law and Moral Philosophy: From Grotius to the Scottish Enlightenment* (Cambridge: Cambridge University Press, 1996), 135–45.

magnified and idealized. But idealization of the office of the sovereign was in reality the precondition for its institutionalization and later its revolutionary transformation.[7] In Britain, the sovereign was from the early days a composite institution: the Crown-in-Council, later the Crown-in-Council-in-Parliament. In continental Europe, it took the form of the 'enlightened absolutism' of the sovereign ruler. In the latter case, governmental modernization led first to the establishment of comprehensive official machinery by bringing the relatively autonomous, and feudal, institutions of local government into a hierarchical arrangement of government. It then led to the officialization of a judiciary that had previously represented feudal interests and finally to the formation of a separate jurisdiction to determine legal disputes of an official nature.[8] This established a formal division between private law and public law in continental Europe. It was an arrangement which the British did not follow,[9] but which, now that an extensive and formalized governmental network has evolved in the United Kingdom, has since been accommodated.[10]

From a European perspective, the development of British public law may be unusual but it is not altogether different. The differences are the product of a peculiar history of governmental development[11] and today they do not hold as much sway. It might also be noted that whenever political conditions warranted, the British were content to work with the discrete concept of public law. Consider, for example, the circumstances leading in 1707 to the establishment of the first chair of public law in Britain at Edinburgh University. The Regius Chair of Public Law and the Law of Nature and Nations was endowed by Queen Anne in accordance with a prospectus drafted to all intents and purposes by Pufendorf and as a reward for the Scots signing the Treaty of Union and acquiescing in the newly-formed state of Great Britain. But it was no mere gift: its establishment served strategic objectives. Based on the harmonizing public law mandate in article 18 of the Treaty, knowledge of 'the political Principles of all Laws; the Substantials of the Law of Nations; and of the Gothick Constitution' became an essential foundation for the study of Scots law.[12] Further, as John Cairns notes, 'natural-law theorizing could play a part in explaining the possibilities of the political communities of two sovereign entities each agreeing to dissolve to create a new sovereign polity'.[13] The study of 'how government should be conducted on the grounds of utility or public interest', he suggests, 'must have been made more pressing by the Union'.[14] This broader concept of public law was invoked to serve pressing 'reasons of state'.

---

[7] See ES Morgan, *Inventing the People: The Rise of Popular Sovereignty in England and America* (New York: Norton, 1989).

[8] PH Reill, *The German Enlightenment and Rise of Historicism* (Berkeley: University of California Press, 1975); S Lestition, 'The Teaching and Practice of Jurisprudence in Eighteenth Century East Prussia: Konigsberg's First Chancellor, RF von Sahme (1682–1753)' (1989) 16 *Ius Commune* 27–80.

[9] See, e.g., AV Dicey, *Introduction to the Study of the Law of the Constitution* (London: Macmillan, 8th edn. 1915), Ch.12.

[10] See, e.g., H Woolf, 'Droit Public – English Style' 1995 PL 57–72.

[11] For analysis of the reasons for the different trajectory of development see Ch.3 below.

[12] Francis Grant (1715); cited in JW Cairns, 'The Origins of the Edinburgh Law School: the Union of 1707 and the Regius Chair' (2007) 11 *Edinburgh Law Review* 300–48, at 314.

[13] Ibid. 235.   [14] Ibid.

During the eighteenth century, 'modern' natural law provided the conceptual language through which the legitimacy of the emerging secular state could be explained.[15] Natural jurisprudence was particularly useful because it formed a loosely-structured discourse rather than a precisely-formulated doctrine, facilitating its conversion into a type of political jurisprudence in which sovereign authority over a defined territory and people was justified as promoting peace and sociability.[16] Public law was shaped in accordance with Pufendorf's tripartite scheme expressed in the endowment of the Regius Chair: public law in the sense of the positive rules that establish and regulate the institutions of the state; the modern law of nature which expounded the political precepts underpinning the authority of the institutions of state; and the law of nations, as the rules that regulate the interactions of sovereign states in the international arena.

III. Bodin's Concept of Fundamental Law

Pufendorf's work is of pivotal importance to the eighteenth century debates, but the emerging concept of public law had already been specified in 1576 in Jean Bodin's *Les Six livres de la République*.[17] For understandable reasons, most scholars have focused on the first of the six books in which he argues that every viable state must possess a single, supreme centre of authority containing all governmental powers, this being the essence of the emerging phenomenon of sovereignty. This was a significant innovation but to neglect the other five books is to underestimate Bodin's ambition. The objective of the books that follow is to present an analysis, by way of historical comparisons of the main forms of government, of the various factors that cause states to grow, flourish, and decline, and thence to derive prudential maxims that enable rulers to maintain their state.

Treated as a whole, the *République* provides a systematic account of the 'fundamental laws' at work in the public realm: Book I stipulates the constitutive rule and Books II–VI specify the regulative rules of public law. Using historical illustrations, Bodin sketches the 'political laws' of governmental development. Incorporated in his discussions are claims that have become powerful tropes of modern political thought. These include: power corrupts;[18] the necessity of ensuring a separation of

[15] Tuck, above n.5; Q Skinner, 'The State' in T Ball, J Farr, and RL Hanson (eds), *Political Innovation and Conceptual Change* (Cambridge: Cambridge University Press, 1989), 90–131(Skinner refers to the school as 'natural law absolutism').

[16] That it was itself an intensely political exercise is illustrated by the language of Tooke's translation of Pufendorf's work into English (which, e.g., failed to draw a distinction between sovereignty and government and substituted nation for state): see D Saunders and I Hunter, 'Bringing the State to England: Andrew Tooke's translation of Samuel Pufendorf's *De officio hominis et civis*' (2003) 24 *History of Political Thought* 218–34, esp. 229–30.

[17] J Bodin, *The Six Bookes of a Commonweale*, R Knolles trans. [1606], KD McRae ed. (Cambridge, MA: Harvard University Press, 1962).

[18] Ibid. 414: 'the power of command in sovereignty has this mischief in it, that often it makes a good man evil; a humble man proud; a merciful man a tyrant; a wise man a fool; and a valiant man a coward'.

the legislative and executive power;[19] that relative equality in wealth distribution promotes the stability of the state;[20] that wars sustain democracies;[21] that most self-styled democracies are disguised aristocracies;[22] and that 'the less the power of the sovereignty is (the true marks of majesty thereunto still reserved), the more it is assured'.[23]

These precepts of civil prudence are essential elements of public law. But important clues to the nature of public law are also revealed in the way Bodin re-specifies juristic method. First, rejecting the authority of Roman law, he argues that knowledge of public law is not found through a scholastic method of exegesis but acquired through historical investigation. Public law is a type of historico-political discourse. Secondly, Bodin marks an important shift in orientation by beginning his investigation not with an account of the *sovereign* but with the *commonwealth* (or the *state*). It is a study not of rulers but of the political constitution of a people or nation. Bodin's objective is to show the importance of the ruler acquiring knowledge of the people. By emphasizing the relationship between the people and their institutions of government, Bodin relocates the power relationship at the core of the governing process from that of the highest power of command (Book I) to that generated by a field of forces (Book VI, harmonic proportion). Bodin shifts the focus of inquiry from positive law (the power of command) to public law (the precepts of political right). The subject forms a coherent whole, he suggests, only when the frame of reference is extended from the structure of official legal texts to include those informal understandings that condition the exercise of public authority. Public law concerns all the rules, principles, practices, and maxims that establish, sustain, and regulate the activity of governing the state.

IV. Rousseau's Concept of Political Right

If Bodin was the first to provide a systematic understanding of the autonomy (Book I) and method (Books II–VI) of public law, a sharper insight into its nature is acquired by scrolling forward almost 200 years to consider the work of Jean-Jacques Rousseau. Rousseau's political writings form an extended essay on the nature of state-building understood as a juristic exercise.

As is evident from its subtitle, *les principes du droit politique*, *Du Contrat Social* is directly concerned with the 'political laws, which constitute the form of

---

[19] Ibid. 277: 'them that give power of command unto a Senate…go about the destruction of the commonwealth, and utter ruin of the state'.

[20] Ibid. 569: 'Among all the causes of sedition and changes of commonwealths there is not greater than the excessive wealth of some few subjects, and the extreme poverty of the greatest part.'

[21] Ibid. 422: 'Whereby it is to be perceived, nothing to be more profitable for the preservation of a popular state, than to have wars.'

[22] Ibid. 705: 'if we shall rip up all the popular states that ever were, we shall find that … they have been governed in show by the people; but in effect by some of the citizens, or by the wisest among them, who held the place of a prince and monarch'.

[23] Ibid. 517.

Government'.[24] Rousseau argues that the principles of a just society derive not from precepts of natural right but from political reasoning. That is, only when natural law has been jettisoned is the space opened up for the emergence of an autonomous concept of 'political right'. Rousseau builds on and radicalizes the work of Pufendorf, who had sought to secularize natural law by removing transcendental moral claims. The immanent norms that Pufendorf had called natural laws are analogous to that which Rousseau labels 'principles of political right'.

Rousseau formulates the task right at the beginning: 'I want to inquire whether in the civil order there can be some legitimate and sure principle of government, taking men as they are, and laws as they can be'.[25] Is there some science of political right that yields the principles that make a governing order legitimate? Although this appears to be a purely philosophical exercise, the final clause of the opening sentence, 'taking men as they are and laws as they can be', suggests it is not. This is not a purely speculative undertaking; it is an attempt to discover practical principles of good government.

Rousseau's solution is to posit a social contract in which humans exchange their natural freedom for a 'higher' political freedom. He argues that Hobbes erred in treating the social contract as an exchange between being free and being governed, that is, as involving a trade-off between liberty (as the absence of constraint) and law (as the rule of the sovereign). Liberty, says Rousseau, is not the mere absence of constraint. It entails self-government which is acquired only in 'obedience to the law one has prescribed to oneself'. The question then is whether it is possible to reconcile liberty and law by establishing a state in which people live under the laws that they themselves have made. Rousseau's conception of the relationship between liberty and law makes the concept of political right (*droit politique*) the key to understanding governing order. The critical question is: how can *droit politique* reconcile freedom and government?

The answer is given in stages. First, Rousseau argues, contra Hobbes, that the sovereign cannot be a single person or a representative office; it must be the people themselves who by an act of association form a collective body. The sovereign is the public person formed by the union of all. This is the principle of solidarity that founds the state. He maintains, secondly, that rather than substituting a *natural equality* for subjection to rule, the social contract replaces *natural inequality* with *political equality*. This is the principle of equality. Thirdly, this political equality is the precondition for the formation of a single will: each acquires the same rights over the others as is granted over himself. That is, all people must be acknowledged as equals and under such conditions all must work to promote the greatest good of all. This is the principle of equal liberty, otherwise known as the 'general will' or will of the sovereign. The general will is not a restriction on, but an expression of, freedom: the principle of equal liberty in conditions of solidarity.

---

[24] J-J Rousseau, *The Social Contract* [1762] in *The Social Contract and other later political writings*, V Gourevitch ed. (Cambridge: Cambridge University Press, 1997), 39–152, at 81.
[25] Ibid. 41.

In Book I of *The Social Contract* Rousseau eloquently outlines the ideal elements of *droit politique*. But specifying its working practices is much more challenging and beyond Book I Rousseau's pessimism comes to the fore. Following Bodin in distinguishing between sovereignty and government, he argues that this establishes a tension that can corrupt and then destroy the ideal constitution. Sooner or later, 'the Prince ends up suppressing the Sovereign and breaking the Social treaty'.[26] We start with grand ideals, but they are soon debased. The best hope, he suggests, is with a type of law 'unknown to our political theorists', but one 'on which the success of all the other laws depends'.[27] It is the type of law that forms 'the State's genuine constitution'.[28] This is the living law which expresses the customs and beliefs of a people and which sustains the nation, a point similar to Bodin's on the importance of precepts of civil prudence.

Rousseau here brings out the ambivalent nature of public law. It is a mistake to regard it, as do many legal and political theorists today, as a pure science of principle. Public law can only be conceptualized by incorporating the basic practices of governing according to certain traditions of conduct.

This claim is reinforced once it is noted that Rousseau offers not one but two versions of the social contract. In addition to that presented in *The Social Contract*, his account of the founding of government in *Discourse on Inequality* can be read as a study of the manner in which this pact was actually framed in historical practice. Here Rousseau argues that if we think of government as originating in a foundation, then the contract made was deceptive and fraudulent: it was drafted by the wealthy for the purpose of exploiting the poor. And in his *Discourse on Inequality*, he again finds hope only in custom.[29]

Rousseau understood the difficulties entailed in devising a science of public law. He suggested that putting the law above man is a problem in politics similar to that of squaring the circle in geometry. If it can be solved, good government results. If not, then wherever people believe that the rule of law prevails, they will be deceiving themselves: 'it will be men who will be ruling'.[30] Rousseau reveals both the challenge and ambivalence of public law. It is easy to outline the normative scheme, the principle expressing equal liberty. That is, it is not difficult to sketch a regime of basic principles, such as the need to institute a separation of powers, to recognize the citizen's basic rights, or to structure the exercise of governmental power through such principles as proportionality and subsidiarity. But this normative scheme does not determine the practice of public law. For this understanding we must examine the ambivalences of the modern state that Rousseau captures in his two versions of the social contract. We must acknowledge the active character of the governing relationship revealed in the tension between the sovereign and sovereignty or between 'the

---

[26] Ibid. 106.   [27] Ibid.   [28] Ibid.

[29] J-J Rousseau, *Discourse on the Origin and Foundations of Inequality Among Men* [1755] in his *The Discourses and other early political writing*, V Gourevitch ed. (Cambridge: Cambridge University Press, 1997), 111–222.

[30] J-J Rousseau, *Considerations on the Government of Poland and on its Projected Reformation* [1772] in his *The Social Contract and other later political writings*, V Gourevitch ed. (Cambridge: Cambridge University Press, 1997), 177–260, at 179.

office of government' and 'the people'. And we must recognize that the practice of public law incorporates techniques of political reasoning that normative theorists seek to suppress.

V. The Modern Science of Public Law

The ambiguities and tensions that permeate the field have given the concept of public law an uncertain meaning. The search for a 'science of political right' is driven by the conviction that there is some mode of right ordering of public life that free and equal individuals would rationally adopt. But this is purely an exercise in imagination which experience suggests is a journey without end: countless normative schemes have been postulated and all have foundered on the rocks of political necessity. In part, this is because political right must negotiate between norm and fact and this has left public law thought with a polarized consciousness.[31] But it is also because the modern state itself expresses 'an unresolved tension between the two irreconcilable dispositions', between the state as *societas*, a structure of rules of conduct, and the state as *universitas*, a corporation established in furtherance of designated purposes.[32]

Many contemporary scholars prefer the aesthetic symmetry of ideal formulations but they only lead to a dead-end in which the exercise of power is equated with its abuse. Jurists who have sought to integrate 'irreconcilable dispositions' into their frameworks bring us closest to grasping the nature of the subject. Such works include Mortati's constitutional analysis which moves beyond the formal framework of norms to embrace a 'material constitution' that amounts to an expression of the institutional arrangement of social forces;[33] Fraenkel's study of the Nazi dictatorship which showed that, through law, the state divided into two co-existing orders of the normative state or *Normenstaat*, structured by statutes and court orders and the prerogative state or *Maßnahmenstaat*, structured in accordance with the exigencies of party rule;[34] and Habermas' argument that the tension between the idealism of constitutional law and the materialism of administrative law is manifested by a drifting apart of philosophical and empirical approaches to the study of law.[35]

[31] See, e.g., Georg Jellinek's attempt to bring the German theory of *Staatsrecht* to culmination in his two-sided doctrine (*Zwei-Seiten Lehre*) of the state: G Jellinek, *Allgemeine Staatslehre* (Berlin: Springer, 3rd edn. 1921).

[32] M Oakeshott, 'On the Character of a Modern European State' in his *On Human Conduct* (Oxford: Clarendon Press, 1975), 185–326, at 200–1.

[33] C Mortati, *La Costituzione in Senso Materiale* (Milan: Guiffrè, 1940). Mortati here follows in a German tradition that can be traced to the work of Ferdinand Lassalle: see F Lassalle, 'Über Verfassungswesen' in his *Gesamtwerke*, E Blum ed. (Leipzig: Pfau, 1901), vol.1, 40–69, at 45: 'the actual power relationships which emerge in every society are the active determinants of all laws and constitutional orientations of the society'. Lineages can be seen in JAG Griffith, 'The Political Constitution' (1979) 42 MLR 1–21.

[34] E Fraenkel, *The Dual State: A Contribution to the Theory of Dictatorship*, EA Shils trans. (New York: Oxford University Press, 1941).

[35] J Habermas, *Between Facts and Norms: Contributions to a Discourse Theory of Law and Democracy*, W Rehg trans. (Cambridge: Polity Press, 1996), 38–41. In similar vein, I have tried to explain British

This fissure runs through the entire discipline and determines its character. If the science of public law is not to be reduced to an anatomical account of the rules of an existing regime or to some normative theory of how things ought to be, then it must offer a positive account that reveals the postulates of evolving practice.[36] The discontinuities that pervade the practice—between the universal and the local, the absolute and the conditional, the formal and the material—can be neither eliminated nor reconciled but only negotiated. This means that the method of public law involves the exercise of prudential judgment. Public law remains a practical discourse which, although orientated to norms, must have regard to consequences; it recognizes 'abstract universals' but does not ignore 'necessary conditions'.[37] It is a reflexive discourse that negotiates the evolving relation between instituted authority (the government/constituted power) and the people (the nation/constituent power). It expresses a special type of political reason. Public law is not in essence *voluntas*; it is *ratio*. But contrary to those who suggest that the tensions of public law can be overcome through an exercise of moral reason, it is a special type of reason: *ratio status*.[38]

Public law is formed only with the establishment of the idea of the state as an autonomous domain, an autonomy clearly expressed in Rousseau's work. Rousseau rejects the Hobbesian idea that liberty stands outside the sphere of law; for Rousseau, concepts such as freedom and security are products of the operation of law within this domain. But by law here is not meant primarily positive law; it is *droit politique*, the code of this public worldview.

This point highlights the significance of the concept of *droit politique*.[39] Operating under the prevailing influence of legal positivism, many today conceive law as a set of posited rules enacted by the law-making institutions of the state.[40] They treat law as an entity that protects liberty by imposing limits on the exercise of power. But from the perspective of political jurisprudence, law is not a bridle on an otherwise unrestrained exercise of power: understood as *droit politique*, law is itself a power-generating phenomenon. Like freedom, power is generated by the operations of *droit politique*. Political power is a special type of power created by the drawing together of 'the people' in an institutional frame. This symbolic power is founded on the 'consent' of the people, rooted in trust, and generated through the imposition of

public law thought as having evolved through tensions between normativist and functionalist styles: M Loughlin, *Public Law and Political Theory* (Oxford: Clarendon Press, 1992).

[36] Cf. Friedrich Hayek, who recognizes the importance of these polarities but seeks to resolve the tension by maintaining that one type of ordering (nomocratic) is correct and the other (telocratic ordering) is a degenerate form: FA Hayek, *Law, Legislation and Liberty: Vol.1 Rules and Orders* (London: Routledge & Kegan Paul, 1973).

[37] GWF Hegel, *Philosophy of Right* [1821], TM Knox trans. (Oxford: Clarendon Press, 1952), §§ 29–33. See A Honneth, *The Pathologies of Individual Freedom: Hegel's Social Theory* (Princeton: Princeton University Press, 2010), 15: 'here [in this section of *Philosophy of Right*] it becomes clear that the term *right* has the double meaning of a "necessary condition" and a "justifiable claim"'.

[38] The development of this mode of reasoning is examined in Ch. 8 below.

[39] The development of this concept by French jurists is examined in Ch. 5 below.

[40] The case for treating law as institution rather than a set of norms is examined in Ch. 6 below, and for the related theme that law is the expression of a concrete-order, see Ch. 7 below.

controls and checks on those who hold positions of authority. As Bodin was the first to explain, in this sphere constraints on power generate power. Similarly, modern constitutional frameworks do not impose limitations on the exercise of some pre-existing power; they are the means by which power is itself generated.

Public law as political jurisprudence operates to ensure that the autonomously conceived domain of the political is able to maintain and enhance its authority. It is founded on a principle of sovereignty, which expresses the autonomy of that political domain, and the authority of this worldview is maintained by a continuous process of institutional development according to a set of principles first outlined by Bodin in the late-sixteenth century.

2

The Political Jurisprudence of Thomas Hobbes

I. Introduction

Thomas Hobbes was a jurist of the first rank and his *Leviathan* stands as the greatest masterpiece of political jurisprudence written in the English language. Commonly regarded as a political philosopher,[1] 'political jurisprudence' is a more precise label for his scholarly field. Hobbes was certainly a philosopher in some sense but he was critical of abstract theorizing and so-called philosophical thinking, believing that true wisdom, 'the knowledge [*scientia*] of truth in every subject', comes only from experience.[2] His general reflections remained fixed on practical matters.[3] He was engaged in a thoroughly practical undertaking which he termed 'civil science' and which, given its juristic orientation, can also be called 'political jurisprudence'.

In this chapter, I will examine the ambition and significance of Hobbes' political jurisprudence. One immediate obstacle is that of his status as a jurist. He is occasionally treated as a founder of legal positivism, but this is only a cursory acknowledgement that overlooks his pivotal role.[4] The reason is that, finding his authoritarianism repugnant and his criticisms of the common law method objectionable, many regard Hobbes' contribution to jurisprudence as discreditable.[5] Modern legal positivists

---

[1] See, e.g., M Oakeshott, 'Introduction to Leviathan' [1946] in M Oakeshott, *Hobbes on Civil Association* (Indianapolis: Liberty Fund, 2000), 1–79, at 3: '*Leviathan* is the greatest, perhaps sole masterpiece of political philosophy written in the English language'.

[2] See T Hobbes, *On the Citizen*, R Tuck and M Silverthorne eds (Cambridge: Cambridge University Press, 1998), 4–5 (hereafter: *De Cive*, DC). Noting in his introduction to *De Cive* that 'the war of the sword and the war of the pens is perpetual', Hobbes suggested that one reason was that 'both parties to a dispute defend their right with the opinions of Philosophers'. Much of what passes for philosophy, he complained, 'has contributed nothing to the knowledge of truth': its appeal 'has not lain in enlightening the mind but in lending the influence of attractive and emotive language to hasty and superficial opinions'.

[3] Cf. GWF Hegel, *Lectures on the History of Philosophy* [1805] (London: Bell, 1894), Pt. I B 3, who notes of Hobbes' books that 'there is nothing speculative or really philosophic in them'. He continues: 'The views that he adopts are shallow and empirical [i.e. there is "nothing properly philosophical" in them] but the reasons he gives for them, and the propositions he makes respecting them, are original in character, inasmuch as they are derived from natural necessities and wants'.

[4] It might be noted, e.g., that contemporary Anglo-American legal positivism takes its cue from HLA Hart, *The Concept of Law* (Oxford: Clarendon Press, 1961), a work which does not address Hobbes' account of law and which treats John Austin's more reductive account as definitive of the older tradition.

[5] This type of assessment dogged Hobbes from the outset. Herman Conring, one of the leading German jurists of the seventeenth century, argued that: 'Hobbes philosophies in the *Elementa* and *De Cive* in an outrageous manner when he grounds sovereignty as a whole in the most powerful authority

also seem embarrassed at the way Hobbes, having defined law as the command of the sovereign, proceeds to accord natural law such a prominent place.[6] But such criticisms reveal more about the construction of modern schools of legal thought than about Hobbes' contribution to jurisprudence. To appreciate Hobbes' significance it is necessary to move beyond the argument of whether he is a natural lawyer or a legal positivist.

Following his own injunction to try and grasp the overall point of a scholar's writing,[7] I will focus on how Hobbes drew a clear distinction between natural law and positive law for the purpose of crafting a rich, ambitious, and comprehensive account of the modern idea of law.

II. Political Jurisprudence

Towards the end of his life, Hobbes claimed to be the founder of a new field of knowledge, that of 'civil science'. This subject, which he defined in contrast to the natural sciences, was concerned with the relations of 'politic bodies', and especially of the rights and duties of sovereigns and subjects.[8] The subject of 'civil science', he

and explains hatred or enmity between human beings as the basis of the government of the state. Which upright person would expound something so preposterous? The author appears to deserve the hatred of all.' Cited in H Dreitzel, 'The reception of Hobbes in the political philosophy of the early German Enlightenment' (2003) 29 *History of European Ideas* 255–89, at 258. More recently, it has often been noted that Hobbes' statements to the effect that 'every man to every man, for want of a common power to keep them in awe, is an Enemy' forms the basis of Carl Schmitt's claim that 'the specific political distinction to which political actions and motives can be reduced is that between friend and enemy': C Schmitt, *The Concept of the Political* [1932], G Schwab trans. (Chicago: University of Chicago Press, 1996), 26. Strauss offers an explanation. He refers to Hobbes as 'that imprudent, impish, and iconoclastic extremist [who] was deservedly punished for his recklessness, especially by his countrymen. Still he exercised a very great influence on all subsequent political thought, Continental and even English, and especially on Locke – the judicious Locke, who judiciously refrained as much as he could from mentioning Hobbes's "justly decried name"'. See L Strauss, *Natural Right and History* (Chicago: University of Chicago Press 1953), 166.

[6] GH Sabine, *A History of Political Theory* (London: Harrap, 3rd edn. 1963), 460–1: 'It would undoubtedly have been easier for Hobbes if he could have abandoned the law of nature altogether, as his more empirical successors, Hume and Bentham, did. He might then have started from human nature simply as a fact, claiming the warrant of observation for whatever qualities...he might have seen fit to attribute to it.' Some argue that, because of his account of this relationship, Hobbes was not in fact a legal positivist: see L Murphy, 'Was Hobbes a Legal Positivist?' (1995) 105 *Ethics* 846–73 (showing Hobbes' affinities with Aquinas); D Dyzenhaus, 'Hobbes and the Legitimacy of Law' (2001) 20 *Law and Philosophy* 461–98 (showing Hobbes' affinities with Fuller and labelling Hobbes an 'anti-positivist'). Coyle states that: 'In the face of the foregoing account of (Hobbes' perception of) the relationship between natural law and the positive laws of a civil society, it may seem perplexing to persist in regarding such an account as positivist'. He does, however, recognize that there is a 'deeper sense in which Hobbes' thought should be regarded as the foundation of the modern positivist tradition'. S Coyle, 'Thomas Hobbes and the Intellectual Origins of Legal Positivism' (2003) 16 *Canadian J. of Law & Jurisprudence* 243–70, 254–5.

[7] It is not, he claimed, 'the bare words, but the scope of the writer that giveth the true light, by which any writing is to be interpreted; and they that insist on single texts, without considering the main design, can derive no thing from them clearly, but rather... make everything more obscure than it is': T Hobbes, *Leviathan* [1651], R Tuck ed. (Cambridge, Cambridge University Press, 1991), Ch.43, 414–15 (hereafter Lev).

[8] Lev, Ch.9.

boasted, is 'no older than my own book, *De Cive*'.[9] It was inspired by dramatic shifts in European thought since the sixteenth century which were to lead to the formation of the modern idea of the state. Governmental ordering was de-personalized: instead of focusing on the figure of the ruler and the conditions that legitimated his rule, attention came to rest on the state. This institution, rather than those who exercised its powers, set the agenda for Hobbes' inquiries: 'I speak not of the men', he explained, 'but (in the Abstract) of the Seat of Power'.[10] Once it was accepted that the ruler's basic responsibility was to maintain the state, rulership was displaced as the central object of political inquiry.[11]

With the emergence of the modern world, received ideas of natural law underwent dramatic changes. The state could no longer be treated as a natural entity: it was created as an act of imagination. Not by Nature, claimed Hobbes, but 'by Art is created that great Leviathan called a Commonwealth or State'.[12] The state was an artefact of 'self-government', an institution created by humans to serve human purposes. The 'laws' by which this institution was established and maintained might be categorized as 'laws of nature', but they were derived from scientific inquiry into human characteristics and their conditions of social existence. The state was established through a process of reasoning about the relations of 'politic bodies'.

Hobbes sought to explain governmental ordering from an inquiry into human nature. If we cannot rest such claims on divine sanction or unchanging custom, he asked, how could obedience to authority be justified? This was the basis of his civil science, an exercise that Rousseau would later refer to as the science of political right.[13] The objective was not to devise some ideal scheme that reconciled order and liberty. Recognizing law's practical character, it drew on a plausible account of human psychology to provide a realistic portrayal of the nature of collective existence. But since the disjuncture between freedom and belonging could be neither eliminated nor reconciled but only negotiated, it followed that a 'science', in any strict sense of the term, could never be established.[14] So-called civil science did not simply entail the explication of principles of political right; it required the exercise of prudential judgment.[15] It is an exercise in political jurisprudence.

---

[9] T Hobbes, *The Author's Epistle Dedicatory to De Corpore* [1656]: see *The English Works of Thomas Hobbes of Malmesbury*, W Molesworth ed. (London: J. Bohn, 1839), vol. I, ix.

[10] Lev, 3.

[11] Lev, 231: 'The office of the sovereign... consisteth in the end, for which he was trusted with the sovereign power, namely the procuration of *the safety of the people*.... But by safety here, is not meant a bare preservation, but also all other contentments of life...'

[12] Lev, 9.   [13] See Ch.1., IV above.

[14] This is a point that Rousseau himself recognized: see Rousseau, *Emile, or On Education*, A Bloom trans. (New York: Basic Books, 1979), 458: 'the science of political right is yet to be born, and it is to be presumed that it will never be born'.

[15] Quentin Skinner points in the right direction when suggesting that Hobbes came to recognize that the proper conduct of civil science rested as much on the art of persuasion as that of reasoning: Q Skinner, 'Hobbes's changing conception of civil science' in Skinner, *Visions of Politics: vol.3 Hobbes and Civil Science* (Cambridge: Cambridge University Press, 2002), 66–86, at 85. See also Q Skinner, *Reason and Rhetoric in the Philosophy of Hobbes* (Cambridge: Cambridge University Press, 1996), Conclusion.

Once it is accepted that Hobbes was engaged in political jurisprudence, the apparent discrepancies that some legal scholars see in his work are resolved. We can make sense of the apparently paradoxical claim that Hobbes belongs to the natural law tradition yet also founds the modern school of legal positivism. We can also appreciate that although Hobbes' account is authoritarian, it is not absolutist. We can, in short, appreciate the sheer ambition of Hobbes' undertaking.

III. Hobbes on Law

The claim that Hobbes was a progenitor of legal positivism is certainly justified.[16] The overriding objective of his work was to establish the authority of the state, conceived as a human artefact. Central to that objective is his assertion that the office of the sovereign possesses the absolute power of law-making. Hobbes defines law as 'the Reason of this our Artificial Man the Commonwealth'.[17] Sovereign is the name given to the person (office) that represents the commonwealth, and it is 'his Command that makes Law'.[18] Law is made by the authority of the sovereign rather than the wisdom of scholars and philosophers: *Auctoritas, non veritas facit legem*.[19]

Law is the command of the sovereign. This concept of positive law (*lex*) should not be confused with right (*jus*). Hobbes argues that many people were confused about the distinction between right and law: right 'consisteth in liberty to do, or to forbeare' whereas law 'determineth, and bindeth'. Law and Right therefore 'differ as much as Obligation and Liberty; which in one and the same matter are inconsistent'.[20] As the supreme law-maker, the sovereign is the sole source of right and wrong, of justice and injustice. Justice, then, is a purely legal concept: justice consists in acting in accordance with those commands. Since positive law provides 'the measure of Good and Evil actions', there can be no such thing as an unjust law.[21]

Once law is acknowledged as the command of the sovereign, it is evident that the sovereign cannot be bound by law. It is not possible 'for any person to be bound to himself', argues Hobbes, 'because he that can bind can release'.[22] The manner in which the political pact is constructed also supports this position. Since the pact is between individuals, the sovereign created by the pact is not a party to it and therefore cannot commit any breach of legal obligation that might arise between its parties. Further, the so-called 'rights' of 'the people' could not act as a counterweight to the will of the sovereign. Since 'the people', as distinct from 'the multitude', come into existence as a result of the pact to create the sovereign, the office of the sovereign

---

[16] See MM Goldsmith, 'Hobbes on Law' in T Sorell (ed.), *The Cambridge Companion to Hobbes* (Cambridge: Cambridge University Press, 1996), Ch.12.

[17] Lev, 187.   [18] Ibid.

[19] T Hobbes, *A Dialogue between a Philosopher and a Student of the Common Laws of England* [1681], J Cropsey ed. (Chicago: University of Chicago Press, 1971), 55.

[20] Lev, 91. DC, 156: 'There is then a great difference between *law* and *right*; for a law is a *bond*, a *right* is a *liberty*, and they differ as contraries'.

[21] Lev, 223.   [22] Lev, 184.

represents the will of the people.[23] For Hobbes, the sovereign is a 'Mortal God' and the source of law.[24] Established by art—by the political pact—the office of the sovereign was in no way dependent on any higher authority.

Hobbes here deliberately breaks with the ancient world of virtue and vice, good and evil. Moral arguments of right and wrong are transformed into political claims of peace and war.[25] The edifice of the state is designed to subordinate all other sources of morality, justice, or law. Its authority could not be qualified by property, international law, common law, or religion. First, the sovereign not only possesses sole dominion over property; he determines what constitutes property.[26] Secondly, Hobbes argues that the norms of the 'international community' of nations could not be binding on states.[27] Thirdly, he challenges Coke's argument that law constitutes a special type of 'artificial reason': it is not the 'wisdom of subordinate judges but the reason of this our artificial man the commonwealth and his command that makes law'.[28] His final argument—about religion—is the most comprehensive. Hobbes' analysis of ecclesiastical questions takes up almost half of *Leviathan*. Adopting an Erastian analysis, he demonstrates that the church's claim to earthly power is based on error; the church is not an independent institution, but part of the commonwealth and entirely subject to the rule of its sovereign.[29]

It seems beyond doubt that Hobbes constructs, in Bobbio's formulation, 'the ideological framework for legal positivism'.[30] Modern legal positivism—the conviction that positive law forms an autonomous system of law that includes its own criteria of right and wrong, just and unjust—has its origins in his work.

Given his position on the authority of positive law, why then did Hobbes take so seriously the claims of natural law? Why in particular does he seem to rest his entire construction of positive law on a foundation of the laws of nature?[31]

---

[23] DC, 75–6, 137.   [24] Lev, 120.

[25] See R Koselleck, *Critique and Crisis: Enlightenment and the Pathogenesis of Modern Society* (Cambridge, MA: MIT Press, 1988), 25.

[26] Lev, 125.

[27] Lev, 244. See further N Malcolm, *Aspects of Hobbes* (Oxford: Oxford University Press, 2002), Ch.13.

[28] Lev, 187: 'For it is possible long study may increase and confirm erroneous sentences: and where men build on false grounds, the more they build, the greater is the ruin: and of those that study and observe with equal time and diligence, the reasons and resolutions are, and must remain, discordant: and therefore it is not that *Juris prudentia*, or wisdom of subordinate judges; but the reason of this our artificial man the commonwealth, and his command, that maketh law'. See also T Hobbes, *A Dialogue between a Philosopher and a Student of the Common Laws of England* [1681], J Cropsey ed. (Chicago: University of Chicago Press, 1971), 54–77.

[29] Lev, Pt III. See JR Collins, *The Allegiance of Thomas Hobbes* (Oxford: Oxford University Press, 2005), 10: 'He [Hobbes] understood the English Revolution not, primarily, as a constitutional struggle over monarchy, nor as an outburst of republicanism, nor as a theological struggle over Calvinism. Hobbes understood the Revolution as a war over the nature of the church as an independent corporate body, and the status of the clergy as an estate of the realm. In this sense, Hobbes interpreted the English Revolution as an ecclesial crisis, and as the culmination of the long Reformation struggle to redefine the political struggle of Christendom by submitting the universal church to the power of emerging modern states.' See further T Hobbes, *Behemoth or the Long Parliament* [c.1668], S Holmes ed. (Chicago: University of Chicago Press, 1990).

[30] N Bobbio, *Thomas Hobbes and the Natural Law Tradition*, D Gobetti trans. (Chicago: University of Chicago Press, 1993), 116.

[31] See DC, Chs 2–4; Lev, Chs 14 and 15.

The simple answer is that Hobbes could not ignore the claims of natural law without radically circumscribing the overall ambition of his civil science. Once his task is conceived as an exercise of political jurisprudence—of addressing the issue of legitimacy and not simply accepting the authority of positive law as a postulate of thought—it is evident that he could not avoid addressing claims of natural law. Much of his political writing was undertaken during a period of conflict and civil war, the period he calls, in the fourth Part of *Leviathan*, 'the kingdom of darkness'. During these turbulent times, a series of pernicious beliefs flourished: 'sovereignty may be divided; civil and spiritual power are distinct; the sovereign is subject to the law; private men can judge if laws are just or unjust; private conscience justifies resistance, not to mention tyrannicide …'.[32] His civil science could not be adequately formulated without taking seriously the revolutionary claims being made in the name of natural law. Hobbes made natural law a central focus of his work,[33] but he did so in order to expose its errors and to rework its precepts for the purpose of rebuilding the authority of sovereign will.

In order to explain this, I first examine his treatment of natural right, then natural law, and finally draw on the relation between natural law and positive law to address more directly Hobbes' political jurisprudence.

IV. Natural Right

The concepts of natural right and natural law perform major roles in Hobbes' scheme. But right and law must be kept distinct, he argues, since one concerns liberty and the other obligation. This general distinction applies to natural right and natural law. We start with his treatment of natural right.

Hobbes belongs to a school of thinkers who place the concept of natural rights at the core of their arguments.[34] Natural rights theories—especially those that a century later were enshrined in the words 'that all men are created equal and endowed by their Creator with certain inalienable rights'[35]—have had a great impact on the drafting of modern constitutional documents. In later schemes, natural rights as the inherent possession of every human being were declared either inalienable—liberties that no government could suppress—or regulated only with the consent of the individual for the purpose of maximizing liberties.[36] But the role of natural rights in Hobbes' scheme is different.

---

[32] S Holmes, Introduction to *Behemoth*, above n.29, xxv–xxvi.

[33] DC, 156: '*Natural law* is the law which God has revealed to all men through his *eternal word* which is innate in them, namely by *natural reason*. And this is the law which I have been attempting to expound throughout this little book.' See further, Lev, 110: 'The Laws of Nature are Immutable and Eternal … And the science of them, is the true and onely Moral Philosophy.'

[34] R Tuck, *Natural Rights Theories: Their Origin and Development* (Cambridge: Cambridge University Press, 1979), Ch.6.

[35] American Declaration of Independence 1776; see also French Declaration of the Rights of Man and the Citizen 1789, arts 1, 2: 'Men are born and remain free and equal in rights.' See Ch.5, VI below.

[36] French Declaration, ibid., art. 2: 'The aim of all political association is the preservation of the natural and imprescriptible rights of man.'

Hobbes develops his argument about the nature of society and government through the frame of natural rights. Leo Strauss claims that Hobbes did more than any other theorist to bring about the shift in modern political theory from duty to rights, for which reason he is the true founder of modern liberalism.[37] That may be so, though 'modern liberalism' is an ambiguous notion. Tuck notes that 'most strong rights theories have in fact been explicitly authoritarian rather than liberal',[38] a point neatly illustrated in the radical twist Hobbes gave to the concept of natural right.

Hobbes argues that the fundamental right of the individual in the state of nature is self-preservation: 'the first foundation of natural *Right* is that *each man protect his life and limbs as much as he can*'.[39] It is a right built into our nature: 'we cannot be blamed for looking out for ourselves', he contends, for 'we cannot will to do otherwise'. The desire for self-preservation thus 'happens by a real necessity of nature as powerful as that by which a stone falls downward'.[40]

Hobbes replaces the Aristotelian claim that man is a social animal with the argument that humans are self-centred, competitive, and driven by their passions and fears. Their fundamental right by nature is freedom to preserve the conditions of their existence. Hobbes' analogy to gravitational force suggests that he was seeking to put this basic natural right on a scientific foundation. The fundamental natural right of self-preservation is 'not a philosopher's thought imputed to mankind', but 'a rational claim immanent in human nature'.[41]

This basic right to preserve one's existence is directly connected to his concept of sovereignty.[42] In a state of nature, 'every man was permitted to do anything to anybody, and to possess, use and enjoy whatever he wanted and could get'.[43] Consequently, 'the effect of this *right* is almost the same as if there were no *right* at all'.[44] The drive for self-preservation and the right of liberty of each individual leads directly to 'a war of every man against every man'.[45] It follows that for the purpose of maintaining this basic natural right, humans must pool their natural rights and vest them in the office of the sovereign. Hobbes argues that this is a necessary corollary of the existence of the fundamental natural right of self-preservation.

Hobbes was the first to draw a clear distinction between natural right and natural law, arguing that the former is not dependent on the latter. Natural rights inhere in humans for the purposes of ensuring their survival. Formulating natural rights in this way reveals the paradox that in order to realize natural rights, humans must agree to relinquish them and vest an absolute right of rule-making in the office of the sovereign.[46]

---

[37] L Strauss, *Natural Right and History* (Chicago: University of Chicago Press 1953), esp. 166–202.
[38] Tuck, *Natural Rights*, above n.34, 3.   [39] DC, 27.   [40] Ibid.
[41] P Zagorin, *Hobbes and the Law of Nature* (Princeton: Princeton University Press, 2009), 28.
[42] Lev, Ch 30.   [43] DC, 28.   [44] DC, 29.   [45] DC, 29.
[46] Hobbes does qualify this point with the statement that 'not all rights are alienable', arguing that 'a man cannot lay down the right of resisting them that assault him by force, to take away his life': Lev, 93. It is sometimes argued that this right of self-defence undermines Hobbes' theory of absolute sovereignty: see, e.g., J Hampton, *Hobbes and the Social Contract Tradition* (Cambridge: Cambridge University Press, 1986), 197–207. But in a systematic account, Susanne Sreedhar shows that Hobbes' account of resistance rights are personal and peculiar, do not conflict with his prohibition on rebellion, and are entirely compatible with his account of absolute sovereignty. In reality, Hobbes takes the potentially powerful

V. Natural Law

Modern modes of thinking have eroded the medieval idea of natural law as disclosing an ordered world replete with meaning. Given Hobbes's scientific approach to matters of law and state, the retention of natural law in his scheme requires explanation. He was very critical of those who invoked the concept of natural law without defining it and he poured scorn on those who argued 'that a particular act is against natural law because it runs counter to the united opinion of all the wisest or most civilized nations'.[47] Such claims are naïve: 'men condemn in others what they approve in themselves, publicly praise what they secretly reject, and form their opinions from a habit of listening to what they are told, not from their own observation'.[48]

Hobbes retained the medieval formulation of natural law as 'the dictate of right reason'. But he placed the precepts of reason on a more scientific footing. Noting that geometry was 'the only science that it hath pleased God hitherto to bestow on mankind',[49] Hobbes saw reason as a type of instrumental calculation. This helped him to reformulate natural law as a set of logical and purposive axioms.

For Hobbes, the laws of nature are axioms 'found out by Reason, by which a man is forbidden to do that which is destructive of life, or takes away the means of preserving the same'.[50] Natural laws yield a catalogue of duties to maintain the fundamental right to self-preservation. Natural law does not prescribe the type of good conduct laid down in Scripture; since these laws are 'immutable and eternal', they predate any divine texts.[51] Natural law does not promote behaviour that is good in itself; it exists for the purpose of regulating action necessary for the maintenance of self-preservation. The main problem with these laws of nature, Hobbes suggests, is that they oblige *in foro interno*, in conscience only.[52] Strictly, they are 'dictates of Reason' not really laws at all for 'they are but Conclusions, or Theorems concerning what conduceth to the conservation and defence of themselves'. Law, by contrast, 'properly is the word of him that by right hath command over others'.[53]

Chapters 2 and 3 of *De Cive* and Chapters 14 and 15 of *Leviathan* list the primary laws of nature in some detail. But their essential purpose is expressed in the first law: 'to seek peace'.[54] Since the state of nature was one of perpetual war generated from the exercise of natural rights, this first law, seeking to ensure self-preservation by promoting peace, must lead to the giving up of the state of nature. It follows that 'the right of men to all things must not be held on to; certain rights must be transferred or abandoned'.[55] The overriding purpose of natural law is to promote peace 'for a means of the conservation of men in multitudes'.[56]

Hobbes retains the concept of natural law within his overall scheme mainly as a 'device … to provide an acceptable foundation of the absolute power of the sover-

conceptual tools of resistance and renders them politically innocuous. Sreedhar concludes that Hobbes' 'delimited set of cases of justified resistance … serves to underscore all of the ways in which subjects are *not* at liberty to disobey the sovereign'. S Sreedhar, *Hobbes on Resistance: Defying the Leviathan* (Cambridge: Cambridge University Press, 2010), 171.

[47] DC, 32.   [48] DC, 33.   [49] Lev, 28.   [50] Lev, 91.   [51] Lev, 110.
[52] Lev, 110.   [53] Lev, 111.   [54] DC, 34.   [55] DC, 34.   [56] Lev, 109.

eign, and thus to ensure the undisputed supremacy of positive law'.[57] His objective was to use natural law, a concept used by many of his contemporaries to justify revolution and resistance to oppression, to demonstrate that laws of nature require the very opposite: unconditional obedience to the sovereign. This is highlighted in his second law of nature: 'stand by your agreements, or keep faith'.[58] Yet this obligation is impossible to realize in the state of nature, where force or fraud prevail: 'Covenants, without the Sword, are but Words, and of no strength to secure a man at all'.[59] These first two basic laws—maintenance of peace and fidelity to agreements—could be realized only by subjecting individuals to the rule of the sovereign.

Hobbes' longer list of the general laws of nature includes gratitude, sociability, mercy, respect, impartiality, proportionality, equality of standing, and fair adjudication of disputes.[60] His point is that humans might adhere to these laws of nature, but they do so only as a matter of conscience and personal morality. For these laws to become obligatory they have to be converted into positive laws by command of the sovereign: 'Thus the practice of *natural law* is necessary for the preservation of peace, and *security* is necessary for the practice of *natural law*'.[61]

Hobbes' argument about natural right and natural law can be summarized. Left to the free exercise of inherent natural rights, individuals end up destroying themselves. The sovereign's law is necessary because natural rights must be given up for the purpose of self-preservation. He recognizes the existence of certain laws of nature, such as mutual respect and fair treatment, which propel humans to sociability. But he argues that these natural laws cannot be realized outside the state. They became 'true' laws—that is, obligatory—only once recognized by civil law. For Hobbes, natural laws form part of a regime of public reason, which means the reason of the sovereign.[62] The difference between Hobbes and natural lawyers thus becomes clear. Natural lawyers say that positive law binds only if it complies with the precepts of natural law. Hobbes, by contrast, maintains that natural law binds only when expressed in the form of positive law.

VI. Natural Law and Civil Law

Hobbes is a legal positivist but he assigns an important role to the precepts of natural law. Some have argued that, by accepting a natural or rational mode of ordering, he is revealed to be a suppressed natural lawyer, but this misconstrues the radical character of his argument. There are two critical issues: first, his claim that natural law

---

[57] Bobbio, above n.30, 123.   [58] DC, 43.   [59] Lev, 117.

[60] See esp. DC, 47–54. For discussion see GS Kavka, *Hobbesian Moral and Political Theory* (Princeton: Princeton University Press, 1986), 343; SA Lloyd, *Morality in the Philosophy of Thomas Hobbes: Cases in the Law of Nature* (Cambridge: Cambridge University Press, 2009), 52–5. For consideration of equality see J Kidder, 'Acknowledgement of Equals: Hobbes's Ninth Law of Nature' (1983) 33 *Philosophical Quarterly* 133–46.

[61] DC, 70.

[62] Lev, 306: 'we are not every one, to make our own private Reason, or Conscience, but the Publique Reason, that is the reason of Gods Supreme Lieutenant'.

and civil law are parts of a common concept, and secondly the question of the sovereign's authority.

Hobbes contends that once the state has been established the 'law of nature and the civil law contain each other and are of equal extent'.[63] Laws of nature, 'being qualities that dispose men to peace and to obedience' undoubtedly form component parts of an orderly regime.[64] But natural laws are dependent on sovereign power for their obligatory force. 'Civil and natural law are not different kinds', he concludes, 'but different parts of Law; whereof one part being written is called Civil, the other unwritten, Natural'.[65]

Hobbes believes that if a dispute arises on which the civil law was silent—perhaps because the legislature has not foreseen the issue—the judge should refer to the precepts of natural law for a solution. He acknowledges that a good judge is impartial, patient, and dispassionate and also has 'a right understanding of that principal law of nature called Equity', which depends 'not on the reading of other men's writings but on the goodness of a man's own natural reason and meditation'.[66] But this hardly constitutes evidence that Hobbes is at heart a natural lawyer. He recognizes that the function of civil law is to promote peace and sociability through an impartially administered regime of rules.[67] When interpreting law, a judge has to have regard to this basic purpose and in this situation the so-called laws of nature provide guidance. They are therefore best understood as prudential precepts.[68] To say that an officer of the state relies on such precepts in interpreting laws is not to acknowledge natural law as an independent set of moral norms; it is to recognize that the judge must be attuned to the nature of the association, to political reason, to 'reasons of state'.[69]

The second issue, the relationship between civil and natural law, concerns the status of the sovereign. Although the sovereign is not bound by positive law, Hobbes

---

[63] Lev, 185.

[64] For an interpretation of Hobbes' account of natural law as founded in reciprocity and generating the obligations of governments to promote the peace and welfare of their citizens see Lloyd, above n.60, esp.Ch.1.

[65] Lev, 185.   [66] Lev, 195.   [67] DC, 159.

[68] Hobbes, *Behemoth*, above n.29, 44: 'To obey the laws is justice and equity, which is the law of nature...Likewise to obey the laws is the prudence of the subject; for without such obedience the commonwealth (which is every subject's safety and protection) cannot subsist.' See further P Pettit, *Made with Words: Hobbes on Language, Mind, and Politics* (Princeton: Princeton University Press, 2008), 165: 'Here I depart form the moralistic view of Hobbesian natural law that is associated with a number of people, most prominently Howard Warrender (1957). My view is much closer to the prudential view of natural law ascribed to Hobbes by John WN Watkins (1973). Debate continues on this issue, but the Watkins stance is now more or less accepted as the "orthodox" one.' The references are to H Warrender, *The Political Philosophy of Hobbes* (Oxford: Oxford University Press, 1957) and JWN Watkins, *Hobbes's System of Ideas* (London: Hutchinson, 1973).

[69] Hobbes did not engage in a detailed examination of what is often called 'reason of state' thinking. The most obvious reason was that his primary objective was to develop a science of politics rather than to offer guidance on the arts of governing. But in all probability he felt it presumptuous to instruct sovereigns on how best to exercise their power. Nonetheless, Malcolm's view that 'a number of themes and lines of argument' in Hobbes' works 'echo the teachings of ragion di stato theory' and 'it seems reasonable to align Hobbes's political theory with that of ragion di stato' seems sound: N Malcolm, *Reason of State, Propaganda, and the Thirty Years' War: An Unknown Translation by Thomas Hobbes* (Oxford: Oxford University Press, 2007), 114, at 118. On reason of state see further Ch.8, III–IV below.

does not confer arbitrary power on the office. He explains in *Leviathan* that the office exists to procure '*the safety of the people*; to which he is obliged by the law of nature'.[70] Again for some, this is evidence that Hobbes bases his account on natural law, but this too rests on a misunderstanding. His objective was to establish a governmental regime that possesses absolute validity. The only effective way of doing this was, as Bobbio notes, to 'place it on the pedestal of natural laws, i.e., on a law which was...rationally deductible from another law of nature evident in itself'.[71] But on the critical question of whether a subject could appeal to a higher law which restricted the sovereign's power, Hobbes is unequivocal: the sovereign must 'render an account to God, the author of that law, and to none but him'.[72] Further, the sovereign 'may ordain the doing of many things...which is a breach of trust, and of the law of nature; but this is not enough to authorise any subject, either to make war upon, or so much as to accuse of injustice, or any way to speak evil of their sovereign'.[73]

Hobbes' argument that the authority of the sovereign rests on natural law precepts does not lead him to recognize the validity of a higher legal norm. His primary objective was to explain that there could be no valid law except that of civil law and that the basic function of civil law was to meet the conditions of civil science.

VII. Hobbes' Political Jurisprudence

Hobbes' civil science was formed as a result of the secularization, rationalization, and (partial) positivization of the medieval idea of natural law. It was founded on the view that collective ordering was not divinely-ordained but the result of a human world we have made. In this constructed world, humans were conceived as free, equal, and rational beings able to devise their own arrangements of collective ordering and to establish regimes of government resting on some notion of consent.

A key objective of Hobbes' civil science was to undermine any lingering authority of the medieval idea of natural law. Natural law—the metaphysical notion that all natural occurrences were subject to universal reason apprehended by our faculty of reason—had to be overthrown. Hobbes felt that this could most effectively be achieved using the instruments of natural law. Herein lies the critical importance of his civil science. He secularized the concept of natural law, rejecting the idea of civil rule as an expression of natural order, and conceived the question of obedience to authority as a rational undertaking. He thereby transformed the concept of natural law, treating it instrumentally as a set of axioms that promoted civil peace. Rather than assuming that humans are governed by God-given reason, he understood them to be creatures possessed of reason but driven by potentially destructive passions.

This transformation of natural law was of critical importance in refashioning the instruments of modern political rule. Hobbes showed that to realize liberty and equality—the foundational precepts of political jurisprudence—humans must first

---

[70] Lev, 231.   [71] Bobbio, above n.30, 143–4.   [72] Lev, 231.   [73] Lev, 172.

be subjected to government. The laws of nature he listed and the conditions for their realization—the promotion of civil peace and enforcement of the laws of sociability—became the immanent laws of civil government. Laws of nature were converted into precepts of political right.

This concept of political right must be distinguished from the concepts of natural right and natural law. As Hobbes says, it is not by nature but by artifice—that is, by political imagination—that the state is created and from this institution of the state all rights and duties are derived. The concept of political right might perform a function similar to that of the medieval concept of natural law: that of generating 'laws' that establish and maintain the authority of rule. But Hobbes' claim about the originality of his civil science is that it broke with traditions of natural law.

Hobbes emphasizes the importance of this break with his argument about the omnipotent nature of sovereign power: since positive law provides 'the measure of Good and Evil actions', there could be no such thing as an unjust law.[74] But he did accept that there could be such a thing as a 'good' law, one that 'is *Needful*, for the *Good of the People*, and withall *Perspicuous*'.[75] A law that benefited the ruler but not the people could not be a good law.[76] 'It is a weak Sovereign, that has weak Subjects', he writes, 'and a weak People, whose Sovereign wanteth Power to rule them at his will'.[77] Sovereign authority is a form of public power exercised for the good of the people, and a well-governed state is one in which, without endangering the public good, civil liberty is maximized. This requires acknowledgement of 'the art of making fit laws'.[78] This is the core of his civil science.

Hobbes' overriding objective was to create 'one firm and lasting edifice'.[79] Without the help of 'a very able Architect' what was likely to result was a 'crazy building' which the people would regard as unstable and which 'must assuredly fall upon the heads of their posterity'.[80] To ensure this did not occur, the sovereign had to be skilled in the arts of government.[81] As Hobbes expresses it, the relationship between sovereign and subject was not regulated by positive law, but by the prudential art of governing. For good political reasons, he calls these 'laws of nature', but they are actually precepts of political right.

This is the beauty of Hobbes' civil science: he invokes the concept of natural right to generate the constitutive rules of the modern state and demonstrates that the precepts of natural law yield the regulative rules of the modern state. For Hobbes, the autonomy of the political domain is founded on liberty, equality, and consent. Convinced of the necessity of authoritarian government, Hobbes accepts that 'the

---

[74] Lev, 223.   [75] Ibid. 239   [76] Ibid. 240.   [77] Ibid.   [78] Ibid. 221.
[79] Ibid.   [80] Ibid.

[81] T Hobbes, *The Elements of Law Natural and Politic (Human Nature and De Corpore Politico)* [1640], JCA Gaskin intro. (Oxford: Oxford University Press, 1994), Pt.II, Ch.28.1: 'And as the art and duty of sovereigns consist in the same acts, so also doth their profit. For the end of art is profit; and governing to the profit of the subjects is governing to the profit of the sovereign ... And these three: 1. the law over them that have sovereign power; 2. their duty; 3. their profit: are one and the same thing contained in this sentence, *Salus populi suprema lex*; by which must be understood, not the mere preservation of their lives, but generally their benefit and good. So that this is the general law for sovereigns: that they procure, to the uttermost of their endeavour, the good of the people.'

power of the mighty hath no foundation but in the opinion and belief of the people'.[82] And he recognizes that, to maintain that authority, the sovereign has to act with restraint as well as engaging in the vital task of shaping the people to make them 'fit for society'.[83]

Hobbes' political jurisprudence—a combination of rhetoric as well as reason, of counsel as well as command[84]—marks a vital stage in the transition to modern public law. His argument for authoritarianism is an essential step in the destruction of the medieval worldview. Only by asserting the sovereign's absolute power to make law could the principle of representation transform hierarchical notions of medieval rulership into the immanent logic of the modern state. The concept of sovereignty thereafter evolves from its initial fixation on some transcendent figure that founded the regime into a representation of the entire political entity.[85] In the process, modern public law acquires its identity not from the figure of the sovereign but from the concept of sovereignty, not from the formal law-giver but from the prudential logic binding together the political entity of the state. In that transition, Hobbes' political jurisprudence performs the crucial role of replacing the moral reason of natural law with a form of political reason that leads to the formation of the modern state as an institution promoting civil peace, security, and prosperity.

---

[82] Hobbes, *Behemoth*, above n.29,16.

[83] DC, 21. See also Lev, 233: 'the Common-peoples minds...are like clean paper, fit to receive whatsoever by Publique Authority shall be imprinted in them'.

[84] See T Sorell, 'Hobbes's persuasive civil science' (1990) 40 *Philosophical Quarterly* 342–51, highlighting the importance of counsel as well as command in Hobbes' scheme.

[85] See B de Spinoza, *Tractatus Theologico-Politicus* [1670], RHM Elwes trans. (London: Routledge, c.1951), 200–13.

3

Leveller Legacies

I. Introduction

In 1646 a political group that came to be known as the Levellers was established, one of a number of radical political organizations that emerged during the course of the English revolution. Within three years they were a spent force and at no stage during the short period of their existence were they able to impose their views over those in authority. Not only did they fail to have their reforms adopted but their proposals were so antithetical to English ruling ideas that it is as though modern British government has evolved to systematically suppress the constitutional issues they raised. Their main legacy is to have offered a route-map of a road not taken.

But this is only part of the story. Leveller ideas may have failed to shape modern British practice but they provide the first clear expression in European thought of the basic precepts of modern constitutional democracy. Their ideas influenced the American and French revolutionaries of the late-eighteenth century and helped shape the arrangements of the modern constitutional settlements that followed. Leveller ideas about constitutional democracy today provide a template against which the legitimacy of modern government is measured.

This chapter examines those constitutional ideas. It first situates the Levellers within the context of English seventeenth-century upheavals, explains their constitutional scheme and examines their attempts to get it established in the English Commonwealth. It then assesses their legacy, first by presenting their ideas as a template of modern constitutional democracy and then by using this template to map the trajectory of modern governmental development. Modern regimes are obliged to manage a tension between two competing rationalities of governing, those of constitutionalism and statecraft. While the Levellers promoted the former, modern British practice became exemplary of the latter. Neither facet can be eliminated, though methods of seeking an accommodation vary. Even though British practice accentuates statecraft, growing dissatisfaction with its performance is leading to a resurgence of interest in constitutional renewal. Leveller ideas have thus acquired a renewed significance. But having been so neglected for the last 350 years, discussion about constitutional modernization in Britain has failed to light upon the basic precepts that the Levellers presented with such clarity. This, then, is an account of the uncertain legacies of the Levellers' constitutional thought.

Political Jurisprudence. Martin Loughlin. © M Loughlin 2017.
Published 2017 by Oxford University Press.

II. The Ideological Context of the English Revolution

Leveller ideas have their origins in the economic, political, and religious upheavals of the late sixteenth and early seventeenth centuries. The growth of commerce had signalled the beginnings of economic modernization and weakened both formal class barriers and rigid medieval ideas of status. These economic changes were reflected in the growing political power of the gentry, who were strongly represented in the Commons. During the first half of the seventeenth century one manifestation of these economic and political changes was the struggle for authority between King and Commons. This constitutional struggle has been extensively documented,[1] though its causes and ideological significance remain issues of controversy.[2]

With respect to these issues, I make two observations about the origins and course of the Leveller movement. The first is that the struggle for authority was not a rebellion from below. It arose from a division within the governing class, especially as younger sons of the landed aristocracy assumed a greater degree of economic and then political power through their influence in the Commons. Great landowners dominated the Lords, while the Commons was controlled by their younger sons and by members of the upper squirearchy, including many lawyers whose interests were directly tied to those of the landed class. Secondly, accompanying these economic and political cleavages was the Puritan religious upheaval, based on a conviction that the work of the Reformation needed to be completed. A wide variety of radical religious sects flourished ranging from aggressive Calvinists to covenanters of various splinter congregations. The latter groups included such iconoclastic and utopian movements as Anabaptists, Ranters, Seekers, Arians, Traskites, Familists, Quakers, and Fifth Monarchists.[3] Consequently, these political struggles were fought out not only in Parliament and then, when civil war broke out in 1642, on the battlefield, but also in pulpits, churches, and religious communities across the land. Political beliefs were refracted through the prism of dogmatic religious convictions.[4]

---

[1] See, e.g., MA Judson, *The Crisis of the Constitution: An Essay in Constitutional and Political Thought, 1603–1645* (New York: Octagon Books, 1971); A Woolrych, *Britain in Revolution, 1625–1660* (Oxford: Oxford University Press, 2002); M Kishlansky, *A Monarchy Transformed: Britain 1603–1714* (London: Penguin, 1996); A Cromartie, *The Constitutionalist Revolution: An Essay on the History of England, 1450–1642* (Cambridge: Cambridge University Press, 2006).

[2] On the controversies over the longer-term socio-economic context see: L Stone, *The Causes of the English Revolution, 1529–1642* (London: Routledge & Kegan Paul, 1972), esp. Ch.2. On the political context cf. JP Sommerville, *Royalists and Patriots Politics and Ideology in England, 1603–1640* (London: Longman, 2nd edn. 1999); G Burgess, *Absolute Monarchy and the Stuart Constitution* (New Haven: Yale University Press, 1996); C Russell, *The Causes of the English Civil War* (Oxford: Clarendon Press, 1990). On the religious context see: WM Lamont, 'The Puritan Revolution: A Historiographical Essay' in JGA Pocock (ed.), *The Varieties of British Political Thought, 1500–1800* (Cambridge: Cambridge University Press, 1993), 119–45.

[3] See esp. C Hill, *The World Turned Upside Down: Radical Ideas during the English Revolution* (London: Temple Smith, 1972).

[4] See, e.g., C Hill, *Intellectual Origins of the English Revolution* (Oxford: Clarendon Press, 1965); M Walzer, *The Revolution of the Saints: A Study of the Origins of Radical Politics* (London: Weidenfeld & Nicolson, 1966); P Lake, *Anglicans and Puritans? Presbyterianism and English Conformist Thought from Whitgift to Hooker* (London: Unwin Hyman, 1988).

During the 1640s, the main division within Parliament was between Presbyterians and Independents. The former, the majority, represented the landed interest and were no supporters of the common people. They were content with Calvinist notions of a state-controlled church and sought to ensure continued control over the church through the supremacy of Parliament. Whereas Presbyterians took wealth to be a sign of God's favour, the Independents believed that the landed class had become addicted to luxury. While accepting a national church, the Independents argued for greater congregational independence, replacing the hierarchy of priests and bishops (supported by tithes) with independent ministers paid by their congregations. The Independents were 'the Saints', the godly elite summoned by providence to complete the work of reformation. But each side was militant: each promoted uniformity and rejected toleration.

This is the economic, political, and religious context in which the Levellers came into being. The movement was drawn mainly from the commercial lower middle classes, often self-employed and fiercely independent. They opposed the landed Presbyterians, but they were drawn from a class that had no significant influence among the Independents in Parliament.[5] The crucible of the Leveller movement was religious upheaval, with both their leaders and recruits drawn from the more radical sects. Against church hierarchy, they asserted the equal dignity of all and contended that collective association should be freely established by individual consent.

The constitutional tensions of the period came to a head in 1640 when the King, needing revenue after having ruled for eleven years without it, felt obliged to convene a Parliament. This Parliament, the Long Parliament, acted decisively to redress grievances and sought to control the King by punishing his agents, notably by executing Archbishop Laud and the Earl of Strafford. This heady atmosphere of political uncertainty, democratic temperament, and radical religious views promoted by the newly-invented cheap printing techniques provided favourable conditions for the organization of the Levellers.[6] In the period between the first and second phases of the civil wars, another forum emerged: the war of pamphlets and petitions. This was the milieu in which the Leveller movement was born.

The first phase of civil war came to an end in 1646 when Parliament was victorious but nothing had been settled. The ending had 'left institutions damaged, but not repaired; governmental authority present but relatively ineffective; and expectations

---

[5] It might be noted, by contrast, that Cromwell, who emerged as a leader of the Independents in Parliament, could identify eighteen relatives among the members of the Long Parliament: see HN Brailsford, *The Levellers and the English Revolution*, C Hill ed. (London: The Cresset Press, 1961), 109.

[6] D Wootton, 'Leveller Democracy and the Puritan Revolution' in JH Burns (ed.), *The Cambridge History of Political Thought, 1450–1700* (Cambridge: Cambridge University Press, 1991), 412–42, at 414–5:'Only a society where Puritanism and commerce had encouraged the spread of literacy amongst the common people could such a campaign have offered any prospect of success. Only where censorship of the press, generally so effective in early modern Europe, had broken down could political leaders seek to express the values and interests of the politically dispossessed. Only where the anonymity of market relations had made possible independence of expression without fear of economic sanction could merchants and artisans afford to lay claim to their rights. Only where petitions, street demonstrations, and voluntary military service showed some prospect of changing the course of political events—only under conditions of civil war—could such a strategy seem worth undertaking.'

raised, but neither answered nor effectively suppressed'.[7] Parliament's success meant the end of the Episcopal organization of the Church of England, and this fuelled the conviction that power now rested in the people. But many expressed concerns about this flowering of populism, arguing that it would lead not only to the destruction of religious discipline but also challenge the existence of social distinctions and ranks. It was 'the space created by this constitutional hiatus, with war finished, but nothing put in its place'[8] that the Levellers sought to fill. They did so by producing a clear manifesto, developing an efficient organization, and devising tactics to ensure its implementation.

III. The Formation of the Levellers

The three main civilian leaders of the Levellers, John Lilburne, Richard Overton, and William Walwyn, all came from radical Puritan backgrounds with links to the Anabaptists. 'The profound beliefs of the Anabaptists in human equality, including the equality of the sexes, their faith in toleration, their horror at the thought of capital punishment, their rejection of any form of priesthood', noted Brailsford, 'all this and much more the Levellers inherited'.[9] Their political convictions undoubtedly had strong religious underpinnings, but the Levellers, arguing that the Elect are the world's weak and dispossessed,[10] converted these into a secular political programme.

The catalyst was their remarkable leader, John Lilburne. A Puritan from the Durham minor gentry, he possessed a powerful sense of injustice, a remarkable lack of self-doubt, and a strong propensity for martyrdom.[11] Lilburne stood trial for his convictions on numerous occasions. First imprisoned by Star Chamber in 1638 for publishing seditious books promoting the Puritan cause, he was whipped and pilloried for his contempt in refusing to take an oath to tell the truth.[12] Freed in 1640, when all Laud's prisoners were released by the Long Parliament, Lilburne in 1642 joined the parliamentary army, rising to the rank of Lieutenant-Colonel. He left at the end of the first civil war because with the formation of the New Model Army he would have been required to take the solemn covenant.[13] In 1646

---

[7] J Scott, *England's Troubles: Seventeenth-century English political instability in a European context* (Cambridge: Cambridge University Press, 2000), 153.

[8] Ibid.　　　[9] Brailsford, above n.5, 33.

[10] Cf. Louis de Saint-Just's comment that *les malheureux sont la puissance de la terre*; cited in H Arendt, *On Revolution* (Harmondsworth: Penguin, 1973), 59. But Leveller convictions about social equality remained framed by the teachings of the gospels: see, e.g., W Walwyn, 'The Power of Love' (1643) in *The Writings of William Walwyn*, JR McMichael and B Taft eds (Athens: University of Georgia Press, 1989), 78–96.

[11] See generally P Gregg, *Free-Born John: The Biography of John Lilburne* (London: Phoenix Press, 2000); MA Gibb, *John Lilburne, The Leveller: A Christian Democrat* (London: Lindsay Drummond Ltd, 1947). For a useful reappraisal, which attempts to strip away Lilburne's propensity for self-promotion, see: JT Peacey, 'John Lilburne and the Long Parliament' (2000) 43 *Hist.J.* 625–45.

[12] 3 St.Tr.1315–68.

[13] This was a covenant, required by the Scots as a condition of helping their fellow Puritans, to preserve the Scottish religion and to remodel the English along Presbyterian lines. Lilburne 'could not find it according to his conscience to do so': Gregg, above n.11, 111.

Lilburne was again arrested, this time by a parliamentary committee of the Lords on a charge of printing scandalous writings. It was his imprisonment by the Lords for refusing to answer their questions that sparked the formation of the Leveller movement.

While Lilburne was in Newgate prison awaiting trial, Overton, with Walwyn's assistance, drafted the manifesto that gave birth to the Leveller movement. The manifesto of 7 July 1646 was called *A Remonstrance of many thousand citizens... to their own House of Commons, occasioned through the illegal and barbarous imprisonment of that famous and worthy sufferer for his country's freedoms, Lt-Col. John Lilburne.*[14] Its argument presents the core elements of the Levellers' constitutional thought.

The *Remonstrance* asserted that we the people choose our representatives in Parliament and the power vested in them is merely a 'power of trust – which is ever revocable' because '[w]e are your principals and you our agents'.[15] Further, that since only the Commons 'are chosen by us the people... therefore in you only is the power of binding the whole nation by making, altering, or abolishing of laws'.[16] This argument is amplified by the claim that the 'continual oppressors of the nation have been kings' and that the Lords, not being chosen by the people but being imposed on the people by Kings, similarly have no authority.[17] The *Remonstrance* also asserted the basic liberties of the people, including freedom of the press and freedom from impressment into military service.[18]

By extending the argument about basic liberties, the *Remonstrance* made a specific innovation. Parliament, it noted, has frequently committed men to prison either without showing cause or for refusing to answer questions or take an oath. This is unlawful for 'ye have no power from us so to do, nor could you have' since 'we could not confer a power that was not in ourselves, there being none of us that can without wilful sin bind ourselves to worship God after any other way than what... in our own particular understandings we approve to be just'.[19] Here the *Remonstrance* not only asserted the right to religious freedom, a right at the core of civil liberty, but the specific legal claim that, under a governmental regime authorized by the people, Parliament can have no authority to encroach on these basic liberties.

The *Remonstrance* contained a dramatic reproach to the Commons: 'Have you shoke this Nation like an Earth-quake to produce no more than this for us?'[20] Why, it asked, are the Commons submitting themselves to the King and Lords, when

---

[14] In discussing the Leveller tracts, I make use of the following collections of primary texts: DM Wolfe (ed.), *Leveller Manifestoes of the Puritan Revolution* [1944] (New York: Humanities Press, 1967); W Haller and G Davies, *The Leveller Tracts, 1647–1653* (New York: Columbia University Press, 1944); and A Sharp (ed.), *The English Levellers* (Cambridge: Cambridge University Press, 1998). When analysing the main constitutions, Wolfe is used as the primary reference. I have occasionally modernized the spelling.

[15] *Remonstrance* in Wolfe, above n.14, 112–34 at 113; Sharp, above n.14, 33–53, at 33–4.

[16] Wolfe, 116; Sharp, 37.

[17] Wolfe, 115, 116; Sharp, 35, 37. The specific point being made was that the Lords therefore had no authority to imprison Lilburne: see Wolfe, 117; Sharp, 38.

[18] Wolfe, 123, 125; Sharp, 45, 47.   [19] Wolfe, 122; Sharp, 44.

[20] Wolfe, 116; Sharp, 36.

patently these institutions have no authority? And it warned against a tendency of the Commons to act as some superior body.[21] Do not get above yourselves, it argued, since you are mere agents of the people: 'The work, ye must note, is ours and not your own, though ye are to be partakers with us in the well or ill-doing thereof. And therefore ye must expect to hear more frequently from us than ye have done.'[22]

Some of these arguments had previously been circulated in pamphlet form,[23] but only with the *Remonstrance* were Lilburne's bold, simple, and direct claims fashioned into a cohesive philosophy.

For publishing the *Remonstrance*, Overton was brought before the Lords and committed to Newgate Prison.[24] But first they dealt with Lilburne. When he was brought before the Lords, in his own words, he not only 'refused to kneel... [b]ut also with my fingers stopped both my ears when they went about to read my pretended charge', and proceeded to argue that the Lords had no jurisdiction in this matter.[25] The Lords determined that his recent pamphlets were 'a high breach of the privilege of Parliament, and high offences against the laws and statutes of this kingdom'. Lilburne was fined £2,000, sentenced to seven years' imprisonment in the Tower, and barred forever from holding any public office. They also ordered that his pamphlets be burnt by the common hangman.

IV. The Course of the Leveller Movement

'Ye must expect to hear more frequently from us than ye have done', was the declaration at the end of the *Remonstrance*. Eight months later came the next manifesto: the *Petition of March 1647*. The *Petition*, which formalized the specific measures by

---

[21] Wolfe, 120; Sharp, 42: 'For we must deal plainly with you. Ye have long time acted more like the House of Peers than the House of Commons. We can scarcely approach your door with a request or a motion, though by way of petition, but ye hold long debates whether we break not your privileges.'

[22] Wolfe, 128; Sharp, 52.

[23] For illustrations, see: [R Overton] Martin Mar-Priest, *The Arraignment of Mr Persecution* (1645), which attacked the Presbyterians and argued for total freedom of conscience and complete separation of church and state; W Walwyn, *Englands Lamentable Slavery* (1645) (in his *Writings*, above n.10, 143–53), a tract 'that conjoined the biblical roots of his political beliefs with his understanding of natural law' (Walwyn entry in the DNB); and J Lilburne, *Englands Birth-Right Justified* (1645), which deals with the role of parliament in preserving the people's traditional liberties and which Frank called 'a mélange of Biblical citation and legal precedent, of personal pique and large principle, of invective and positive political analysis': see J Frank, *The Levellers: A History of the Writings of Three Seventeenth-Century Social Democrats: John Lilburne, Richard Overton, William Walwyn* (Cambridge, MA: Harvard University Press, 1955), 61. See also the tracts of Lilburne, *On the 150th Page* (1645) and W Walwyn, *Toleration justified and persecution condemned* (1646) in Sharp, above n.14, 3–8, and 9–30, respectively.

[24] From prison, Overton wrote *An arrow against all tyrants and tyranny, shot from the prison of Newgate into the prerogative bowels of the arbitrary House of Lords* (1646) in Sharp, above n.14, 54–72. The crux of his argument was that neither the King nor the Lords partook of the sovereign power: 'Therefore the sovereign power, extending no further than from the represented to the representers—all this kind of sovereignty challenged by any (whether of king, Lords or others) is usurpation, illegitimate and illegal, and none of the kingdom's or people's.... [S]eeing the sovereign power is only from the represented to the representers, and cannot possibly legally further extend, the power of the king cannot be legislative but only executive, and he can communicate no more than he has himself.' (ibid. 63)

[25] J Lilburne, *The Legal Fundamental Liberties of the People of England* (1649) in Haller and Davies, above n.14, 399–449, at 411.

which the constitutional assumptions underpinning the *Remonstrance* could be made real, marks the official birth of the Leveller party. Although its tone was more measured—indicative of Walwyn's influence—Parliament again took offence, deeming it seditious because, ignoring the authority of the King and Lords, it was addressed 'To the right honourable and supreme authority of this nation, the Commons in Parliament assembled'.[26] Parliament ordered that the March petition also be burned by the hangman.

At this point, Leveller leaders realized that appeals to the Commons, under the control of the Presbyterians, would achieve nothing in their struggle to uphold their rights against the Lords. They therefore appealed over the heads of members of Parliament directly to the sovereign people. This was an innovation, a moving away from the traditional appeal to the Commons to resolve grievances and into the uncharted waters of direct popular action. But despite this the device they favoured was still the petition. Sanctified by custom, the petition was the easiest way of circumventing restrictions that had been imposed on the press. The process of collecting signatures was also a means of making real the otherwise amorphous idea of public opinion, as well as a method of educating and politicizing supporters.

The thrust of the Leveller argument during this period was that since the 'degenerate representative body of the Commons of England'[27] had refused to listen to the people, they had severed the bonds of trust. The social contract had been ripped up and England was thrust back into a state of nature. In a scathing tract, Overton argued that 'if the betrusted act not for the weal and safety of the betrusters, they depart from their just power' and therefore that 'if I prove forfeiture of the people's trust in the prevalent party at Westminster in Parliament assembled then an appeal from them to the people is not anti-parliamentary, anti-magisterial, not *from* that sovereign power, but *to* that sovereign power'.[28] Overton's case culminated in the claim that by ordering the burning of the March petition, Parliament 'really have burnt the Great Charter of England' and 'if this be not High Treason, and an open and visible forfeiture of their parliamentary being and trust, I would fain know what is'.[29] Consequently, 'halters and gallows is more fit for them than places in Parliament'.[30]

Towards the end of this fiery tract Overton turned directly to the people and, specifically, to the only institution that was capable of implementing their claims, the New Model Army. The Army, he concluded, 'is the only formal and visible Head that is left unto the people for protection and deliverance'.[31] This was a direct plea for the Army's support, though at the same time warning them that 'if you dally with us, and befool our expectations too long, we shall turn our pens, our hearts, and our hands against you, for our affection and concurrence with you is but for our safety and protection'. In short, 'have a care how you interpose your own light'.[32]

The Leveller appeal to the Army marked a new phase in the revolutionary period. At the end of the first phase of the civil war when there was comparative peace the

[26] *To the right honourable and supreme authority of this nation* (1647) in Wolfe, above n.14, 135–41.
[27] R Overton, *An appeal from the degenerate representative body the Commons of England assembled at Westminster to the Body represented, the Free People in general* (1647) in Wolfe, above n.14, 157–88.
[28] Ibid. 163.   [29] Ibid. 171.   [30] Ibid. 172.   [31] Ibid. 184.   [32] Ibid. 187.

Army had time for political debate. In 1647, the Army adopted the Solemn Engagement, a covenant between the soldiers and the people, in which they pledged not to be disbanded until certain military arrangements had been put in place and that conditions for the settlement of the kingdom had been met. This led to the drafting, mainly by Henry Ireton, Cromwell's son-in-law, of *A Representation from the Army*, which declared that they were 'not a mere mercenary army, hired to serve any arbitrary power of a state' but had been established for 'the defence of our own and the people's just rights and liberties'.[33] This was a critical moment. In 1647 both Houses of Parliament were under the control of a Presbyterian majority that wanted to restore the King. Fairfax and Cromwell, as leaders of the Army, came under attack. At the same time there was considerable Leveller agitation within Army ranks. This was expressed in demands to the Army Council,[34] leading to discussions both between Leveller leaders and Cromwell and Ireton and also within the Army Council.[35]

The outcome of these deliberations was the first of three versions of *An Agreement of the People*, drafted by the Levellers and presented to the Army Council at Putney on 29 October 1647.[36] The Agreement became a landmark in constitutional history: 'if we except the laws of the Greek cities, [the Agreement is] the first written constitution ever contrived',[37] 'the first rough draft of a written constitution in the history of democracy',[38] and a document that 'anticipated the fundamentals of the American constitution'.[39] The document formed the basis of the Putney debates which took place between 28 October and 11 November 1647. The debates highlighted serious differences between the Independents (strongly reflected amongst officers) and the Levellers (representing the views of many of the soldiers).[40] These disagreements indicated the degree to which the Levellers had moved beyond claiming religious freedom towards a demand for political equality. They also reveal the extent to which the Levellers had absorbed republican ideals.[41]

Cromwell had cooperated with the Agitators and the Levellers, not least because they assisted him in his struggle against the Presbyterian majority in Parliament. The

---

[33] *A Declaration or Representation of the Army* (14 June 1947) in Haller and Davies, above n.14, 51–63, at 55.

[34] See *The Case of the Army Truly Stated* (15 October 1647) in Wolfe, above n.14, 198–218; Haller and Davies, above n.14, 64–87. See also M Kishlansky, 'The Army and the Levellers: The Roads to Putney' (1979) 22 *Hist. J.* 795–824.

[35] See Brailsford, above n.5, Chs 10–11.

[36] *An Agreement of the People* (published as a pamphlet on 3 November 1647) in Wolfe, above n.14, 225–34; Sharp, above n.14, 92–101.

[37] FD Wormuth, *The Origins of Modern Constitutionalism* (New York: Harper, 1949), 43.

[38] Brailsford, above n.5, 255. [39] Woolfe, above n.14, 223.

[40] The Leveller views at Putney were represented mainly by Colonel Thomas Rainsborough, John Wildman and William Petty. For excerpts, see Sharp, above n.14, 102–30, including the famous debate over voting rights between Ireton ('no person has a right to this that hath not a permanent fixed interest in this kingdom') and Rainsborough ('I think the poorest he that is in England has a life to live as the greatest he ...'); both at 103. On the context and significance of the debates see: M Mendle (ed.), *The Putney Debates of 1647: The Army, the Levellers and the English State* (Cambridge: Cambridge University Press, 2001).

[41] SD Glover, 'The Putney Debates: Popular versus Elitist Republicanism' (1999) 164 *Past & Present* 47–80.

crunch came, however, once he felt that discussion about democracy, especially within the Army, was likely to undermine discipline. The turning point was the King's flight on 11 November 1647 from Hampton Court to the Isle of Wight on the pretext that Levellers were planning to murder him. The general alarm that the event raised enabled army discipline to be restored and put Cromwell back in control.[42] The King's flight led eventually to the second civil war beginning in the summer of 1648 as the Scots army under the Duke of Hamilton invaded. The Scots, however, were put to rout at Preston.

By 1648 the Levellers had reached their highest point of party organization, but their claims began to sound more ambivalent. Having failed to get the full support of the Army at Putney for the establishment of a new constitution to be ratified by the people, they returned to the practice of petitioning Parliament. After six years of civil war they contended that the issue of authority had to be resolved by removing the constitutional role of the King and Lords. It is, they suggested, 'impossible for us to believe that... the safety or freedom of the Nation' can be achieved while we are 'governed either by 3 or 2 Supremes, especially where experience has proved them so apt to differ in their judgements concerning freedom or safety'.[43] They also held meetings with the Independents in the course of which it was agreed that a Convention should be called of representatives of both the Army and the people to draw up a second *Agreement of the People*, which could then be ratified by the 'well affected' of the nation. At this critical moment the Grandees clearly needed the Levellers' support. It seemed as if the military power wielded by Cromwell and Ireton could be combined with Leveller constitutional ideas to bring about a new constitutional settlement.

But this was not to be. On 2 December, when it appeared that Parliament might agree a settlement on the King's terms, the Army arrived in London and four days later Pride's Purge took place.[44] When Colonel Pride's soldiers blocked the door of the Commons and allowed only those members favoured by Army leaders to take their seats, Cromwell's pre-eminent position was entrenched. The Army had determined that the old constitution could not be restored: Charles was immediately brought to London, placed on trial, and on 30 January 1649 executed. But although their discussions with the Army Council continued into early January, the Levellers realized that they had been deceived; while the Purge had destroyed the power of the old Parliament, this was not going to lead to the dissolution of Parliament or to the reconstitution of governmental authority. On 4 January 1649 the Commons resolved that 'the people are under God the original of all just power' and that 'the Commons of England in Parliament assembled, being chosen by and representing

---

[42] Following the King's escape, a half-hearted rebellion by some Leveller-inspired regiments was quickly put down at Ware, with three ringleaders being summarily sentenced to death, but allowed to cast lots so that only one was executed: see Brailsford, above n.5, Ch.14; M Kishlansky, 'What Happened at Ware?' (1982) 25 *Hist. J.* 827–39.

[43] *To the Right Honourable, the Commons of England* (Petition of September, 1648) in Wolfe, above n.14, 279–90 at 284; Haller and Davies, above n.14, 147–55, at 149.

[44] See D Underdown, *Pride's Purge: Politics in the Puritan Revolution* (Oxford: Clarendon Press, 1971).

the people, have the supreme power in this nation'.[45] Although this resolution reads as if it has been directly copied from the *Remonstrance*, it did nothing to vindicate the Leveller programme. Who, they asked, had authorized Colonel Pride to choose this Parliament on behalf of the people?

In mid-December, Lilburne reported that Army leaders—and especially Ireton, 'the cunningest of Machiavellians'—had 'cozened and deceived us'.[46] They therefore decided immediately to publish this second *Agreement of the People* before the Grandees were able to modify it further.[47] But events moved in a different direction: following the execution of the King the Rump Parliament abolished the House of Lords and the office of the King and established a Council of State. Although not opposed to the King's execution, Lilburne expressed concern about the process: were not the Royalists now being subjected to precisely the same illegitimate treatment before a special court of Parliament to which he had himself been exposed? The Levellers therefore continued to agitate, arguing that the Army and the Rump had no greater authority from the people than the Long Parliament had possessed.

This agitation led, on 28 March 1649, to the arrest of the Leveller leaders: Lilburne, Walwyn, Overton, and Thomas Prince. After their arrest, they arranged for the publication, on 1 May 1649 of the third and final *Agreement of the People*.[48] This was their most fully developed programme. Whereas the first had focused on general principles and the second on specific grievances, this Agreement sought to blend both. It was also the most radical of the Leveller constitutions. Since the authors wrote it while they were in the Tower, they obviously had no concerns about being arrested and they had no reason to try to modify their argument in the hope of winning support from within the Army leadership.

By this stage, however, the game was up. On 24 April 1649, a minor mutiny in one of the regiments stationed in London was put down and its Leveller ringleader, Robert Lockyer, executed. In May another Leveller rebellion occurred among the troopers of Scoop's Horse, and this Cromwell dealt with at Burford.[49] Leveller resistance within the army was over. In October of that year came what should have been the dramatic climax of Lilburne's political career. Having concluded that his recent pamphlets offered sufficient evidence to convict him of treason, the Council of State put Lilburne on trial at the Guildhall. But Lilburne managed to convince the jury that they were judges not only of fact but also of law, and pleaded with them to do that which was just. And then, as the trial report states: 'The people with a loud voice cried, Amen, Amen, and gave an extraordinary great hum; which made the Judges look something untowardly about them, and caused Major-General Skippon to

---

[45] For the resolution see Brailsford, above n.5, 460.

[46] Lilburne's account is to be found in his *Legal Fundamental Liberties*, above n.25, at 423; the relevant excerpts are also to be found in Wolfe, above n.14, 411–24, at 420.

[47] [Second Agreement] *Foundations of Freedom; or An Agreement of the People* (15 December 1648), in Wolfe, above n.14, 293–303.

[48] [Third Agreement] *An Agreement of the Free People of England* (1 May 1649) in Wolfe, above n.14, 400–10.

[49] See Brailsford, above n.5, Ch.24. (The Army took 340 prisoners and the court martial chose four from their leaders to be sentenced to death.)

send for three more fresh companies of foot-soldiers'.[50] The jury found him not guilty.[51] That night, there were bonfires across London and on 8 November Lilburne and his three fellow prisoners were released. The Leveller leaders were free, but as a political force they were entirely spent.

After release, Overton, Walwyn, and Prince appear to have taken the Engagement, the pledge requiring all citizens to state that they would be true and faithful to the laws of the Commonwealth. Some of their leaders, such as John Wildman, later converted to the republican theories which James Harrington set out in 1656 in *Oceana*.[52] Lilburne's story is even more surprising: ordered to take the Engagement, he complied but explained away his oath by saying that he defined the Commonwealth as the people and its fundamental laws rather than the governmental system established by the Council of State. Then in 1652 he was banished from England for scandalizing a Member of Parliament and was threatened with execution should he ever return. But return he did in 1653 and, again facing death, was once more acquitted by a jury.[53] Then he was imprisoned and having converted to Quakerism during his confinement remained a prisoner till his death in 1657.

V. Leveller Constitutional Thought

It is easy to romanticize this story of heroic failure. The main characters are larger-than-life, the cause is principled, and the prose is fresh, direct, and compelling. But this should not obscure the point that Leveller political tactics were inept. Wootton has convincingly argued that the movement had three critical flaws. Knowing that army officers were sceptical of their egalitarianism, they failed to develop any independent military strength. Drawing support both from religious sects who wanted toleration and soldiers who wanted fair treatment, they could not stop their support ebbing away the moment Cromwell offered both toleration and regular pay. Finally, notwithstanding their principled claims, they 'had no effective strategy for consolidating power and preparing the background for elections'.[54] The Levellers did not seem to realize, as did some of their radical contemporaries, that the reforms they were advocating would be unlikely to bring about the desired change.[55] For these

---

[50] 4 St.Tr. 1270–470, at 1395.

[51] For a detailed analysis of this trial see: HW Wolfram, 'John Lilburne: Democracy's Pillar of Fire' (1952) 3 *Syracuse Law Rev.* 213–58.

[52] Frank, above n.23, 224–7. In 1685 Wildman, having advocated the assassination of James II, was obliged to flee to Holland, though after the 1688 Revolution he was elected to the Convention Parliament. The reference is to J Harrington, *The Commonwealth of Oceana* [1656], JGA Pocock ed. (Cambridge: Cambridge University Press, 1992).

[53] 5 St.Tr. 407–49.   [54] Wootton, above n.6, 415–16.

[55] See, e.g., C Hill, *Milton and the English Revolution* (London: Faber, 1977), 170: 'Milton rejected the Leveller plea for a wider franchise, on the realistic ground that it would *increase* the power of the men of property, by bribery and corruption, to return their own nominees. Given the influence of landlords and parsons, in the absence of a secret ballot, a free vote of the electorate proposed by the Levellers would probably have established a Royalist government, and would certainly not have established a democracy.'

reasons historians have often marginalized their role in the English Revolution.[56] And in view of the idealistic twentieth century appropriation of the Levellers by various causes, this has not been without justification.[57]

But it is more surprising that political theorists have ignored their arguments. Wootton speculates that this may be because of the uncertain status of the English civil war: was it the first modern political revolution or the last of Europe's religious wars? This combined with the fact that the Levellers 'did not write in Latin, quote authorities, or define their own relationship to established traditions of political theory'.[58] And of course modern British political thought has mainly focused on the ends rather than the forms of government.[59]

Whatever their status in history or political theory the Levellers, I suggest, made a major contribution to political jurisprudence. In order to justify this claim, it is necessary to show how the Levellers were the first to present in a systematic form the foundational elements of modern constitutional democracy. Certainly, they were influenced by earlier political movements.[60] But their importance lies in the fact that, despite having to formulate their ideas in the maelstrom of revolutionary upheaval, they were able to mould political ideals into a practical constitutional scheme. From the general body of Leveller writing, including the various Petitions and the three *Agreements*,[61] eleven fundamental principles of constitutional democracy can be identified.

The first and most basic is that political power originates with the people. Leveller tracts were all drafted on the assumption of the intrinsic freedom and equality of the individual. As bearers of natural freedoms, the people might properly give up some of their liberties for 'the peace and prosperity of the Commonwealth', but only on the basis of consent.[62] Consequently, the *Third Agreement* opened with a novel formulation that has become an almost universally adopted trope of modern constitution-making: '*We the free People* of England... agree to ascertain our

---

[56] One historian who does not underestimate their role, nevertheless argues that 'any notion of a "Leveller Party" is misleading... The movement never established a large-scale organisation of its own. Its leaders were at their most powerful speaking on behalf of constituencies which were not precisely theirs. The most important of these were the London gathered churches from 1645, and the army from 1647. They were consequently to be "betrayed" and "abandoned" by both in turn.' See Scott, above n.7, 270–1.

[57] See esp. B Worden, 'The Levellers in history and memory, c.1660–1960' in Mendle, above n.40, 256–82 at 257: 'Might it not be equally well asked why the Levellers, whom few people before the twentieth century thought a worthy subject of historical investigation, have come to be taken so seriously'.

[58] Wootton, above n.6, 416.

[59] This conviction is best expressed in Alexander Pope's, *Essay on Man*, Epistle 3: 'For forms of government let fool's contest/whate'er is best administered is best'. Cf. D Hume, 'That politics may be reduced to a science' in his *Political Essays*, K Haakonssen ed. (Cambridge: Cambridge University Press, 1994), 4–15.

[60] The most obvious direct influences can be found in Calvinist resistance theories of the late sixteenth century: see Q Skinner, *The Foundations of Modern Political Thought* (Cambridge: Cambridge University Press, 1978), Vol.2, Pt.3; RN Kingdon, 'Calvinism and Resistance Theory, 1550–1580' in Burns (ed.), above n.6, 193–218.

[61] On the differing formulations of the three agreements see: I Gentles, 'The *Agreements of the people* and the political contexts, 1647–1649' in Mendle, above n.40, 148–74.

[62] *Third Agreement*, Wolfe, 402.

Government...'.[63] This expresses the principle of *popular sovereignty*,[64] a principle expressing a conviction about the authorizing power, but not prescribing any particular form of government.[65]

Secondly, the Levellers contended that those occupying the office of government have authority only because they have been authorized to decide on behalf of the people. In the words of the *Third Agreement*: 'That the supreme authority of England...shall be and reside henceforth in a Representative of the people consisting of four hundred persons'. This is the principle, consequential on the first, of *representation*. There is no liberty, they argued, if law-giving power is not in the hands of the people or their representatives.[66] During the 1640s this meant that neither the King nor the Lords appointed by Kings possessed authority. Supreme authority, as the *Remonstrance* and the various Petitions made plain, vested only in the 'Commons in Parliament assembled', a rather different institution to that of the 'King-in-Parliament'.

Since it is 'a Truth which you cannot but acknowledge'[67] that the people are the principals and government their agents, government must be an office of trust. To ensure that representatives act in accordance with the wishes of the people and that the people have an equal say in the business of government, appropriate mechanisms of authorization and recall must be in place. This leads to the third principle, that of *democracy*. Concerned about the disparities in traditional arrangements, in each of the Agreements the Levellers advocated proportionate representation.[68] And in addition to proposing the rationalization of constituency size, they also advocated universal manhood suffrage.[69]

---

[63] Ibid. (emphasis supplied).

[64] D Wootton, 'The Levellers' in J Dunn (ed.), *Democracy: The Unfinished Journey, 508BC to AD 1993* (Oxford: Oxford University Press, 1993), 71–89, at 71: 'The Levellers are the first modern political movement organized around the idea of popular sovereignty'. The idea was nevertheless in wide circulation at the time: see, e.g., MA Judson, 'Henry Parker and the Theory of Parliamentary Sovereignty' in *Essays in History and Political Theory in Honor of Charles Howard McIlwain* (Cambridge: Harvard University Press, 1936), Ch.5.

[65] ES Morgan, *Inventing the People: The Rise of Popular Sovereignty in England and America* (New York: Norton, 1989), 56: 'The sovereignty of the people was not a repudiation of the sovereignty of God. God remained the ultimate source of all governmental authority, but attention now centered on the immediate source, the people. Though God authorized government, He did it through the people, and in doing so He set them above their governors.'

[66] *Remonstrance* (Wolfe, 113): 'if you or any other shall assume, or exercise any Power, that is not derived from our Trust and choice thereunto, that Power is no less than usurpation and an oppression'.

[67] *Remonstrance* (Wolfe, 113).

[68] *Second Agreement*, cl.II (Wolfe, at 295–6): 'That the people of England being at this day very unequally distributed, by Counties, Cities or Boroughs for the election of their Representatives, be more indifferently proportioned and to this end... [the Agreement then prescribes a precise allocation of constituency representation across England and Wales]'. See also *First Agreement*, cl.II (Wolfe, 226–7); *Third Agreement*, cl.I (Wolfe, 403).

[69] *Third Agreement*, cl.I: 'all men of the age of one and twenty years and upwards (not being servants, or receiving alms, or having served the late King in Arms or Voluntary Contributions) shall have their voices; and be capable of being elected to that Supreme Trust' (Wolfe, 402–3). Cf. Second Agreement, cl.II.3 (Wolfe, 298), imposing a property restriction of an estate worth £50. For debate about the Leveller commitment to democracy see CB Macpherson, *The Political Theory of Possessive Individualism: Hobbes to Locke* (Oxford: Oxford University Press, 1962), Ch.3; JC Davis, 'The Levellers and Democracy' (1965) 40 *Past & Present* 174–80; K Thomas, 'The Levellers and the Franchise' in GE Aylmer (ed.), *The*

The fourth principle, closely connected, is a distinctive feature of Leveller thought. Operating on the maxim 'power corrupts', they proposed the establishment of a range of devices to ensure that office-holders could never forget their office was held on trust for the purpose of promoting the public good.[70] These included annual parliaments[71] and to ensure that oligarchical rule could not be established it was proposed that no member of one Parliament could be elected to the next[72] and no Member of Parliament may hold public office or maintain a legal practice.[73] This is the principle of *accountability*. It is also expressed in the *Second Agreement* by a proposal to make government officials—and the Council of State to be established 'for the managing of public affairs'—appointed by and answerable to the Parliament.[74] But in the *Third Agreement* the idea of a Council of State is removed altogether and during periods of parliamentary adjournment the business is to be conducted by a parliamentary committee.[75] This concern over the usurpation of power by any faction even extended to the elimination of the power of patronage from the office of government by making the great majority of executive officers directly elected.[76]

These first four principles established the basis of a system of representative, responsible, accountable, and democratic government. Before addressing the remaining principles, I want to consider a general assumption underpinning the Leveller scheme. Most importantly, Leveller writings recognize the complex point that the sovereign state should be conceived to be both absolute and limited. Political power must first be conceptualized as absolute in the sense that the authority of the people to fashion the political world is unbounded and not limited by history, custom, or inherited religious beliefs.[77] But they also recognized that this political world of public autonomy, being a constructed world, is itself bounded by the conditions of its establishment. The most important condition for the establishment of this

---

Interregnum: The Quest for Settlement, 1646–1660 (London: Macmillan, 1972), 57–78; CB Macpherson, *Democratic Theory: Essays in Retrieval* (Oxford: Oxford University Press, 1973), Ch.12.

[70] In their own language, such institutional constraints are necessary 'for avoiding the many dangers and inconveniences apparently arising from the long continuance of the same persons in Authority': *Third Agreement*, cl.V (Wolfe, 403).

[71] *Third Agreement*, cl.VIII (Wolfe, 404). The *First Agreement* (cl.III) had specified 'a Parliament once in two years' (Wolfe, 227), though the *Remonstrance* referred to the need to maintain 'our free choice of a Parliament once every year' (Wolfe, 129).

[72] *Third Agreement*, cl.IV (Wolfe, 403)

[73] *Third Agreement*, cl.III (Wolfe, 403); see also *Second Agreement*, cl.V (Wolfe, 299).

[74] *Second Agreement*, cl.IV (Wolfe, 299).   [75] *Third Agreement*, cl.VIII (Wolfe, 405).

[76] Petition of January 1648, *To the Supreme Authority of England, the Commons Assembled in Parliament*, cl.11: 'that some chosen Representatives of every Parish proportionably may be the Electors of Sheriffs, Justices of the Peace, Committee-men, Grand jury men, and all ministers of Justice whatsoever, in the respective counties' (Wolfe, 263, at 269). The radical character of this proposal is highlighted by Brailsford, 321: 'It meant first of all decentralisation, the self-government of every parish, hundred and county, instead of the nomination of its rulers from Westminster. More important still, it deposed the landowning ruling class, who had hitherto filled every administrative and judicial post as a matter of course.'

[77] See, e.g., Petition of January 1648, cl.2: 'That as we conceive all Governors and Magistrates, being the ordinance of man before they be the ordinance of God, and no authority being of God but what is erected by the mutual consent of a People …' (Wolfe, 265).

modern world is the recognition of the intrinsic equality and liberty of the individuals who comprise it. These are the conditions of private autonomy.

This conception of sovereignty acknowledges the complexity of political power. Political power is not located in the authority of the established institutions of government to impose their commands; that is merely the distributive aspect of power. The essence of power is to be found in the way it is generated, and it is generated by the drawing together of a people in ties of allegiance to a particular constitution of authority.[78] If authority is ultimately a product of the consent of 'the people', they have to transcend their manifest differences and material inequalities to participate in a collective exercise of imagination. This may require those in positions of authority to promote certain stories of peoplehood.[79] But it also requires recognition that the conditions of establishment are not just limitations on political power; they simultaneously enable the building of the modern state.[80] The constitutional framework is not so much an imposed constraint on governmental power as the architectural form through which such power can be generated.

These general observations provide the basis for understanding the remaining features of the Leveller constitutional scheme. Given the period in which they were writing, it is not surprising that Leveller tracts did not fully embrace this approach to the constitution of sovereignty. Their demands are primarily expressed as classical liberal claims to freedom from government rather than the more republican possibility of promoting freedom through government. But having argued for a system of representative, responsible, accountable, and democratic government, the Levellers did identify the enabling conditions of modern constitution-building.

In explaining the fifth principle, their distinctive name is relevant. The Levellers acquired their name from their opponents, who used it as a term of abuse and a

---

[78] This argument, drawing on the work of Hannah Arendt, is what elsewhere I have called a relational conception of sovereignty: Loughlin, IPL, Ch.5.

[79] The Levellers used similar arguments of peoplehood when they invoked the myth that the entire structure of English government was the product of the 'Norman yoke', which had suppressed the fundamental liberties of the English people as expressed in their ancient Anglo-Saxon constitution: see, e.g., *Remonstrance* (Wolfe, 112–30, at 123, 124–5, 128); C Hill, 'The Norman Yoke' in his *Puritanism and Revolution* (London: Secker & Warburg, 1958), 50–122; RB Seaborg, 'The Norman Conquest and the Common Law: The Levellers and the Argument from Continuity' (1981) 24 *The Historical J.* 791–806. Although this is hardly the argument of 'moderns', it should be noted that the Levellers adopted a radical version of this myth. In contradistinction to those who, like Sir Edward Coke, claimed that the common law protected those fundamental freedoms, the Levellers argued that the common law itself, with its Latin and law-French complexities, was itself part of the Norman oppression: see, e.g., J Lilburne, 'England's Birth-Right Justified' (1645) in W Haller (ed.), *Tracts on Liberty in the Puritan Revolution* (New York: Columbia University Press, 1934), vol.3, 257–307. Pocock thus considered that 'in reality, no two attitudes of mind could have been more deeply opposed' than those of Coke and the Leveller leaders: JGA Pocock, *The Ancient Constitution and the Feudal Law* (Cambridge: Cambridge University Press, rev. edn 1987), 126. It might also be noted that Milton went even further and argued that Parliament was 'a Norman or French word, a monument of our ancient servitude; the name should be abolished, and perhaps the thing too': Hill, above n.55, 114. This point may explain why, throughout the Agreements, the Levellers eschew the word 'Parliament' and refer instead to 'the Representative': e.g., *Third Agreement*, cl.IV (Wolfe, 403): 'That no Member of the present Parliament shall be capable of being elected of the next Representative'.

[80] See S Holmes, *Passions & Constraint: On the Theory of Liberal Democracy* (Chicago: University of Chicago Press, 1995), Ch.4.

means of discrediting them.[81] But although embracing the term, they did not propose social or economic levelling.[82] This was the aim of what were sometimes called the 'True Levellers', Gerrard Winstanley's Diggers.[83] What the Levellers stood for was not the equal distribution of property but the elimination of all legal and political privileges.[84] In the name of equality, the Levellers promoted political levelling. They acknowledged the principle of public autonomy—the *autonomy of the public domain*.

Despite being formed by a leadership with radical religious convictions, the Levellers were a secular constitutional movement. They advocated the separation of church and state, arguing that the state must not tax the people to prop up an established church, so tithes and other forms of clerical maintenance must be abolished.[85] Similarly, the state must not impose Ministers on any parish,[86] and no one should be excluded 'from bearing office in the Commonwealth for any opinion or practice in religion'.[87] The state must be secular precisely because it was supreme. The sole basis on which supremacy is to be yielded is that the state only exists to address matters of public welfare and concern. This sixth principle thus reinforces the autonomy of the public domain but reveals its correlative principle, that of *private autonomy*. Because the state is an expression of the equality and freedom of all, it can have no power to interfere in matters of conscience.

This sixth principle of private autonomy reveals the core of the claim to civil liberty—freedom of conscience and religious worship, on which foundation the rights to freedom of speech, freedom of expression, and freedom of association are established.[88] But the Levellers went further than simply stating that as a matter of prudence the state should not interfere in these matters. Their Agreements state that the powers delegated to government cannot include the power to encroach on the

---

[81] In 1647 Marchamont Nedham referred to the King as having christened the Agitators 'by the name of Levellers, a most apt title for such a despicable and desparate knot to be known by, that endeavour to cast down and level the enclosures of nobility, gentry and propriety': Nedham in *Mercurius Politicus*, 16 November 1647; cited in Brailsford, 309. This attack was also extended in Nedham, *The Case of the Commonwealth of England Stated* (London, 1650). But note Scott's argument that Nedham may himself also have been the author of a notorious Leveller tract, *Vox Plebis, or, The People's Out-cry Against Oppression, Injustice, and Tyranny* (1646): see J Scott, *Commonwealth Principles: Republican Writing of the English Revolution* (Cambridge: Cambridge University Press, 2004), 82–4.

[82] See *Third Agreement*, cl.XXX: 'We therefore agree and declare, that it shall not be in the power of any Representative ...[to] level men's estates, destroy property, or make all things common' (Wolfe, 409); *Second Agreement*, cl.VI.8 (Wolfe, 301).

[83] See Hill, above n.3, Ch.7; A Bradstock (ed.), *Winstanley and the Diggers, 1649–1999* (London: Frank Cass, 2000).

[84] See *Third Agreement*, cl.XIII: 'That all privileges or exemptions of any persons from the laws, or from the ordinary course of legal proceedings, by virtue of any tenure, grant, charter, patent, degree or birth, or any place of residence, or refuge, or privilege of Parliament, shall be henceforth void and null; and the like not to be made nor revived again.' (Wolfe, 406); *Second Agreement*, cl.VI.5 (Wolfe, 300).

[85] *Third Agreement*, cl.XXIII (Wolfe, 408).   [86] *Third Agreement*, cl.XXIV (Wolfe, 408).

[87] *Third Agreement*, cl.XXVI (Wolfe, 408); this clause includes a proviso—'excepting such as maintain the Pope's (or other foreign) supremacy'—that makes it plain that the objection is not to religious worship but to lines of earthly allegiance.

[88] W Walwyn, 'A Parable' (1646) in *Writings*, above n.10, 245–62, at 262: 'if ever men shall kindly be brought to be of one mind, I see it must be by liberty of discourse, and liberty of writing; we must not pretend to more fallible certainty than other men'.

individual's basic liberties,[89] over what Overton called a person's 'self-propriety'.[90] Institutionalization of the principle of private autonomy thus yields a seventh principle—that of basic liberties, or what today would be termed *basic rights*. Although this principle has at its core the right to full religious freedom, immunity is established for political rather than religious reasons. As the previous century of religious wars in Europe had shown, entangling questions of faith with affairs of state had weakened the state's authority; 'nothing having caused more distractions, and heart burnings in all ages', notes the *Third Agreement*, 'than persecution and molestation for matters of conscience'.[91] Placing matters of conscience beyond the public domain avoided basic conflicts that undermined the unity of a people, and thereby formed a vital method of effective state-building.

The eighth principle also concerns state-building: the necessity of maintaining a *separation of governmental powers*. This principle is most clearly expressed in the *Second Agreement*: 'That the Representatives intermeddle not with the execution of Laws, nor give judgement upon any man's person or estate, where no Law hath been provided'.[92] Parliament should make the laws but not be involved in their execution or interpretation. This was new,[93] and the reason it was not developed further is to be found in the proviso to the clause: 'saving only in calling to an account, and

---

[89] The *Third Agreement* states that the Parliament 'are in the extent and exercise of power to follow the direction and rules of this agreement' (cl.VII; Wolfe, 404). It then states (cl.X; Wolfe, 405): 'That we do not empower or entrust our said representatives to continue in force, or make any laws, oaths or covenants, whereby to compel by penalties or otherwise any person to any thing in or about matters of faith, religion, or God's worship or to restrain any person from the profession of his faith, or exercise of religion according to his conscience'. And amplifying this principle, cl.XVI (Wolfe, 406) states: 'That it shall not be in the power of any Representative to punish, or cause to be punished, any person or persons from refusing to answer to questions against themselves in criminal cases'. On the importance of this provision, see LW Levy, *Origins of the Fifth Amendment: The Right Against Self-Incrimination* (New York: Oxford University Press, 1968), esp. Ch.9 ('Lilburne and the Abolition of the Oath'); JL Rauh, Jr, 'The Privilege against Self-Incrimination from John Lilburne to Ollie North' (1988) 5 *Constitutional Commentary* 405–10.

[90] Overton, *An Arrow to All Tyrants* (12 October 1646; Sharp, 55): 'To every individual in nature is given an individual property by nature, not to be invaded or usurped by any. For every one, as he is himself, so he has a self-propriety, else he could not *be* himself.... No man hath power over my rights and liberties, and I over no mans'... Each man can delegate only those powers which will not undercut his inherent rights or involve him in self-injury. Macpherson, *Possessive Individualism*, above n.69, uses this text to emphasize 'the proprietorial quality of the Levellers' individualism...What makes a man human is his freedom from other men. Man's essence is freedom. Freedom is proprietorship of one's own person and capacities' (at 141). This is an economistic interpretation that underplays the relative autonomy of political discourse.

[91] *Third Agreement*, cl.X (Wolfe, 405).

[92] *Second Agreement*, cl.VI.6 (Wolfe, 300); see also *Third Agreement*, cl.XIV (Wolfe, 406)

[93] See, e.g., MJC Vile, *Constitutionalism and the Separation of Powers* (Oxford: Oxford University Press, 1967), 49. After citing from a Lilburne pamphlet complaining that 'the House itself was never...betrusted with a Law executing power', Vile comments: 'This is a new and vitally important element, which resulted from the experience of the Long Parliament during the Civil War. The assertion of the generality of law is thousands of years old, but this was something more. Not only was law to be couched in general terms, but also the *legislature* must be restricted to the making of law, and not meddle itself with particular cases. This was indeed a major step in the development of the separation of powers. The Levellers also made the same demand for the exclusion of placemen from the legislature which was to characterize the eighteenth century, and which is an essential aspect of the doctrine.'

punishing public officers for abusing or failing in their trust'.[94] The Levellers were so apprehensive about executive power that, rather than confining it to its own sphere, they sought to ensure it remained subject to the strictest supervision by either the electorate or by Parliament. The necessity of separation is therefore expressed mainly in the argument that legislative and executive/judicial powers should never be combined.[95] Parliament should not act, as it then did, as a tribunal as well as a legislature. By separating the formulation and application of laws, the conception of law as a set of rules of conduct binding all equally is strengthened and people's faith in their system of government is enhanced.

One principle implicit in the division of powers but needing to be specified is the necessity of maintaining the *independence of the judiciary*. Leveller advocacy of judicial independence was of the first importance, though it tended to be wrapped up in more general arguments over the need for radical reform of the legal system. They distrusted courts and despised lawyers, arguing that the Normans had 'erected a trade of judges and lawyers, to sell justice and injustice at his own unconscionable rate'[96] and claiming it was 'a badge of slavery to our Norman Conqueror, to have our laws in the French tongue'.[97] They therefore demanded codified laws in plain English, legal fees to be precisely specified, the abolition of barbarous punishments, and the decentralization of national courts with a return to local justice in the hundreds.[98] In the *Second Agreement* they demand that Parliament 'rid[] this kingdom of those vermin and caterpillars, the Lawyers, the chief bane of this poor Nation'.[99] Judicial independence was a necessary but not sufficient condition of equality before the law. Without basic reforms making the law clear, precise, and accessible, independence in itself could not achieve much.

The last three principles—basic rights, separation of powers, and independence of the judiciary—form a broader tenth principle: *democracy requires a strong civil society*. The argument that government will abuse its authority unless it is checked also applies when governmental power is exercised by the people's representatives. 'My enmity', wrote Overton, 'is only against Tyranny, where ever I find it, whether

---

[94] *Second Agreement*, cl.VI.6 (Wolfe, 300).

[95] This claim, rooted in Lilburne's argument that parliamentary committees had no authority to determine specific disputes, was most vigorously expressed in the Petition of January, 1648, cl.4 (Wolfe, 266): No particular cause, whether criminal or other, which comes under the cognizance of the ordinary courts of justice, may be determined by this House, or any committee thereof; or any other, than by those courts, whose duty it is to execute such laws as this honourable House shall make.

[96] *Remonstrance*, in Wolfe, at 125.   [97] Petition of January 1648, cl.5 (Wolfe, 266).

[98] See D Veall, *The Popular Movement for Law Reform, 1640–1660* (Oxford: Clarendon Press, 1970), Ch.4, esp. 100–1. The general point about the positive consequences of codification is well made in A de Tocqueville, *Democracy in America* [1835], H Reeve trans. (New York: Vintage Books, 1990), vol.1, Ch.16, at 277: 'The French codes are often difficult to comprehend, but they can be read by everyone; nothing, on the other hand, can be more obscure and strange to the uninitiated than a legislation founded on precedents. The absolute need of legal aid that is felt in England and the United States, and the high opinion that is entertained of the ability of the legal profession, tend to separate it more and more from the people and to erect it into a distinct class. The French lawyer is simply a man extensively acquainted with the statutes of his country; but the English or American lawyer resembles the hierophants of Egypt, for like them he is the sole interpreter of an occult science.'

[99] *Second Agreement*, Wolfe, 303. Note also Lilburne's characterization of lawyers as 'horsleeches': see Frank, above n.23, 89.

in Emperor, King, Prince, Parliament, Presbyters, or People'.[100] An active civil society keeps government within boundaries. Democracy can be extended beyond its most basic meaning to authorize government and encompass the idea that government is a complex arrangement of rights and duties, institutions and practices. This theme, that Society must be defended,[101] was expressed in Leveller opposition to monopolies and their promotion of free trade.[102] It is also evident in their argument that a free press is essential 'to preserve any Nation from being liable to the worst of bondage'.[103]

The final constitutional principle was that of *the constitution as a body of fundamental law*. During the revolutionary period, it was commonplace to make an appeal to some inchoate notion of fundamental law. Even the coup d'état of Pride's Purge was explained away at the time by reference to the need to uphold a 'higher' law.[104] However, in *The Case of the Army Truly Stated*, drafted (primarily by John Wildman) in October 1647, the Levellers were more explicit. They argued that it must be 'positively and resolvedly insisted upon, that a law paramount be made, enacting it to be unalterable by Parliaments'.[105] This formulated the idea of fundamental law as a species of positive law, clarified in the *Third Agreement*, which specifies both the powers (e.g., art.9) and limitations (e.g., arts 10, 11, 14, 16–17) of the Representative and then states that 'it shall not be in the power of any Representative... to take away any part of this Agreement' and that 'all Laws made... contrary to any part of this Agreement are hereby made null and void'.[106]

With this innovation, the Leveller appeal to 'native rights'[107] was transformed into a concept of basic rights (the seventh principle above) at the same time as drawing a distinction between ordinary legislation and fundamental constitutional law. The Agreement might not have made provision for formal amendment and, not surprisingly given their views on the lawyers of their times, it did not award the judiciary the task of ensuring compliance with the constitution.[108] But it did capture

---

[100] R Overton, *Divine Observations Upon the London- Ministers Letter against Toleration* (1646), 16: cited in Frank, above n.23, 68.

[101] See M Foucault, *Society Must be Defended*, D Macey trans. (London: Penguin, 2003), which expresses particular interest in the Levellers' arguments (107–9).

[102] See, e.g., *The March Petition*, in Wolfe, 136–7, 139 (cl.6); *The January Petition*, 1648, in Wolfe, 263–72, at 268 (cl.9): 'That therefore all Monopolies whatsoever... be forthwith abolished, and a free trade restored'.

[103] *The Humble Petition*, 19 January 1649, in Wolfe, 326–30, at 328, which contains the fullest Leveller statement linking freedom of the press with the claims of civil liberty.

[104] J Goodwin, *Right and Might Well Met* (1648); cited in JW Gough, *Fundamental Law in English Constitutional History* (Oxford: Clarendon Press, 1955), 102–3.

[105] *The Case of the Army Truly Stated* in Wolfe, 198–222, at 212.

[106] *Third Agreement*, cl.30 in Wolfe, at 409–10.

[107] *First Agreement*, in Wolfe 226–34 at 228. By 'native rights' is meant the historic rights of the English people reflected in the customs and practices of the governing arrangements.

[108] This latter role was not clearly specified until Alexander Hamilton's classic statement in *The Federalist* No. 78, the terms of which echo the Leveller argument: 'No legislative act... contrary to the Constitution can be valid. To deny this, would be to affirm that the deputy is greater than his principal; that the servant is above his master; that the representatives of the people are superior to the people themselves.' But Hamilton continues: 'A constitution is, in fact, and must be regarded by the judges as, a fundamental law. It therefore belongs to them to ascertain its meaning as well as the meaning of any particular act proceeding from the legislative body. If there should happen to be an irreconcilable

the distinction between the constituent power of the people and the constituted authority of government that underpins modern constitutionalist thought.[109]

By extrapolating these constitutional principles from their remarkable writings, the Levellers present themselves as the world's first clear exponents of constitutional democracy. There is disagreement amongst historians about the significance of the English revolution: was it a modernizing movement that promoted republican ideas or was it entangled in the backward-looking arguments of sects seeking to restore the purity of Christianity and those seeking to protect the ancient constitution against modernizing abuses?[110] The political significance of the Levellers inevitably gets caught up in these wider debates, and there is no doubting Wolfe's assessment that they 'were last-ditch idealists, born centuries too soon, impatient, impulsive, unwilling or unable to gauge the barriers that barred their way to their utopian England'.[111] But as exponents of a constitutional framework for governing, the Levellers were thoroughly modern. 'Whatever our forefathers were', proclaimed the *Remonstrance*, 'we are men of the present age and ought to be absolutely free from all kinds of exorbitancies, molestations or arbitrary power'.[112] The constitutional scheme they devised would play no positive role in the shaping of the modern British system, though it did exert a guiding influence on those who, following revolutionary upheaval in the latter-half of the following century, drafted the world's first modern constitutions.[113] This brings us then to another question: why did the emerging British constitution deviate so far from Leveller constitutionalism?

VI. Leveller Principles and British Practice

Leveller principles run counter to British constitutional practice. Whether we focus on their major proposals, such as the need to adopt a formal constitution or the necessity of maintaining a strict separation of church and state, or on more specific

---

variance between the two . . . the Constitution ought to be preferred to the statute, the intention of the people to the intention of their agents.' J Madison, A Hamilton, and J Jay, *The Federalist Papers* [1788], I Kramnick ed. (London: Penguin, 1987), 438–9. Note also that in *Marbury* v. *Madison* 5 US (1 Cranch) 137 (1803), the decision establishing judicial review, Marshall CJ referred to a written constitution as 'forming the fundamental and paramount law of the nation'.

[109] See M Loughlin and N Walker (eds), *The Paradox of Constitutionalism: Constituent Power and Constitutional Form* (Oxford: Oxford University Press, 2007); M Loughlin, IPL, Ch.6; M Loughlin, 'The Concept of Constituent Power' (2014) 13 *European J. of Political Theory* 218–37.

[110] This question is also bound up with the shift in meaning of the idea of revolution in modern times, on which see especially, R Koselleck, 'Historical Criteria of the Modern Concept of Revolution' in his *Futures Past: On the Semantics of Historical Time*, K Tribe trans. (New York: Columbia University Press, 2004), Ch.3.

[111] Wolfe, above n.14, 386.   [112] *Remonstrance* (Wolfe, 130).

[113] The precise influence of the Levellers on American thinkers remains speculative: see, e.g., Morgan, above n.65, esp. Ch.10; SH Beer, *To Make a Nation: The Rediscovery of American Federalism* (Cambridge MA: Harvard University Press, 1993), 310–12; MK Curtis, 'In Pursuit of Liberty: The Levellers and the American Bill of Rights' (1991) 8 *Constitutional Commentary* 359–93. On connections between Levellers, American and French drafters see G Jellinek, *The Declaration of the Rights of Man and of the Citizen: A Contribution to Modern Constitutional History*, M Farrand trans. (New York: Holt, 1901), which promotes the thesis that the French Declaration is for the most part copied from the American declarations, and that the American declarations and constitution in turn was greatly influenced by the 'remarkable document' [the *Second Agreement*] that the Levellers drafted for Cromwell's army council at Putney (at 63).

demands, such as annual parliaments or the requirement that a member of parliament cannot serve consecutive terms, Leveller principles cut across the grain of British experience. It took almost two centuries before rotten boroughs were finally eliminated, and universal manhood suffrage was not achieved until the twentieth century. Post-revolutionary constitutional arrangements evidently evolved along a very different track. Since Britain today conceives itself as a liberal democratic regime, this requires explanation.

This is a huge subject and my objective is only to demonstrate that a different philosophy of governing from that developed by the Levellers drove the evolving British constitutional practice. Contrary to those who today assert the authority of British 'constitutionalism',[114] I argue that British practice has been so consistent that one might be forgiven for thinking it was inspired by a deliberate policy of suppressing the principles of constitutionalism expounded by the Levellers.

This started immediately with Cromwell who, lacking popular support for the Commonwealth, had to impose his authority from above. Following his death in 1658, the revolution unravelled. In 1660, the monarchy was restored and the Commonwealth expunged from the official record.[115] But if the constitution of the Commonwealth fudged the question of popular support, the Restoration settlement moved even further from Leveller commitments. The Convention Parliament of 1660 restored both the King and the established Church, and the Church then reaffirmed the King's divine right. And even though adherence to popular sovereignty did not dictate a particular form of government, it was felt too dangerous to acknowledge a doctrine that had been invoked throughout the revolutionary period.

Yet the doctrine did resurface. During the Exclusion crisis the Whigs tried to alter the line of succession and in the 1688 Revolution they succeeded in doing so. For these purposes some notion of popular sovereignty had to be revived. The Whigs managed this process by adopting a highly attenuated form of the doctrine; ignoring basic questions of ultimate authority, they claimed that the people's will was that expressed by Parliament. Having determined that James had forfeited his crown, the Convention Parliament of 1688 altered the line of succession and invited William and Mary to reign jointly, with full executive authority vested in William. Since these changes could not be justified by existing law and practice, the constitutional issues were deliberately kept ambiguous, and these revolutionary actions

---

[114] See, e.g., D Feldman (ed.), *English Public Law* (Oxford: Oxford University Press, 2004), Ch.1A Fundamental Principles: 'Constitutional law in the United Kingdom... is dominated by three principles: the legislative supremacy of Parliament, the rule of law, and the separation of powers. Traditionally, the first of these has been regarded as much the most important... More recently, some scholars and judges have attached relatively more weight to the other two principles'(1.58). These latter principles have recently been promoted by 'the courts as custodians of the common law constitution' (1.117). For an elaboration of the idea of the common law constitution see TRS Allan, *Law, Liberty, and Justice: The Legal Foundations of British Constitutionalism* (Oxford: Clarendon Press, 1993).

[115] At the restoration, no statute was enacted to declare void all the legislation that had been passed between 1649 and 1660; the lack of legal authority was simply assumed. The assumption was that Charles I had been murdered, and Charles II therefore began his reign on 30 January 1649, even though it was only from 30 May 1660 that he was able to enjoy the fruits of his regal authority.

defended as being necessary to restore the proper workings of the ancient constitution.[116]

The 1688 settlement led to Whig supremacy in government for the next eighty years, a time when the main practices of modern parliamentary government were shaped. The Act of Settlement 1701 had in fact gone a considerable way towards prescribing in law a constitutional framework which would separate legislative and executive power but this was undone before it could take effect, enabling the practices of parliamentary government to evolve.[117] Parliamentary government was then strengthened by the Septennial Act 1715 which, contrary to the Leveller principle of annual parliaments, extended their life from three to seven years. This made Parliament less dependent on popular opinion, helped to shift executive power from the King to ministers, enabled the formation of a more consistent state policy, and ensured that Parliament—both Lords and Commons—was placed firmly under aristocratic control.[118]

Through this unusual system of rule, authority was wrested from the person of the King[119] and a sense of the people as the originating source of authority was finessed.[120] Rulers might need to respond to the people's concerns but they were not their agents. A Parliament controlled by the landed class, in which the people were only represented virtually, maintained a monopoly of speaking as the *vox populi*. Once this arrangement was set in place, all efforts at extending the franchise were resisted on the ground that Parliament should not use its statutory power to tamper with the 'matchless constitution'. And after 'the people' had asserted their claims during the American and French revolutions, resistance turned to outright hostility, putting back the cause of modest electoral reform in Britain for over forty years.

Crucial to this evolving system was the role of political parties. These came into existence not as expressions of democratic sentiment but as vehicles for managing Parliament. In place of the seventeenth century narrative whereby Parliament battled with the Crown for power, the Whig and Tory parties stridently competed for control of Parliament while being united in loyalty to the Crown.[121] Political

---

[116] See, e.g., W Blackstone, *Commentaries on the Laws of England* (Oxford: Clarendon Press, 1765) Vol.1, 204–11. See further M Loughlin, 'Constituent Power Subverted: From English Constitutional Argument to British Constitutional Practice' in Loughlin and Walker (eds), above n.109, 27–48, at 44.

[117] Regency Act 1706. See C Roberts, *The Growth of Responsible Government in Stuart England* (Cambridge: Cambridge University Press, 1966), Ch.10; Loughlin, FPL, Ch.9.VI.

[118] See J Cannon, *Parliamentary Reform, 1640–1832* (Cambridge: Cambridge University Press, 1973), 431–54, arguing that the Commons was essentially an annex of the Lords: the number of MPs who were sons of peers in 1690 was 32, and in 1754 it was 77.

[119] This process was reinforced by the Act of Settlement 1700, which had settled the crown on the Protestant heirs of Sophia, Electress of Hanover and made title to the crown subject to parliamentary approval. When Georg Ludwig of Hanover succeeded to the throne as George I in 1714, there were nearly sixty persons with stronger hereditary claims.

[120] In *The Secret History of the Scepter* (1715), Daniel Defoe argued that the sceptre (the symbol of executive power) had been grasped from the hand of the monarch by the House of Commons: 'the King would keep the Crown upon his head, and perhaps being a martial prince would take the management of the Sword into his own hand; but for the Scepter, that was their province': cited in Roberts, above n.117, at 411.

[121] W Bagehot, *The English Constitution* (1867) (Oxford: Oxford University Press, 2001), 16: 'It has been said that England invented the phrase "Her Majesty's Opposition", that it was the first government

argument took place not over the nature of the constitution but over the policies of the governing parties,[122] and the main constitutional understandings concerning parliamentary conduct, relations between Government and Parliament, and between Parliament and the people gradually evolved.[123] Consequently, the old regime of 'mixed government', of maintaining checks and balances within the structure of government, was replaced with the notion of balance between the parties. Such arrangements could only have been devised with governing authority entirely under the control of the landed class. They could never have been set to work in a more democratic environment.

Once parliamentary government had been established, the principle of parliamentary sovereignty, implicitly recognized in the Bill of Rights of 1688, could be formulated as a discrete legal concept. This doctrine had little in common with the Levellers' conception of parliamentary rule. In 1765, Sir William Blackstone devised a formulation that would acquire unassailable authority. He noted that 'in times of madness and anarchy' (i.e. 4 January 1648) the Commons had once passed a vote stating that what is passed by 'the commons in parliament assembled' shall have the force of law.[124] But he went on to explain how under Restoration legislation, when 'the constitution was restored in all its forms', it was made an offence to affirm this heresy.[125] Blackstone's conception emphasized the unity of the constituent parts of King, Lords and Commons, acting as the 'king in parliament'. His formulation, both illiberal and partial,[126] was a key element of a modernizing strategy. By projecting the idea of law as a species of command rather than an expression of ancient custom, all appeals to the 'fundamental liberties of the freeborn Englishman' were made redundant. By anchoring this idea of law in an Anglican conception of sovereign power for whom the enemy was Dissent,[127] all residual constitutional claims

---

which made a criticism of administration as much a part of the polity as administration itself.' See also AS Foord, *His Majesty's Opposition, 1714–1830* (Oxford: Oxford University Press, 1964), who shows that, although the expression was first used only in 1826, it was apt enough to define an important constitutional concept that had evolved over the previous century.

[122] See JCD Clark, 'A general theory of party, opposition and government, 1688–1832' (1980) 23 *Historical Journal* 295–325.

[123] Note in particular the triumph of the representative role of the MP, championed by Edmund Burke, which runs directly contrary to Leveller aspirations of mandate and recall. Burke explained that while he might owe his constituents the courtesy of listening to their opinions, they had no authority to impose instructions and mandates; although the member for Bristol, his duty was to act for the best interests of the whole country: 'Speech to the Electors of Bristol, 1774' in E Burke, *Speeches and Lectures on American Affairs* (London: Dent, 1908), 68–75.

[124] See above nn.43–4.

[125] Blackstone, *Commentaries*, above n.116, vol.1, 155.

[126] See E Barker, 'Blackstone on the British Constitution' in his *Essays on Government* (Oxford: Clarendon Press, 1945), 121–54 at 130–1: 'In part his illiberalism...was inevitable and involuntary. He was a lawyer. He was stating the legal theory of the constitution...But his illiberalism was also in some measure voluntary. A member of the established Church, and a beneficiary of the established political system of rotten boroughs, he did not escape partiality.'

[127] This Anglican conception was based on the conviction that 'religious disunity affronted God, threatened national security as well as the salvation of the people, and disrupted the peace of local communities': W Prest, *Albion Ascendant: English History, 1660–1815* (Oxford: Oxford University Press, 1998), 76. Note also that in addition to the Test and Corporations Acts, the Blasphemy Act 1698

rooted in the natural rights discourse of the radical religious sects of the Puritan revolution were purged.[128]

This overview shows how far removed from Leveller ideas was the modern constitutional settlement that evolved during the eighteenth century. The principle of the authorizing power of the people had been usurped by the constituted power (the King-in-Parliament), any active sense of democracy had been rejected, representation was virtual rather than actual, and public accountability mechanisms were almost non-existent since the system of government operated through patronage and electoral manipulation.[129] Although judicial independence had been instituted,[130] the system was leading to a fusion rather than a separation of legislative and executive power. Underpinned by the principle of parliamentary sovereignty, there could be no notion of constitutional law as higher law, or of basic rights since rights were simply entitlements conferred by positive laws. Nor, more generally, was there any clear sense of a public-private distinction since the system of government was bound up with landed wealth and civil status depended on adherence to religious orthodoxy.

When viewed though present-day juridical spectacles and measured against Leveller principles, this British inheritance is easy to criticize. But this would be to commit a normativist error. The decades following the 1688 Revolution not only marked the moment when modern constitutional practice was set in place; it was also the period in which the country changed from an agricultural to an industrial and commercial economy, when the English State was extended to form Great Britain,[131] when a relatively weak insular state was transformed into a major European power, and when the governing foundations were laid that enabled Britain rapidly to establish itself as the world's dominant trading economy and leading imperial power.

The link between constitutional arrangements and the growth of imperial power is not circumstantial. Scott has convincingly argued that these transformations were able to be effected through the formation after 1688 of an Anglo-Dutch state. This was first achieved through the 'construction of a functional English army' and bringing England into what some historians call the second Hundred Years' War that ended with the defeat of Napoleon, and then through a financial revolution that extended the tax base, created a new system of deficit financing and established the Bank of England modelled on the Dutch example of the Bank of Amsterdam.[132]

had made it an offence punishable by up to three years' imprisonment to deny the doctrine of the Trinity, the truth of Christianity, or the authority of Scripture.

[128] JCD Clark, *The Language of Liberty 1660-1832* (Cambridge: Cambridge University Press, 1994), 83–4.

[129] See Prest, above n.127, 125–7.

[130] Act of Settlement 1700, s.3. See also EP Thompson, *Whigs and Hunters: The Origins of the Black Act* (Harmondsworth: Penguin, 1977), 259: 'What is remarkable (we are reminded) is not that the laws were bent but the fact that there was, anywhere in the eighteenth century, a rule of law at all. To ask for greater justice than that is to display mere sentimentalism.'

[131] By the Treaty of Union 1707 between England and Scotland the kingdom of Great Britain was established and then in 1800, by the Act of Union with Ireland, the United Kingdom of Great Britain and Ireland was formed.

[132] Scott, above n.7, 474–86.

These changes built a powerful fiscal-military state, the details of which Brewer presents in a study that places finance, administration, and war—the 'hidden sinews which animated the British body politic'—at the centre of post-1688 developments.[133] War was the harbinger of constitutional modernization and 'the parliamentary monarchy was the centrepiece of the newly constructed English state'.[134] Parliament became the principal instrument of modern British state-building: 'The [seventeenth century] struggle was against arbitrary government not absolutism; for participation in government, not its abolition' and after 1688 'parliament was to show that it had the capacity to build the state'.[135]

One consequence of this pattern of development in Britain was that the growth of nineteenth-century nationalism, which in many parts of Europe was both populist and progressive, was more ambiguous. British symbols of national identity did not evolve from historic claims to the 'rights of the freeborn Englishman'; they were constructed from the symbols of monarchy, the established Church, and its accompanying aristocratic and anti-populist institutions and commitments.[136] This was reinforced with the formation of the British Empire and the extension of the imperial claims of the English. When the Levellers talked of the 'universality of the people' as the originating source of power,[137] they meant actual people living in their historic communities. But with the formation of the United Kingdom through treaties between 'equal' nations which in effect incorporated Scotland and Ireland into English forms of government, the idea of 'the people' or 'the nation' became a much more ambivalent notion, one that the governing elite had good reasons to stifle.

British practice has evolved as a discourse of governing. This does not mean that adherence to constitutional forms is not a vital aspect of governing; rather that the relationship between authority and right—between government and law—assumes a different form. 'In all governments', noted Hume, 'there is a perpetual intestine struggle, open or secret, between *authority* and *liberty*; and neither of them can ever absolutely prevail in the contest'.[138] But whereas constitutionalism treats positive law as the foundation of the activity of governing, statecraft treats law primarily as a tool of governing.

Modern British constitutional practice operates within a tradition of statecraft explicated by such practitioners as Halifax,[139] Bolingbroke,[140] and Burke.[141] It was

---

[133] J Brewer, *The Sinews of Power: War, Money and the English State, 1688–1783* (New York: Knopf, 1989), xvi.

[134] Scott, above n.7, 483.   [135] Scott, above, n.7, 495.

[136] See L Colley, *Britons: Forging the Nation, 1707–1837* (London: Pimlico, 1992); D Cannadine, 'The Context, Performance and Meaning of a Ritual: The British Monarchy and the "Invention of Tradition", c.1820–1977' in E Hobsbawm and T Ranger (eds), *The Invention of Tradition* (Cambridge: Cambridge University Press, 1983), 101–64.

[137] *Remonstrance* (title page); Wolfe, 112.

[138] D Hume, 'Of the origin of government' in his *Political Essays*, above n.59, 20–3, at 22.

[139] See, e.g., Viscount Halifax, 'The Character of a Trimmer' [1684] in his *Complete Works*, JP Kenyon ed. (Harmondsworth: Penguin, 1969), 49–102.

[140] Viscount Bolingbroke, 'The Idea of a Patriot King' [1738] in his *Political Writings*, D Armitage ed. (Cambridge: Cambridge University Press, 1998).

[141] See Ch.4 below.

forged by managing the tensions between authority and liberty, monarchical authority and popular control, and state and society. Monarchical government may have been constrained by law, fiscality, and constitutional practice, notes Pocock, but it also retained 'a far-reaching consultative machinery keeping it in contact with the shires, boroughs, parishes' and this machinery 'constituted a symbiosis of state and civil society which renders it unnecessary to think of them as parallel, let alone opposed entities'.[142] The modern British constitution is a constitution forged by statecraft.

This aspect of British governing practice explains why the Levellers' constitutional ideas had to be suppressed and the success of this policy also explains the striking fact that the Levellers spawned no followers. The only organization that might be claimed as their descendants were the Chartists of the 1830s and their story is instructive. An association uniting those protesting against poverty and economic privation with those concerned to reform the traditional, undemocratic constitutional arrangements, the Chartists found their alliance fatally undermined by Peel's introduction of social and economic reforms *without* undertaking a parallel process of constitutional reform.[143] This became a feature of the British parliamentary approach to reform over the following 150 or so years. It was evident in the twentieth century Labour movement's rejection of constitutional reform for the promotion of their policy objectives in favour of utilizing the inherited tools of the parliamentary state.[144] In this sense, Scott is right to claim that the British continue to live in Restoration times.[145]

VII. Conclusion

The basic precepts of constitutional democracy, the most influential legitimating discourse of modern government, was first presented by the Levellers in the course of the mid-seventeenth century English revolution. This achievement is commonly overlooked, not only because they were so quickly defeated by Cromwell but also because their ideas gained no currency during the subsequent course of British constitutional development. Leveller ideas acquired an intellectual vibrancy only via the American and French revolutionary movements of the late-eighteenth century.

Leveller constitutionalist discourse was vigorously suppressed precisely because it was antithetical, first to the policy of the Commonwealth, later to the policy of Anglo-Dutch state-building and then, throughout the eighteenth and nineteenth centuries, to the evolving imperial policies of British statecraft. From post-1688

---

[142] JGA Pocock, *Barbarism and Religion: Vol.2 Narratives of Government* (Cambridge: Cambridge University Press, 1999), 165.

[143] See G Stedman Jones, *Languages of Class: Studies in English Working Class History 1832–1982* (Cambridge: Cambridge University Press, 1983), Ch.3.

[144] Though not promoting the cause of constitutional modernization, the classic account of Labour's adherence to the traditions of parliamentarism is R Miliband, *Parliamentary Socialism: A Study in the Politics of Labour* (London: Merlin Press, 2nd edn. 1972).

[145] Scott, above n.7, 496.

developments there emerged an alternative and equally powerful discourse to that of constitutionalism, the discourse of governing. This discourse, otherwise known as statecraft, is antagonistic to constitutionalism, most basically over the question of whether societies need to be governed. Centring on the autonomous, rights-bearing individual who contracts to establish a framework of limited and accountable government, constitutionalism schematizes government in a juridical form. The discourse of statecraft, by contrast, recognizes the primacy of the governing relationship as a power relationship in which elites rule through a range of devices, including techniques that discipline and control subjects, and which in certain crucial respects escape the juridical frame of constitutionalism.[146]

Statecraft accepts the law-conditioned character of governmental authority, but subjects the autonomous 'world-making' aspects of constitutional discourse to a heavy dose of historical realism. The 'foundational' character of rights has to be modified by the necessity of rendering such claims compatible with competing claims of others and of collective well-being. The functional differentiation of governmental tasks is a useful technique of state-building only to the extent that 'separation' does not lead to deadlock. The autonomy of judicial reasoning cannot be taken too literally since 'the constitution is not a suicide pact'[147] and judges are servants of the state. The 'strong' civil society conducive to democracy is strong precisely because it has been disciplined.

These competing discourses have together shaped modern governmental authority. The tensions are played out in a number of registers: right and utility, liberty and order, equality and hierarchy, autonomy and heteronomy, legitimacy and efficacy, law and discipline, norm and fact, concept and practice. Neither can exist without the other: constitutionalism because it presents itself, as Leveller discourse shows, as an anti-governmental philosophy in a world of government; statecraft because constitutional frameworks have to generate the power needed to govern effectively. In modern constitutional regimes, the discourse of governing fills the silences and gaps that permeate all constitutional frameworks.[148] But in the British system of governing, the constitution is essentially an accretion of governing practices. It works not through adherence to the constitutional framework but because of a series of political tensions between the governing elite and the people, between central and local government, between government and opposition, between government and parliament.

The problem today is born of a gathering sense that British practices are not working well. The list of concerns is extensive. Modern party discipline has eroded the authority of conventional understandings: *ésprit de patrie* is overtaken by *ésprit de partie*, the problem of 'elective dictatorship'. Centralizing forces have shattered the central-local compact. The decline of ideologically-driven party politics has

---

[146] See further Ch.1,V. above.

[147] *Terminiello* v. *City of Chicago* 337 US 1 (1949), 37 Jackson J (diss): 'There is danger that, if the court does not temper its doctrinaire logic with a little practical wisdom, it will convert the constitutional Bill of Rights into a suicide pact.'

[148] See M Loughlin, 'The Silences of Constitutions' (2018) 16 *International J. of Constitutional Law* (forthcoming).

destabilized the contest between government and opposition which drives the parliamentary system. Growing national sentiment in several parts of the United Kingdom has weakened a collective sense of 'the people'. And the gulf between political elites and the people has undermined faith in the political processes in general. Constitutional modernization has now been placed onto the political agenda but in a regime in which constitutional and governmental rationalities are pulling in different directions, this is a complex undertaking. Bringing these discourses into some form of creative tension remains a key challenge, but their distinctive rationalities first need to be understood.

4

Burke on Law, Revolution, and Constitution

I. Introduction

Edmund Burke occupies an ambiguous position in legal, political, and constitutional thought. A lawyer by training, he gained his reputation primarily as a man of letters and a skilled parliamentarian. Possessed of great intellectual and literary talents, many have nonetheless questioned whether his was a coherent political philosophy. Burke excelled at the essay form and these essays vary considerably in tone and mood. Written according to the shifting events of his times, they reveal ambiguities about his political convictions, his philosophical beliefs, and his jurisprudential thought. Depending on context, Burke can appear in the guise of conservative, liberal, and radical. Is he a realist, a historicist, and a consequentialist thinker or is he an idealist, even a Romantic? The sheer range and variety of his political writings might suggest that his genius was founded not on his political philosophy but on his singular grasp of the practical engagement of politics.

In this chapter, I outline the main themes of Burke's political jurisprudence. These can be distilled from his position on the four great matters of world affairs that most occupied his attention: the revolutions in North America and in France, and the status of Ireland and India within the British Empire. One immediate question is whether he maintains a consistent position over these controversies. Burke supports the independence claims of the American colonists, advocates an extension of English legal and political privileges to the Irish, and opposes the oppressive governmental regime instituted by the East India Company in India. His arguments on these issues are decidedly liberal. But when it comes to the revolutionary overthrow of the *ancien regime* in France his denunciation is vehement. The work for which he is most famous, *Reflections on the Revolution in France*, acquired classic status in modern political thought as the epitome of conservatism. Can his positions on these issues be reconciled?

Burke himself thought so, though not all commentators are convinced. He evidently changed his view on particular issues. Consider, for example, his assessment of the Glorious Revolution. In *Thoughts on the Cause of the Present Discontents* in 1770, he recognized that the Revolution of 1688 had fundamentally altered the English system of government, not least by depriving the Crown of many useful

Political Jurisprudence. Martin Loughlin. © M Loughlin 2017.
Published 2017 by Oxford University Press.

prerogatives.[1] But in 1791 in *An Appeal from the New to the Old Whigs*, he denies that the Revolution brought about any radical break, claiming it was justified on the basis that 'the people, who have inherited its freedom . . . are bound in duty to transmit the same constitution to their posterity'.[2] Such discrepancies have caused some to believe that there are two Burkes: the liberal youth and the conservative man. Although his essays are different in emphasis, I suggest they share an underlying consistency of thought.

This consistency was clouded by the reception of his ideas. Burke is best known to us today as a conservative who stoutly defended the virtues of traditional hierarchical ordering, but this was not the case in the nineteenth century. Under the influence of his biographer, John Morley, he was refashioned as a liberal and a positivist, one whose thought shaped the ideas of John Stuart Mill and his disciples.[3] To get to the core of Burke's distinctive contribution, layers of accretion must be stripped away and his work examined in the context of his times.

My objective is to sketch the main themes of his political jurisprudence which I take to be law, revolution, and constitution. In common with many thinkers of his time, Burke was strongly influenced by Montesquieu, with whom he shared a belief that the complex relationship between law and society is shaped by the cultural and historical life of a nation. His ideas were also moulded by the works of Bacon, Locke, and Hume, from whom he acquired a firm belief in the importance of experience in political matters. But alongside this practical, evolutionary mode of thinking Burke retained a Christian belief in the workings of natural law. He blended historical sensibility and moral principle in a manner opposed to the Cartesians of his day,[4] and presented a compelling account of the proper relationship between thought and action, theory and practice.

II. Constitution

Burke's arguments on how governments acquire authority should first be considered. Government should be evaluated according to the degree to which it attends to the needs of its people. Authority flows not from its formal constitution, but from the ends it is able to realize. All governmental power is acquired by artifice and since the very existence of government offends the principle of the natural equality of mankind, it can only be justified by how it benefits the people's welfare.[5] This is Burke's cardinal rule.

---

[1] See E Burke, 'Thoughts on the Cause of the Present Discontents' in *The Writings and Speeches of Edmund Burke, vol. II: Party, Parliament and the American Crisis, 1776–1774*, P Langford ed. (Oxford: Clarendon Press, 1981), 241–323, at 262–3, 299–300.

[2] E Burke, *An Appeal from the New to the Old Whigs*, JM Robson ed. (Indianapolis: Bobbs-Merrill, 1962), 59.

[3] J Morley, *Edmund Burke: A Historical Study* (London: Macmillan, 1879).

[4] See, e.g., E Burke, 'Speech on American Taxation, 19 April 1774' in *The Writings and Speeches of Edmund Burke, vol. II: Party, Parliament and the American Crisis, 1776–1774*, P Langford ed. (Oxford: Oxford University Press, 1981), 406–501, at 458: 'I do not enter into these metaphysical distinctions; I hate the very sound of them.'

[5] See, e.g., E Burke, 'Speech on Fox's India Bill, 1 December 1783' in *The Writings and Speeches of Edmund Burke, vol. V: India: Madras and Bengal 1774–1785*, PJ Marshall ed. (Oxford: Oxford

This rule is most clearly outlined in *An Appeal from the New to the Old Whigs*, where he states that 'political problems do not primarily concern truth or falsehood' but 'relate to good or evil'. Consequently, 'what in the result is likely to produce evil, is politically false: that which is productive of good, politically is true'.[6] This method of measuring any political tenet according to its practical consequences provides the bedrock of principle running through all Burke's works. It is on this foundation that he argues for reforms to the government of Ireland, defends the claims of the American colonists, criticizes the East India Company's regime in India, and vehemently opposes the revolution in France. 'I cannot think that what is done in France', he declares in 1792, 'is beneficial to the human race'. But if that did prove to be the case, then neither the British constitution nor any other should prevail against it.[7]

Burke held that the rights of government are prescriptive in nature,[8] but this does not mean his views on constitutional ordering were entirely conservative. He did not believe that a constitution's authority rests purely on its ancient lineage. Rather, his argument is that the prescriptive constitution proves its worth not by virtue of its longevity but from the good outcomes it produces. Consequently, a long-established constitution does not render irrelevant any discussion of a government's legitimacy but a government is not illegitimate simply because it has not been authorized by its present generation of subjects. Burke's argument about the prescription of the constitution is directed primarily against radical natural rights claims, particularly the claim that each generation has the right to determine its own governing arrangements. Any claim based on natural rights, he maintains, is irrelevant as soon as people enter into civil society and form governing arrangements. Thereafter, the justification of government rests only on the benefits it bestows.

The existence of a long-standing constitution does not therefore end all discussion of its authority but such a constitution has authority only through its proven value over many generations. Given the fickleness of human reason, an arrangement which is the work of 'many minds, in many ages' makes it one intrinsically worthy of respect.[9] Of the British constitution, the epitome of a prescriptive constitution, he states:

It is no simple, no superficial thing, nor to be estimated by superficial understandings. An ignorant man, who is not fool enough to meddle with his clock, is however sufficiently confident to think he can safely take to pieces, and put together at his pleasure, a moral machine of another guise, importance and complexity, composed of far other wheels, and springs, and balances, and counteracting and co-operating powers. Men little think how immorally they act in rashly meddling with what they do not understand.[10]

University Press, 1981), 378–451, at 385: 'all political power which is set over men . . . being wholly artificial, and for so much a derogation from the natural equality of mankind at large, ought to be some way or other exercised ultimately for their benefit'.

   [6] Burke, *An Appeal from the New to the Old Whigs*, above n.2, 99.

   [7] E Burke, 'Heads for Consideration on the Present State of Affairs, November 1792' in *The Writings and Speeches of Edmund Burke, vol. VIII: The French Revolution 1790–1794*, LG Mitchell ed. (Oxford: Oxford University Press, 1998) 386–402, at 402.

   [8] See P Lucas, 'On Edmund Burke's Doctrine of Prescription'; Or, an Appeal from the New to the Old Lawyers' (1968) 11 *Historical J*. 35–63.

   [9] Burke, *An Appeal from the New to the Old Whigs*, above n.2, 134.

  [10] Burke, *An Appeal from the New to the Old Whigs*, ibid.

The criterion of a good constitution, then, is the goodness of its results, but Burke is also saying that 'good results' in the treacherous field of the political are not easily calibrated. It is for this reason that the inherited arrangements of government should not lightly be tampered with. Blind adherence to the existing constitution is not required but radical change is ruled out. We can dispose of accretions that no longer deliver good government but we must never lose sight of the fundamentals and always work with the grain.

This principle of prescription in government, of adherence to the inherited constitution, does not entail stasis. 'A state without the means of some change', he maintains, 'is without the means of its conservation'.[11] Progress is marked by sensitive incremental reform of the constitution.

Does Burke's argument mean that the revolutionary changes of the sort brought about by the French Revolution on the basis of natural rights must always be opposed? He answers in the affirmative, reasoning that a constitution is not created at a particular moment in time when a people agree the fundamental principles of its government. Rather, the constitution is a pact that subsists through time: the constitution 'is a partnership not only between those who are living, but between those who are living, those who are dead, and those who are to be born'.[12] Constitutions change through time, but these changes must be gradual, evolutionary, and fixed on the objective of promoting the public good.

III. Rights, Reform, and Revolution

Burke's view on the authority of the constitution provides the basis for understanding his position on many of the contentious political issues of his times. This is most vividly illustrated with respect to his stance on Irish and American affairs.

Burke consistently promoted the cause of reform in Ireland. Seventeenth century upheavals in Ireland had entrenched Protestant rule in an overwhelmingly Catholic country. He argued that no one could contend that the existing regime, in which Catholics were barred from participation in political affairs and Irish Protestant rule was sustained by bargaining with the English government, was in the best interests of the Irish people. Reform was required not because of a Romantic notion of self-government, but because the English needed the support of the Irish to ensure their own security. Basic political reforms, including Catholic emancipation, were needed to ensure that Ireland remained within the British Empire.[13] His position on Irish affairs conformed to his general political philosophy. In *Thoughts on the Cause of the Present Discontents* (1770), he noted that 'the people have no interest in disorder' and that 'where popular discontents have been very prevalent, it may well be affirmed

---

[11]   E Burke, *Reflections on the Revolution in France* [1790], CC O'Brien ed. (London: Penguin, 1968), 106.

[12]   Burke, *Reflections*, ibid.194–5.

[13]   See J Conniff, 'Edmund Burke's Reflections on the Coming Revolution in Ireland' (1986) 47 *J. of the History of Ideas* 37–59.

and supported that there has been generally something found amiss in the constitution, or in the conduct of government'.[14]

Burke's views with respect to the disputes that arose in the American colonies are consistent with this. He had initially been in favour of the Declaratory Act of 1766, which declared the right of Parliament to tax the colonies; indeed, he may even have been responsible for its drafting.[15] But the Act 'had been intended as a claim of right, not a statement of policy'.[16] Sovereign right, he contended, must never be confused with government policy and he soon realized that taxation of the colonists was not prudent politics. Explaining that a nation is not governed 'which is perpetually to be conquered', he argued for restraint on the part of the British Parliament.[17] The question is 'not whether you have a right to render your people miserable, but whether it is not in your interest to make them happy'. He adds that it 'is not what a lawyer tells me I *may* do, but what humanity, reason, and justice tell me I ought to do'.[18]

Such matters could not be resolved by legal formalities of right and duty; they were determined according to the political logic of prudence and the maintenance of peace. Having established that prudence dictated restraint, however, Burke was not slow to convert the matter into an issue of principle. Liberty-loving settler colonists who carried their common law rights with them were not prepared to submit to taxation by an institution in which they were not represented. According to Burke, the Americans were justified in claiming that this reduced them to the status of slaves, even if the ironic aspect of their claim seems to have escaped them.

Burke's support of this right of rebellion is sustained, however, only once prudential requirements are converted into a general principle. His argument runs as follows. The right to liberty enshrined in the common law is that from which the constitutional laws of England derive. Far from being bequeathed by statute, it is the right on which the foundation of governmental authority rests. Only if government subverts this basic right without evident utility are people justified in rebelling. Burke makes these claims with the doctrine of Parliamentary sovereignty, especially a Parliament stuffed with the King's placemen, directly in his sights. But his argument comes perilously close to upholding the claim of natural rights that elsewhere he decries as abstract metaphysical nonsense.

Given his stance on the American conflict, in what circumstances might the overthrow of the established government be justified? When might the abuse of governmental authority lead to the establishment of a *right* of rebellion? His explanation is

---

[14] Burke, 'Thoughts on the Present Discontents', above n.1, at 255.

[15] See RM Hutchins, 'The Theory of the State: Edmund Burke' (1943) 5 *Review of Politics* 139–55, at 142.

[16] R Bourke, *Empire and Revolution: The Political Life of Edmund Burke* (Princeton: Princeton University Press, 2015), 495.

[17] E Burke, 'Speech on Conciliation with America, 22 March 1775' in *The Writings and Speeches of Edmund Burke, vol. III: Party, Parliament, and the American War 1774–1780*, WM Elofson and JA Woods eds (Oxford: Clarendon Press, 1996), 106–69, at 119.

[18] Burke, 'Conciliation with America', ibid. at 135.

based on a doctrine of necessity implicit in Locke's ideas of reason of state, an influence most clearly seen in Burke's account of the English Revolution of 1688.[19]

Burke believes that a claim of necessity can only be invoked in the most extreme case when action is unmistakably needed and would redound to the benefit to the entire society. He justifies the 1688 Revolution in accordance with this test, arguing that the overthrow of James II was only 'a small and a temporary deviation from the strict order of a regular hereditary succession'.[20] The adoption of William of Orange as King 'was not properly a *choice*', he maintains, but 'an act of *necessity*, in the strictest moral sense in which necessity can be taken'.[21] The Crown was therefore 'carried somewhat out of the line in which it had before moved; but the new line was derived from the same stock' and 'it was still a line of hereditary descent'.[22] Consequently, the 'principles of the Revolution did not authorize them to elect kings at their pleasure, and without attention to the antient fundamental principles of our government'.[23] Neither was the overthrow the result of mere misconduct. 'No government could stand a moment', he claims, 'if it could be blown down with anything so loose and indefinite as an opinion of *misconduct*'.[24] On the contrary, only a 'grave and overruling necessity obliged them to take the step they took'.[25]

For Burke, such a revolutionary act would always be 'an extraordinary question of state' and 'wholly out of the law'. It was 'a case of war and not of constitution' and therefore a question 'of dispositions, and of means, and of probable consequences, rather than of positive rights'. But he was keen to emphasize that this remedy 'was not made for common abuses' and therefore 'not to be agitated by common minds'.[26] Governments 'must be abused and deranged' before revolution could be contemplated: 'a revolution will be the very last resource of the thinking and the good'.[27] Burke was here at pains to emphasize that revolutionary action is not generated by general theories of government and constitution, or by abstract concepts of right. The legitimacy of revolutionary action must be assessed by reference to specific political circumstances,[28] the relevant criteria being whether it is driven by necessity and undertaken with a minimal degree of disruption to the established order.

IV. The Revolution in France

Can Burke's justification for revolutionary action be reconciled with his infamous views about the significance of the French Revolution? In earlier disquisitions, he expressed sympathy with popular insurrection on the basis that because the people

---

[19] D Armitage, 'Edmund Burke and Reason of State' (2000) 61 *J. of the History of Ideas* 617–34. On Locke's right of rebellion, see Ch.8.VI–VII below.
[20] Burke, *Reflections*, above n.11, 101.　　[21] Burke, *Reflections*, 101–2.
[22] Burke, *Reflections*, 106.　　[23] Burke, *Reflections*, 110.　　[24] Burke, *Reflections*, 112.
[25] Burke, *Reflections*, 113.　　[26] Burke, *Reflections*, 116.　　[27] Burke, *Reflections*, 116–7.
[28] See BJ Taylor, 'Reflections on the Revolution in England: Edmund Burke's Uses of 1688' (2014) 35 *History of Political Thought* 91–120.

are not easily roused, if driven to action they are invariably right.[29] But the tone in *Reflections on the Revolution in France* is decidedly different. After initially blaming the Revolution on the King's advisers, the blame falls entirely on the cabal that expresses its revolutionary spirit. Most striking is his assessment of the role of 'the people', which deviates considerably from earlier formulations.

Burke first rails against the perfidy of the King's advisers who had reassured him that by convening the Estates General 'he had nothing to fear but the prodigal excess of their zeal in providing for the support of the throne'.[30] These counsellors are held responsible for having seen 'the medicine of the state corrupted into its poison'.[31] Through their ineptitude in promoting the 'perilous adventures of untried policy' the French people were motivated to 'rebel against a mild and lawful monarch, with more fury, outrage, and insult than ever any people has been known to rise against the most illegal usurper, or the most sanguinary tyrant'.[32]

His immediate target here is probably right: statecraft indeed failed through 'rash and ignorant counsel'.[33] But his views on the people seem an over-reaction: was this really a mob of unprecedented fury and outrage? This essay was written in 1790 at an early stage of the Revolution during which the French King was still untouched. And we might note that, despite vigorously justifying the achievements of the Glorious Revolution in the *Reflections*, he entirely overlooks the precedent of the English civil war of the 1640s, a bloody conflict that led to the execution of a King. Ignoring this, he complains only of the great destruction effected by the French mob and of learning 'cast into the mire and trodden down under the hoofs of a swinish multitude'.[34]

But Burke's most vehement outrage is reserved for those who have misguided the people. This is the 'literary cabal' that forged a plan 'for the destruction of the Christian religion',[35] otherwise referred to as 'a cabal calling itself philosophic' which conjured the 'true actuating spirit' of the people's actions.[36] These are mere 'men of theory' who lack 'any practical experience in the state'.[37] A great proportion of the National Assembly may have been lawyers, but Burke points out that they were not jurisconsults experienced in affairs of state; they are 'inferior, unlearned, mechanical, merely instrumental members of the profession'.[38] These mechanicals 'could not be expected to bear with moderation . . . a power which they themselves, more than any others, must be surprised to find in their hands'.[39] They were 'men formed to be instruments, not controls'.[40] Once they had acquired the reins of power, their natural tendency was towards centralization and standardization with the result that 'every landmark of the country' was abolished 'in favour of a geometrical and arithmetical

---

[29] Burke, 'Speech on Conciliation with America, 22 March 1775', above n.17, at 120; Burke, 'Thoughts on the Present Discontents', above n.1, at 252–3.

[30] Burke, *Reflections*, above n.11, 125.   [31] Burke, *Reflections*, 126.

[32] Burke, *Reflections*, 125, 126.   [33] Burke, *Reflections*, 127.

[34] Burke, *Reflections*, 173. Conor Cruise O'Brien, Burke's editor, notes that Burke's opponents were quick wrongly to quote him as referring to '*the* swinish multitude'. The indefinite article is important since Burke may have been referring to a specific event: *Reflections*, 385, n.66.

[35] Burke, *Reflections*, 211.   [36] Burke, *Reflections*, 185.   [37] Burke, *Reflections*, 128.

[38] Burke, *Reflections*, 130.   [39] Burke, *Reflections*, 130.   [40] Burke, *Reflections*, 132.

constitution'.[41] The power of the city of Paris became 'one great spring of all their politics ... the centre and focus of jobbing', through which 'the leaders of this faction direct, or rather command, the whole legislative and the whole executive government'.[42]

Burke maintains that this group, 'the politicians of metaphysics', had 'opened schools for sophistry and made establishments for anarchy'.[43] The French nation had thereby been delivered over to anarchy and the tyranny of the multitude. His prediction that such a destruction of constitutional order could lead only to the establishment of a ruthless dictatorship has been widely admired. Whether this is attributable to Burke's insight and wisdom in the arts of government or to his thoroughly jaundiced view of the Revolution remains an open question.

V. Revolutions Contrasted

The French Revolution, Burke contends, arose from a combination of forces: the weakness of the forces of conservation and the strength of the impetus to revolution. But if the responsibility lies in part with the ineptitude of counsellors and a conspiracy of the professional and intellectual elites, a similar argument could surely be made with respect to the American Revolution.

Why did Burke adopt a radically different position on these events? He maintained that his interpretation of the two revolutions was consistent, explaining in his *Appeal from the New to the Old Whigs* that he had 'always firmly believed that they [the Americans] were purely on the defensive ... standing ... in the same relation to England as England did to King James the Second in 1688'.[44] In this attempt to dissuade his fellow Whigs from expressing sympathy for the ideals of the French Revolution, he asserts that the American colonists were right to stand up against encroachments upon their established rights. In France, by contrast, it is 'not the people, but the monarch [who] was wholly on the defensive ... to preserve some fragments of the royal authority against a determined and desperate body of conspirators, whose object it was ... to annihilate the whole of that authority'.[45] In other words, Burke argues that the American Revolution had been caused by the British Crown's subversion of the principles of its own constitution, whereas the French Revolution was an attempt by the National Assembly to subvert the principles of the French Constitution.

There is something to this claim, but it overlooks an important point. While supporting the American cause, Burke should surely have objected to the natural rights terminology used in the American Declaration of Independence. This suggests another reason for his contrasting positions on these two revolutionary movements. Only at the time of the French Revolution did Burke fully appreciate that the American Revolution was not simply a revolution to preserve the common law

---

[41] Burke, *Reflections*, 144.   [42] Burke, *Reflections*, 314.   [43] Burke, *Reflections*, 348.
[44] Burke, *An Appeal from the New to the Old Whigs*, above n.2, 39.
[45] Burke, *An Appeal from the New to the Old Whigs*, ibid. 41–2.

rights of the freeborn Englishman and that it also lit a beacon for the Enlightenment claim that legitimate government must be founded on the natural and inalienable rights of man.

Significantly, Burke's essay of 1790 concerns 'the revolution in France' rather than 'the French Revolution'. The revolutionary zeal exhibited by the French was not theirs alone: the missionary creed of the Rights of Man was explicitly designed for export. As Thomas Paine proclaimed, America had taken a stand not only for herself but on behalf of the modern world: the American Revolution was the moment and the place 'where the principles of universal reformation could begin'.[46] This earlier revolution marked the beginning of the end of regimes of monarchical government based on military objectives,[47] and replacement by government 'founded on a moral theory, on a system of universal peace, on the indefeasible hereditary Rights of Man'.[48] Whereas monarchical government was founded on hierarchy, the legitimating principle of the new regimes was equality. Government legitimated by divine will or sacred custom was now challenged by government authorized by the consent of free and equal citizens.

The main principles underpinning this 'universal reformation' are that the individual possesses inherent natural rights, that the office of government must ensure the maintenance and full enjoyment of these rights, and that we safeguard these rights in the civil state through the device of a written constitution specifying the terms of the bargain between rulers and ruled. 'Man did not enter into society to become *worse* than he was before, nor to have fewer rights than he had before', argues Paine, 'but to have those rights better secured'.[49] The modern regime of government that Paine proclaims is firmly founded on the 'rights of man'.

Burke's shrill assessment of the situation in France in 1790 is revealed in his essay's full title: *Reflections on the Revolution in France, and on the proceedings in certain societies in London relative to that event*. His rhetoric is directed primarily at the British, partly as a warning to the governing class about the consequences of the failure of statecraft, but mostly to agitators at home. The apparent improvements achieved by the French National Assembly, he proclaimed, 'are superficial, their errors fundamental'.[50] They could not be models for us, rather, the reverse; we should be recommending to our neighbours the example of the British constitution. 'Standing on the firm ground of the British constitution, let us be satisfied to admire, rather than attempt to follow their desperate flights, the aeronauts of France'.[51]

Burke later referred to the French Revolution as the world's first 'total revolution'. As he notes in his *Letters on a Regicide Peace*, 'France, on her new system, means to form a universal empire, by producing a universal revolution'.[52] Britain was not at

---

[46] T Paine, *Rights of Man* [1791–2] in his *Rights of Man, Common Sense and other Political Writings*, M Philp ed. (Oxford: Oxford University Press, 1995), 83–331, at 210.

[47] Of monarchical government, Paine, ibid. 212, noted: 'War is their trade, plunder and revenue their objects'.

[48] Ibid. 213.   [49] Ibid. 119.   [50] Burke, *Reflections*, above n.11, 375.

[51] Burke, *Reflections*, 376.

[52] E Burke, 'Third Letter on a Regicide Peace' in *Selected Works of Edmund Burke: vol.3, Letters on a Regicide Peace* (Indianapolis: Liberty Fund, 1999), 191–306, at 248.

war 'with an ordinary community which is hostile or friendly as passion or as interest may veer about; not with a State that makes war through wantonness, and abandons it through lassitude'. Instead the British 'are at war with a system, which by its essence is inimical to all other Governments'. We were at war 'with an armed doctrine'.[53] He claimed that if the war to prevent Louis XIV from imposing his religion had been just, similarly 'a war to prevent the murderers of Louis XVI from imposing their irreligion upon us is just; a war to prevent the operation of a system . . . is a just war'.[54] His opposition to the French Revolution was an opposition to a fanatical sect spouting a revolutionary doctrine. And only later in life did he come to realize that, far from being simply a dispute over the common law inheritance, the American Revolution had been the first wave of a wholly new political doctrine.

VI. Law

Government rests ultimately on the consent of the people and for Burke so too does law. The people are presumed to consent to the laws laid down by the legislature but they cannot be assumed to consent to laws that do not operate for the overall good. This much Burke makes clear in his views on Ireland. To contend otherwise is to connive in oppression. His argument is underpinned by natural law, conceived as a 'means of promoting the progress of society through the pursuit of personal liberty'.[55] Laws enacted by legislatures are, in the final analysis, declaratory: they must be devised with the object of promoting human flourishing. The office of government exists purely to secure and conserve these human values.

Burke's convictions about the foundation of lawful authority are most clearly revealed in his lengthy speech on the impeachment of Warren Hastings over his conduct as Governor-General of Bengal. Burke had long believed that the British had established in India 'an oppressive, irregular, capricious, unsteady, rapacious, and peculating despotism'[56] and that this 'spirit of conquest' corroded the foundations of lawful authority. In his prosecution of the case against Hastings he argues that the natural rights of a people are universal and not subject to geography.[57] All law and all sovereignty is derived from God: 'if the laws of every nation, from the most simple and social of the most barbarous people, up to the wisest and most salutary laws of the most refined and enlightened societies, from the Divine laws handed down to us in Holy Writ, down to the meanest forms of earthly institution, were attentively examined, they would be found to breathe but one spirit, one principle, equal distributive justice between man and man, and the protection of one individual from the encroachments of the rest'.[58] This is the entire basis of any claim to sovereignty.

---

[53] Burke, 'First Letter on a Regicide Peace' in *Select Works*, ibid. 59–152, at 76.
[54] Burke, 'First Letter on a Regicide Peace', 122.   [55] Bourke, above n.16, 574.
[56] Burke, 'Speech on Fox's India Bill', above n.5, 425.
[57] E Burke, 'Speech on the Opening of Impeachment, 15–19 February, 1788' in *The Writings and Speeches of Edmund Burke, vol. VI: India*, PJ Marshall ed. (Oxford: Clarendon Press, 1991), 264–471, at 353.
[58] Burke, 'Impeachment Speech' ibid. 363–4.

For Burke, the authority of a divine creator is the basis for the universal and natural foundation of law. He closed his speech at Hastings' impeachment by pleading with the Lords to impeach Hastings 'in the name and by virtue of those eternal laws of justice which he has violated'. 'I impeach him', he states, 'in the name of human nature itself, which he has cruelly outraged, injured, and oppressed, in both sexes, in every age, rank, situations, and condition of life'.[59]

Can these beliefs be reconciled with his views on the prescriptive authority of government and the primary importance of prudence in politics? A strict natural rights doctrine would maintain that any claim to legal title must have some foundation in right, possession acquired through force or fraud never being valid. Yet Burke's position is more nuanced. He maintains that 'Time' must be permitted to 'draw his oblivious veil over the unpleasant modes by which lordships and demesnes have been acquired in theirs, and in almost all other countries upon earth'.[60] He accepts in effect that an original evil is transformed into good by virtue of a higher natural necessity: the need for order and the security of the state and its citizens. Burke considered it 'prudent to relativize at least part of what classical and Christian natural-law theory had held to be absolute and immutable'.[61] And history, he asserts, 'is a preceptor of prudence'.[62]

Prudence is 'not only the first in rank of the virtues political and moral, but ... the director, the regulator, and standard of them all'.[63] Principle must be subservient to prudence. But Burke recognizes that 'without the guide and light of sound, well-understood principles, all reasonings in politics, as in everything else, would be only a confused jumble of particular facts and details, without the means of drawing out any sort of theoretical or practical conclusion'.[64] There is, then, a crucial ambiguity in his thought on law and authority. Burke refuses to make a purely conventionalist or historicist argument and calls on principles to fortify his position. But in the end he cannot offer anything more than a rhetorical account of the basis of his universal principles.

VII. Conclusion

Burke distills his political jurisprudence from a variety of sources. He treats society as an organic unity, maintaining that this sense of unity has through time shaped the distinctive character and situation of a people. He recognizes the power of reason,

[59] Burke, 'Impeachment Speech', 459. See further WH Greenleaf, 'Burke and State Necessity: The Case of Warren Hastings' in R Schnur (ed.), *Staatsräson: Studien zur Geschichte eines politischen Begriff* (Berlin: Duncker & Humblot, 1975), 549–67.

[60] 'Letter to Richard Burke, post 19 February 1792' in *The Writings and Speeches of Edmund Burke*, vol. IX: *The Revolutionary War 1794–97 and Ireland*, RB McDowell ed. (Oxford: Clarendon Press, 1991), 640–58, at 653.

[61] RW Kilcup, 'Burke's Historicism' (1977) 49 *J. of Modern History* 394–410, at 401.

[62] Burke, Letter to Dr William Markham, 9 November 1771; cited in Bourke, above n.16, 3.

[63] Burke, *An Appeal from the New to the Old Whigs*, above n.2, 20.

[64] Cited in D Herzog 'Puzzling through Burke' (1991) 19 *Political Theory* 336–63, at 345.

but only when it works within this historical framework. And he rejects the type of metaphysical reasoning exhibited in natural rights doctrines. 'Nothing universal', he suggests, 'can be rationally affirmed on any moral, or any political subject'. The lines of morality in the realm of the political 'admit of exceptions' and 'demand modifications'. For this reason, prudence is the highest virtue in political jurisprudence.[65] Prudence—*artifices officiorum*—'requires a very solid and discriminating judgment, great modesty and caution, and much sobriety of mind in the handling'. It can be reckoned only in the context of a particular situation, 'else there is a danger that it may totally subvert those offices which it is its object only to methodize and reconcile'.[66]

There is some consistency in Burke's method but also a tension between conservatism and liberalism. He defends the old order of nobility, the 'age of chivalry', and the retention of 'the decent drapery of life' that bolsters the hierarchical ordering of society through the power of myth. Yet there is considerable ambivalence in his view of the historical role of the bourgeoisie, revealing a liberalism that comes to the fore in his writings on political economy. This is illustrated by his attack on the East India Company's regime in India, where he defends the emerging liberal values of a disciplined, rational commercialism against the vices of monopolistic abuse.

These tensions in Burke's writing reflect the tensions within modern liberalism itself. Burke could see that the movement of progressive societies was not simply from status to contract. Contractual relations could work well only when commercial principles operate within a social order founded on status and hierarchy. The political pact invoked by liberal theorists using equality as an image of unity also establishes a system of government founded on hierarchy. Burke recognized that this pact is not created at some mythical constitutional moment: it is intergenerational. In doing so he exposed the profound if ambivalent principle that political equality is acceptable to liberals only when it is redefined to make it compatible with a social order based on hierarchy.

---

[65] Burke, *An Appeal from the New to the Old Whigs*, above n.2, 20.
[66] Burke, *An Appeal from the New to the Old Whigs*, ibid. 99.

5

Droit Politique

I. Introduction

Seeking to justify the forms of government under which we live is of universal interest, but it excites attention only at certain historical moments. One such moment
occurred in eighteenth-century Europe with the flourishing of the Enlightenment
movement. Although its ripples were felt across Europe, its epicentre lay in France.
It was not just a French concern,[1] and neither was there a simple unity to
Enlightenment thought.[2] But it was French scholars who advanced furthest in developing rationalist schemes,[3] and in this chapter I examine the impact of French
jurists of the Enlightenment who sought to reveal the scientific principles that would
reconcile order and liberty in an arrangement of legitimate government. The challenge they faced was, in Rousseau's formulation, to stipulate *les principes du droit
politique*. I will explain how Enlightenment scholars elaborated these principles and
consider the extent to which the 'science of political right' propounded by scholars
of the French Enlightenment has continued to shape ideas about the legitimacy of
the modern French state.

II. The Concept of *Droit Politique*

One distinctive mark of the Enlightenment is to have joined, 'to a degree scarcely
ever achieved before, the critical with the productive function and converted the
one directly into the other'.[4] In challenging the authority of traditional ordering,

---

[1] A Macintyre, *After Virtue. A Study in Moral Theory* (London: Duckworth, 2nd edn. 1985), 37:
'One ... reason why the unity and coherence of Enlightenment sometimes escapes us is that we too often
understand it as primarily an episode in *French* cultural history'.

[2] P Gay, *The Enlightenment: An Interpretation* (New York: Knopf, 1966), 3: 'There were many philosophes in the eighteenth century, but there was only one Enlightenment. A loose, informal, wholly
unorganized coalition of cultural critics, religious skeptics, and political reformers ... the philosophes
made up a clamorous chorus, and there was some discordant voices among them, but what is striking is
their general harmony, not their occasional discord.'

[3] G Hawthorn, *Enlightenment and Despair: A History of Social Theory* (Cambridge: Cambridge
University Press, 2nd edn. 1987), 12–13: 'it was in France almost exclusively that theories were proposed which attempted to extend the empirical method of the physical sciences to society while retain-
ing the total view made possible by schematic rationalism'.

[4] E Cassirer, *The Philosophy of Enlightenment*, FCA Koelln and JP Pettegrove trans. (Princeton:
Princeton University Press, 1951), 278.

Political Jurisprudence. Martin Loughlin. © M Loughlin 2017.
Published 2017 by Oxford University Press.

Enlightenment scholars had to devise new legitimating principles for modern societies. Living through a period of economic, social, and technological change, they began to conceive 'the political' as a domain of thought and action quite distinct from the economic and social networks shaping emerging modern societies. The identification of the political as an autonomous way of viewing the world was the first and most basic assumption of the movement.

The second assumption was that this distinctive worldview could only be formulated in the language of law. Jurists presented contrasting accounts of political order and consequently relied on different conceptions of authority, liberty, equality, solidarity, rights, and so on. They nevertheless all shared the language of right and law (*le droit et la loi*). These two basic assumptions combine in a third, derivative, claim: namely, that sustaining the autonomy of the political depends on adopting an autonomous account of legality. This somewhat paradoxical declaration provides the foundation for the concept of *droit politique*.

Droit politique flourishes when the intrinsic structural relationship between the legal and the political is acknowledged,[5] but a great achievement of French thought has been its ability to reconcile apparent opposites. As an autonomous worldview, the political presents itself as an unlimited domain but the political has to operate in accordance with its own fundamental laws. This is so often overlooked in modern public law that the very idea of *droit politique* has been marginalized. One reason is that politics and law are today seen as quite separate: politics, concerned with the struggle over human interests, is a material phenomenon, whereas law is purely normative. This is a modern distortion.

To say that 'the political' is a distinct way of looking at the world is not a claim about the practice of politics. Politics (*la politique*) is a set of practices within an established regime, whereas 'the political' (*le politique*) is the ground on which an autonomous worldview is founded.[6] 'If we make a rigid distinction between what belongs to the realm of economics or politics (defined in modern science's sense of the terms), or between what belongs to the juridical or the religious in an attempt to find within them signs of specific systems', notes Claude Lefort, 'we forget that we can arrive at that analytical distinction only because we already have a subjective idea of the primal dimensionality of the social, and that this implies an idea of its primal *form*, of its political *form*'.[7] That is, the political emerges through the formation of human groups whose mode of association has intrinsic value only through

    [5] See C Gusy, 'Considérations sur le "droit politique"' (2009) 1 *Jus Politicum*: http://juspoliticum. com/article/Considerations-sur-le-droit-politique-26.html (though this account remains in the foothills of the concept).
    [6] This distinction is recognized in a certain strand of French scholarship: see C Castoriadis, *Philosophy, Politics and Autonomy*, DA Curtis ed. (New York: Oxford University Press, 1991), esp.156–62; C Lefort, *Democracy and Political Theory*, D Macey trans. (Cambridge: Polity Press, 1988); P Lacoue-Labarthe and J-L Nancy, *Retreating the Political*, S Sparks ed. (London: Routledge, 1997); J Rancière, *Aux bords du politique* (Paris: La Fabrique, 1998); P Rosanvallon, *Pour une histoire conceptuelle du politique* (Paris: Éditions du Seuil, 2003).
    [7] Lefort, above, n.6, 218.

preserving the group's existence. In this sense, the autonomy of the political rests on a rudimentary inclusionary/exclusionary distinction.[8]

The origins of the political lie in existential expressions of insecurity, triggered by a breakdown of civil peace or the threat of war. But collective association can only preserve its sense of unity by establishing institutions that express a common will. The political forms an autonomous domain by generating common understandings, practices, and norms, and strengthening the authority of its worldview through the medium of right and law.

Conversely, the authority of law is bolstered by political monopoly over the use of force. Modern law is the product of the monopolization of legitimate physical force in a given territory, presenting itself as an expression of the will of a ruling power. But this refers only to the phenomenon of positive law conceived as an instrument of the ruling authority. Enlightenment scholars, by contrast, were seeking something different. They sought to stipulate the conditions, precepts, practices, and norms that establish and maintain the right ordering of the regime. Their aim was to specify the fundamental laws of the political domain. In this sense, law, meaning *droit politique*, is not the instrument of an existing power but rather the medium through which that power maintains its authority.

III. Origins

Although *droit politique* comes into its own in Enlightenment thinking, its foundations had been laid by the *politique* jurists.[9] Foremost among this group was Jean Bodin, whose monumental study of 1576, *Six livres de la république*, broke with the medieval worldview. Bodin's great achievement was to have recognized with singular clarity a fundamental truth: that a nation becomes a political unity only through the integrative exercise of conceiving itself as a state. The essential criterion for conceiving itself as a state, he explained, is the establishment of absolute collective authority. This is what he calls sovereignty.

There are different views about Bodin's originality. Some scholars find it in his claim that the modern idea of the state depends on establishing a supreme centre of authority incorporating all governmental powers[10] the origin of the modern idea that law is an expression of the will of the sovereign. Some find original his argument that the sovereign possesses *potestas legibus soluta*, unlimited power to act free from the constraints of law,[11] seeing Bodin as a theorist of absolutism.[12] Others

---

[8] This correlates to the distinction Carl Schmitt made between friend and enemy: C Schmitt, *The Concept of the Political*, G. Schwab trans. (Chicago: University of Chicago Press, 1996).

[9] See, e.g., WF Church, *Constitutional Thought in Sixteenth-Century France: A Study in the Evolution of Ideas* (Cambridge, MA: Harvard University Press, 1941), Ch.4.

[10] J Bodin, *The Six Bookes of a Commonweale*, R Knolles trans. 1606, KD McRae ed. (Cambridge, MA: Harvard University Press, 1962), 84.

[11] Bodin, *Six Bookes*, 14. C Schmitt, *Political Theology: Four Chapters on the Concept of Sovereignty*, G. Schwab trans. (Chicago: University of Chicago Press, 2005), 8–9.

[12] See, e.g., P Eleftheriades, 'Law and Sovereignty' (2010) 29 *Law and Philosophy* 535–69.

suggest that Bodin's rebuttal of the right of resistance to sovereign authority demonstrates his antipathy to constitutional schemes founded on a division of governmental powers.[13] But Bodin's genius rests primarily on the way he conceived of collective human existence in politico-legal terms. Drawing on the ancient Greek distinction between the household (*oikos*) and the polity (*polis*), he distinguishes between the 'natural' hierarchy of superior and inferior and a public domain founded on what is held in common and the creation of governing arrangements as an expression of human will.[14] This exercise in imagination provides the foundation for the political as a distinctive worldview.

In 1576, during pressing political circumstances in France, Bodin undoubtedly felt the necessity of emphasizing the importance of a supreme central office of authority.[15] His account, which recognizes that the sovereign might be either the prince or the people, is more concerned to explain the nature, significance, and function of sovereignty than to specify who exercises the powers of the office. Crucial to his analysis is the distinction between sovereignty and government. Sovereignty is absolute, perpetual, and indivisible, while government is conditional, limited, and divisible. Sovereignty is conceptual, government empirical. Sovereignty is constitutive, while the issue of who actually exercises the sovereign powers of rule is merely regulative.

In Books II–VI, Bodin analyses the main forms of government which have emerged, his purpose being to derive empirical conclusions—prudential maxims—about those practices of government that strengthen or weaken the authority of the state. But his overall purpose is juridical: it is to specify the 'fundamental laws' at work in the public realm. From these books, then, a constitutional thesis can be derived. In Chapter 6 of Book IV, for example, he explains that, whether the state is monarchical or republican, its powers of government should be directly exercised by the sovereign only in the rarest of cases. Nothing has corrupted a state more than the attempt by the sovereign, whether prince or people, to assume the authority of a Senate, the command of magistrates, or to remove the processes of justice from their ordinary course. From this account, Bodin derives the principle that 'the less the power of the sovereignty is (the true marks of majesty thereunto still reserved), the more it is assured'.[16] The underlying reason is clearly stated: 'hard it is for high and stately buildings long to stand', he explains, 'except they be upholden and stayed by most strong shores, and rest upon most sure foundations; all of which consisteth in the Senate or council, and in the good duties of the magistrates'.[17] For Bodin, the political domain is sustained through the establishment of robust institutional arrangements.

---

[13] See, e.g., JH Franklin, *Jean Bodin and the Rise of Absolutist Theory* (Cambridge: Cambridge University Press, 1973).

[14] Bodin, *Six Bookes*, above n.10, I. 2.

[15] The reference is to St Bartholomew's Day massacre of 1572. But note also how Bodin explains in the preface to his first edition of the *Six Bookes* that he has written this treatise because the 'ship of state, rocked by a violent tempest, is in imminent danger of foundering' owing to the fact that certain writers had displayed ignorance of 'laws and of public right' that established and maintained the state, ibid. A69.

[16] Ibid. 517.   [17] Ibid.

Bodin's originality extends beyond an account of the modern concept of sovereignty. He demonstrates: that the political can be asserted as an autonomous domain only through an act of imagination; that this autonomous domain is founded on the concept of the state; that the state possesses the quality of sovereignty; that the sovereign state provides the symbol of political unity needed to sustain the authority of its governing institutions; and that these institutions need adequate equilibration—Bodin called it harmonic proportion[18]—to maintain their authority. In Book I, Bodin gives us a modern definition of law as the will of the sovereign, and through his studies of governmental forms in Books II–VI he provides a blueprint of the fundamental laws of the political domain. These are neither causal laws of the natural sciences nor the divine laws of a revelatory God: they are a distillation of the practices of right ordering of the state, *les principes du droit politique*, the constitutional arrangements that sustain the sovereign authority of the state.

IV. *Droit Politique* in Enlightenment Thought

During the seventeenth century, 'at the precise moment when the concept of public law was taking shape', William Church notes that 'jurists were abandoning analysis of all things political and governmental'. Although public law continued to develop during the long reign of Louis XIV, it was with 'a minimum of direct influence from the jurists, who instead concentrated more and more upon the vast, complex body of private law'.[19] This began to change during the first half of the eighteenth century, when two scholars produced works that would bring the science of political right to maturity. Despite the antithetical character of their views, Montesquieu and Rousseau provide us with the framework of Enlightenment thought on this subject, and their ideas exerted a powerful influence over the leading figures of the late-eighteenth century Revolution.[20]

Lawyers today, especially in the Anglo-American world, commonly invoke Montesquieu as the inventor of the 'doctrine' of the separation of powers.[21] But that contribution was not especially original or profound; by the mid-eighteenth century the idea that constitutional government needed to differentiate between governing tasks was well understood. This is not to underestimate Montesquieu's originality, but it is in the more understated aspects of his work that his real achievement lies. An

---

[18] Ibid. Book VI, Ch. 6.

[19] WF Church, 'The Decline of the French Jurists as Political Theorists, 1660–1789' (1967) 5 *French Historical Studies* 1–40, at 5.

[20] N Hampson, *Will and Circumstance: Montesquieu, Rousseau and the French Revolution* (London: Duckworth, 1983); C Blum, *Rousseau and the Republic of Virtue: The Language of Politics in the French Revolution* (Ithaca: Cornell University Press, 1986).

[21] Given Montesquieu's influence over the framers of the American Constitution, this is entirely understandable: see J Madison, A Hamilton, and J Jay, *The Federalist Papers*, I Kramnick ed. (London: Penguin, 1987), no. 47, at 303: 'The oracle who is always consulted and cited on this subject [the separation of powers] is the celebrated Montesquieu. If he be not the author of this invaluable precept in the science of politics, he has the merit at least of displaying and recommending it to the attention of mankind.'

appraisal of Montesquieu's significance as a political jurist must start with his conceptions of the political and the state.

Political philosophers of his time commonly built their theories of order from first principles derived from an original social contract. This has the benefit of avoiding both theological speculation and complex historical inquiry, but it is not Montesquieu's method. Instead, he derived his conclusions empirically from 'the nature of things'.[22] On the basis of historical inquiry, he claimed that, contrary to Hobbes, the state of nature does not amount to a state of war. War arises once societies have already been formed; only in society do people feel the will to power and it is this power-impulse that leads to war. Far from being a condition for the formation of society, war is the product of its formation. He uses this point to highlight another: it is the threat of war, both within and between societies that makes law a necessity.[23]

Montesquieu explains that laws exist in order to regulate three main types of social relations: *civil right*, the relations between citizens, *political right*, the relations between governors and governed, and the *right of nations*, the relations between states. These three come together through the union of individual wills, a union that becomes the institution of the state.[24] Having explained the social conditions leading to the formation of the state, he turns to his major task: to specify the character of a state's laws. This is the ambition behind his major work on *L'Esprit des Lois*.

Montesquieu's aim is not simply to classify the types of laws made by particular regimes: those, the positive laws, are merely the products of that regime. Rather, he wants to discover the 'laws' at work in the formation of those regimes. As he explains in the preface, 'I have set down the principles, and I have seen particular cases conform to them as if by themselves, the histories of all nations being but their consequences, and each particular law connecting with another law or dependent on a more general one'. His many years studying the history of government were devoted to discovering what produces positive law, 'the chain connecting [the principles] with the others'.[25]

Montesquieu sought a new understanding of the concept of law. Before *L'Esprit des Lois*, law was conceived as command, whether the product of the will of a divine creator or, when Bodin broke with the medieval world, as the command of the sovereign. Montesquieu showed that law is not command but an expression 'of the necessary relations arising from the nature of things'.[26] The significance of this claim is in his argument that each type of order formed in the world operates according to its own fundamental laws.

---

[22] Montesquieu, *The Spirit of the Laws*, A Cohler, B Miller, and H Stone trans. and eds (Cambridge: Cambridge University Press, 1989), Bk 1, Ch.1.

[23] Montesquieu, Bk 1, Ch.3: 'As soon as men are in society, they lose their feelings of weakness; the equality that was among them ceases, and the state of war begins. Each particular society comes to feel its strength, producing a state of war among nations. The individuals within each society begin to feel their strength; they seek to turn to their favour the principal advantages of society, which brings about a state of war among them. These two sorts of states of war bring about the establishment of laws among men.'

[24] Montesquieu, Bk 1, Ch.3.   [25] Montesquieu, Preface.   [26] Montesquieu, Bk 1, Ch.1.

The laws of the physical world are certainly different from those that regulate human interaction. And within human conduct, there are different modes of interaction. 'Not all political vices are moral vices', he explains, 'and not all moral vices are political vices, and those who make laws that run counter to the general spirit should not be ignorant of this'.[27] Legislation—positive law—is not isolated, some arbitrary or abstracted will; it is, as Hegel (praising Montesquieu's discovery) noted, 'a subordinate moment in a whole, interconnected with all the other features which make up the character of a nation and an epoch'.[28] A study of positive law is important, but it should not be confused with a deeper inquiry: the search for the fundamental laws of the political domain.

Many scholars have shown that Montesquieu's so-called doctrine of the separation of powers entails no strict separation but merely a blending or balancing of governmental powers.[29] To appreciate why, we must move beyond a liberal interpretation that shows his objective was to indicate law's importance in curtailing political power. His true purpose was to demonstrate that, in order to *generate* political power, the political must be framed by the legal. He recognized that the authority needed to govern modern societies requires institutional arrangements of some complexity. Just as Bodin had shown that there could be no universal form of scientific jurisprudence (in his day, one derived from Roman law),[30] so Montesquieu demonstrates that authority cannot be maintained by imposing a strict legal uniformity.[31] Condorcet would later criticize Montesquieu for failing to speak of the justice or injustice of the laws.[32] But the reason is that, although governing must be conducted in a 'spirit of moderation',[33] the precepts of *droit politique* can only be generated contextually through evolving relations of historically-constituted political formations.

Rousseau moved the argument on, specifically criticizing Montesquieu for having devoted so much attention to 'the positive laws of settled government' that he could not specify the principles of political right.[34] Historical inquiry, Rousseau maintained, can only replicate historical injustices and legitimate existing power formations.[35] Rather than locating the origins of political order in war and insecurity, Rousseau begins his inquiry into *droit politique* by first seeking the principles

---

[27] Montesquieu, Bk 19, Ch.11.

[28] GWF Hegel, *Philosophy of Right*, T.M. Knox trans. (Oxford: Oxford University Press, 1952), §.3.

[29] C Eisenman, 'L'Esprit des lois et la séparation des pouvoirs' (1984–5) 2 *Cahiers de philosophie politique* 3–34; M Troper, *La Séparation des pouvoirs et l'histoire constitutionelle français* (Paris: Librairie générale de droit et jurisprudence, 1980); MJC Vile, *Constitutionalism and the Separation of Powers* (Oxford: Clarendon Press, 1967), Ch.4.

[30] J Bodin, *Method for the Easy Comprehension of History*, B Reynolds trans. (New York: Columbia University Press, 1945).

[31] Montesquieu, Bk 29, Ch.18.

[32] See C Larrère, *Actualité de Montesquieu* (Paris: Presses de Sciences Po, 1999), 9; cited in DW Carrithers et al (eds), *Montesquieu's Science of Politics* (Lanham: Rowman & Littlefield, 2001), 14.

[33] Montesquieu, Bk 29, Ch.1

[34] J-J Rousseau, *Emile, or Education* [1762], B Foxley trans. (Indianapolis: Liberty Fund, 2010), 377.

[35] J-J Rousseau, *Discourse on the Origin and the Foundations of Inequality among Men* in his *The Discourses and other early political writing*, V Gourevitch ed. (Cambridge: Cambridge University Press, 1997), 111–88.

of legitimate government. The essence of the political, he suggests, cannot be derived merely from the desire to have order: if law is defined as the will of the sovereign then legal study cannot yield the principles of legitimate political order. The challenge of discovering *les principes du droit politique* is to understand how law can be transformed from an instrument that bolsters the hierarchical relationship of sovereign and subject into a medium by which liberty and equality can be realized.

Some claim that Rousseau makes the legal and the political subservient to the social and that, far from providing an account of the political as an autonomous domain, he seeks 'the eclipse of political authority' in favour of community.[36] In fact, Rousseau sought a conception of the political in rational terms. This would be a practical exercise in discovering the principles of political right, principles that were not extricated from historical experience but could only be validated by their efficacy in real societies.[37]

Like Hobbes before him, Rousseau invokes the idea of a social contract. But he felt that Hobbes was mistaken in presenting the foundational pact as a trade-off between liberty (the absence of constraint) and law (the will of the sovereign). For Rousseau, the modern state is legitimate only when its foundation in natural liberty is replaced by political liberty. Liberty for Rousseau is not the mere absence of constraint: liberty entails self-government. In this new state political liberty and law are not opposed but reconciled since people live under laws they themselves have made. This claim makes the concept of political right the key to understanding legitimate government. The question then arises: how can political right reconcile freedom and government? As has been explained,[38] Rousseau argues that the sovereign established by the pact is 'the people' and the general will of this sovereign people is to maintain conditions of equal liberty.

Once the principle that maximum equal liberty is the fundamental law of the modern state is established,[39] the concept of law is transformed. Law is no longer a restriction on, but an expression of, freedom. The objective of the foundational political pact, Rousseau suggests, is to transform humans from 'stupid and bounded animals' into 'intelligent beings'. This can be achieved only in accordance with this basic law and whoever refuses to obey must be constrained to do so. But this means only that he 'shall be forced to be free'.[40]

Having identified the basic law, Rousseau specifies its operating principles. He explains that since sovereignty expresses the general will, its exercise cannot be

---

[36] SS Wolin, *Politics and Vision: Continuity and Innovation in Western Political Thought* (Princeton: Princeton University Press, exp. edn. 2008), 273, 330–6.

[37] J-J Rousseau, *The Social Contract* [1762] in *The Social Contract and other later political writings*, V Gourevitch ed. (Cambridge: Cambridge University Press, 1997), 39–152, at 41. 'I want to inquire whether in the civil order there can be some legitimate and sure principle of government, taking men as they are, and laws as they can be'.

[38] See above Ch.1, IV.

[39] E Cassirer, *The Question of Jean-Jacques Rousseau*, P Gay trans. (New Haven: Yale University Press, 1963), 63: 'Law in its pure and strict sense is not a mere external bond that holds in individual wills and prevents their scattering; rather it is the constituent principle of these wills...It wishes to rule subjects only inasmuch as, in its every act, it also makes and educates them into citizens.'

[40] Rousseau, *Social Contract*, 53.

transferred, represented, or divided. Sovereignty cannot be possessed or represented by any agent; it permeates the entire order and expresses the autonomy of the political. Laws are 'nothing but the conditions of the civil association', the people subject to them are their author, any state ruled by laws is a republic, and 'every legitimate government is republican'.[41] The constitution is a living organism unified by a synthesis of individual actions that encompass the entire complex of institutional order.

Rousseau's analysis does not focus on positive law but on what he calls 'political laws' or 'fundamental laws'. These are the laws that regulate 'the action of the entire body acting upon itself, that is to say the relation ... of the Sovereign to the State'.[42] His objective is to specify a similar type of law (*droit politique*) to that of Montesquieu. Both Bodin and Montesquieu had tried to identify the principles of political right working from historical experience which for Rousseau is mistaken. Yet he does follow Bodin in recognizing the critical distinction between sovereignty as the exercise of law-making power and government as the office responsible for the execution of the law. Rousseau's specific innovation was to show that, in order to prevent the development of legalized domination, sovereign law-making authority must remain with the people rather than be allocated to the (representative) office of government. The fundamental law of the political domain, he maintained, was the realization of equal liberty in conditions of solidarity.

V. The Revolution in France

French political jurists might not have agreed on the principles of political right but by the mid-eighteenth century they had made considerable advances in devising a common conceptual framework through which these principles could be expressed. They recognized the autonomous character of the political domain and the need to devise an immanent structure of public law based on the concepts of state, sovereignty, and constitution. It remained to show how principles of political right could be embedded in the framework of modern nation-states. This was a challenge that Rousseau sought to finesse through his remarkable figure of the Lawgiver (*le législateur*), a 'superior intelligence' able to design an ideal constitution without performing a governmental role within it.[43] With the Revolution of 1789, this ceased to be a purely philosophical problem and became a vital test of political reality.[44]

---

[41] Rousseau, *Social Contract*, 67–8.   [42] Rousseau, *Social Contract*, 80.

[43] Rousseau, *Social Contract*, 68–72.

[44] F Furet, *Interpreting the French Revolution* (Cambridge: Cambridge University Press, 1981), 31: 'Rousseau may well have been the most far-sighted genius ever to appear in intellectual history, for he invented, or sensed, so many of the problems that were to obsess the nineteenth and twentieth centuries. His political thought set up well in advance the conceptual framework of what was to become Jacobinism and the language of the Revolution, both in his philosophical premises (the fulfilment of the individual through politics) and because the radical character of the new consciousness of historical action is in keeping with his rigorous theoretical analysis of the conditions necessary for the exercise of popular sovereignty. Rousseau was hardly "responsible" for the French Revolution, yet he unwittingly assembled the cultural materials that went into revolutionary consciousness and practice.'

The French Revolution, 'the most important single event in the entire history of government', is of universal significance. 'It razed and effaced all the ancient institutions of France, undermined the foundations of all other European states, and is still sending its shock-waves throughout the rest of the world'.[45] Although Rousseau had predicted in 1762 that 'the crisis is approaching and we are on the edge of a revolution',[46] no political jurists before 1789 had advocated revolution; their various schemes had been 'designed to stave off rather than promote revolution'.[47] But when it came the basics of the political, and not just the elements of political right, were subjected to intense debate.

It is impossible to examine this period of upheaval and conflict without getting entangled in continuing ideological battles, not least over the question of whether 1789 marks 'the year zero of a new world founded on equality'.[48] But my objective is only to consider the prospect of sound principles of political right being incorporated into the new constitutional arrangements of the revolutionary period.

For this purpose, it might be said that the Revolution began on 17 June 1789. This was the moment when the meeting of the Third Estate declared itself to be the National Assembly. This momentous declaration had been drafted by Emmanuel-Joseph Sieyes, and it was he who in *Qu'est ce que le Tiers État?* most concisely explained its significance.[49] Faced with the imminent bankruptcy of the state the King had convened a meeting of the Estates-General. Sieyes argued that this moment was symptomatic of a deeper bankruptcy of the entire political order. Rather than convene the Estates-General, a constituent assembly should have been established to consider fundamental constitutional reform. Prime responsibility for the dire state of affairs, he suggested, lay with the nobility. By virtue of their entrenched feudal privileges, the nobility had in effect seceded from the nation. Far from being active producers of the nation's resources, they had become its most avaricious consumers. Far from being a vital part of the nation, they had become in effect its enemies. As de Tocqueville later put it, 'the nobility ceased to be an aristocracy' charged with the affairs of governing and had become 'a caste'.[50]

In *Qu'est ce que le Tiers État?* Sieyes, capturing the sentiment of the assembly, proclaimed the third estate as the nation.[51] Their declaration demanded that sovereign

---

[45] SE Finer, *The History of Government, vol. 3: Empires, Monarchies and the Modern State* (Oxford: Oxford University Press, 1997–9), 1517; E Burke, *Reflections on the Revolution in France*, CC O'Brien ed. (London: Penguin, 1986), referring to the 1789 Revolution as 'the most astonishing [event] that has hitherto happened in the world'.

[46] Rousseau, *Emile*, above n.34, 145.

[47] R Wokler, 'The Enlightenment Science of Politics' in C Fox, R Porter, and R Wokler (eds), *Inventing Human Science: Eighteenth Century Domains* (Berkeley: University of California Press, 1995), 323–45, at 326.

[48] Furet, above n.44, 2.

[49] E-J Sieyès, 'What is the Third Estate?' in his *Political Writings*, M Sonenscher trans. (Indianapolis: Hackett, 2003), 92–162.

[50] A de Tocqueville, *The Ancien Régime*, J Bonner trans (London: Dent, 1988), 69.

[51] M Forsyth, *Reason and Revolution: The Political Thought of the Abbé Sieyes* (Leicester: Leicester University Press, 1987) 3: 'he [Sieyes] is, more than any other, the man who articulates the political theory of the French Revolution'. See further, J-D Bredin, *Sieyès: Le clé de la revolution française* (Paris: Éditions de Fallois, 1988).

authority be transferred from the King to the nation. These dramatic claims initiated a radical political and legal revolution. The newly-established National (Constituent) Assembly on 4 August 1789 removed the privileges of the aristocracy and the clergy, resulting in the abolition of feudalism and the establishment of the principle of equality before the law. The Assembly then established a committee to prepare a draft constitution and, as an intended preamble to that constitution, on 26 August adopted a *Declaration of the Rights of Man and the Citizen*. This proclaimed that 'men are born and remain free and equal in rights' (art 1), that the aim of 'political association is the preservation of the natural and imprescriptible rights of man' (art 2), that 'sovereignty resides essentially in the nation' (art 3), that law is 'the expression of the general will' (art 6) and that, without a defined separation of powers, a society 'has no constitution at all' (art 16).

These principles of legitimate constitutional ordering owe much to the influence of Rousseau, though Sieyes, their principal architect, does not mention him by name. He argues, contrary to Bodin and Montesquieu, that a nation is not some cultural artefact defined by laws and customs and sanctioned by history. The nation (the state) has its origin in a social contract that transforms an aggregate of isolated individuals into a unified body politic possessed of a single general will. The nation comprises the entire body of citizens and its will is sovereign. 'The nation exists prior to everything; it is the origin of everything. Its will is always legal. It is the law itself'.[52] The nation exists prior to the constitution, and its government serves only at the pleasure of the national will. It follows from Sieyes' argument that the nation is not bound by any prior constitutional order. 'A nation cannot alienate or prohibit its right to will and, whatever its will might be, it cannot lose the right to change it as soon as its interest requires it'.[53] The nation determines the constitutional form of the state by a pure exercise of sovereign will.

In these matters, Sieyes closely follows Rousseau. Where he departs from him is over the formation of the national will. Rousseau had maintained that 'sovereignty cannot be represented' and that 'the moment a people gives itself representatives it is no longer free'.[54] Sieyes, by contrast, argues that a constitution can only be made by representatives. In contrast with the constitutions of the ancient republics Rousseau extolled, a political division of labour was a necessity in a modern state.[55] For Sieyes, the basic law—the general will—is not some ideal collective will: it is formulated by representatives as a 'common will'.[56] A representative body must take the place of an assembly of the entire nation and be charged with making a constitution. That

---

[52] Sieyes, above n.49, 136.   [53] Sieyes, above, n.49, 137.

[54] Rousseau, *Social Contract*, Ch.15.

[55] For discussion of Sieyes on representation see M Sonenscher, Introduction to Sieyes, above n.49, vii–xxii; WH Sewell, Jr, *A Rhetoric of Bourgeois Revolution: The Abbé Sieyes and What is the Third Estate?* (Durham: Duke University Press, 1994), Ch.3.

[56] Sieyes, above n.49, 138. Michael Sonenscher argues that Sieyes' system of representative government is strongly influenced by Montesquieu's argument about the importance of intermediary powers: see M Sonenscher, *Before the Deluge: Public Debt, Inequality, and the Intellectual Origins of the French Revolution* (Princeton: Princeton University Press, 2007), 94–7.

body's common will is as valid as that of the nation itself.[57] The national assembly—and its constitution committee, of which Sieyes was a member—becomes the sole and rightful bearer of the nation's sovereign will.

But the Revolution soon veered out of control. A Constitution was drafted in 1791, with many of its provisions bearing the marks of Sieyes' influence. This was a bourgeois constitution whose purpose was to distance the legislature from the sovereign people, not least by creating a division between an active and passive citizenry.[58] The 1791 Constitution was replaced in 1793, but an implicit alliance between Jacobins and the Parisian sans-culottes campaigning for direct democracy and controls on the economy[59] ensured that the 1793 Constitution was suspended soon after it was ratified. Thereafter came the Terror, the Constitution of Year III, Napoleon's coup d'état in 1799 and a Constitution of Year VII, again mainly written by Sieyes. This last Constitution proved irrelevant when Napoleon was named First Consul, then in 1802 First Consul for life, and finally in 1804 proclaimed Emperor.

What influence did principles of *droit politique* have on the key political actors? Alexis de Tocqueville and, following him, François Furet both moved the debate about the Revolution away from the social and economic towards its political significance. Their recognition of the importance of political culture as a set of symbolic practices throws into relief the juristic implications of the revolutionary debates. Tocqueville argued that, although the Revolution had initially advanced the people's interests, it came to promote the idea of a 'pure democracy'. 'In the beginning they quoted and commented on Montesquieu', he wrote, but 'in the end they talked of no one but Rousseau'.[60] Furet similarly has suggested that 'Rousseau is hardly "responsible" for the French Revolution, yet he unwittingly assembled the cultural materials of revolutionary consciousness and practice'.[61] Often based on a misunderstanding of Rousseau's thought, much revolutionary discourse offered 'an unlimited promise of equality', a 'matrix of universal history', and signified that society 'was ridding itself of the symbolic powers of the State, along with the rules that it imposed'.[62] To these aspects, and especially to the failure of the Revolution to establish a stable constitutional form, I now turn.

VI. The Jacobin Discourse of Natural Right

Constitutional deliberations after 1789 had established the principle of civil equality but had been unable to settle on a system of government. A monarchical constitution drafted in 1791 proved short-lived and was replaced by a republican

---

[57] Sieyes, above n.49,139: 'A body of extraordinary representatives is a surrogate for an assembly of that nation . . . it is a surrogate for the Nation in its *independence* from all constitutional forms'.

[58] Of 24 million citizens, only 4.3 million were designated as active, and only active citizens could vote for the Legislative Assembly. Sieyes attacked the exclusion of women, but he had no compunction about excluding, alongside the nobility, vagabonds, beggars, and servants: Sewell, above n.55, 148.

[59] See M Sonenscher, *Sans-Culottes: An Eighteenth-Century Emblem in the French Revolution* (Princeton: Princeton University Press, 2008).

[60] Tocqueville, *Old Regime*, vol 2, book 1, Ch.5: cited in Furet, above n.44, 45.

[61] Furet, above n.44, 31.   [62] Furet, above n.44, 5, 24.

constitution of 1793. This constitution, ratified in a referendum on universal male suffrage in August, was suspended two months later and, in response to war and the insurrection in the Vendée, a series of emergency measures was instituted. These included the formation of the Committee of Public Safety and the establishment of the Revolutionary Tribunal to judge suspects as 'enemies of the people'. These emergency responses were quickly extended into a system of government,[63] which subsequently descended into the dictatorial regime of violence and fear known as the Terror. Over a period of ten months from September 1793 to 9 Thermidor (27 July 1794), an estimated 500,000 arrests and 16,600 executions took place.[64]

As the Revolution unfolded it became the theatre for many unresolved issues over the principles of political right. Rousseau's construction of 'the general will' had highlighted a tension between the fundamental principles of popular sovereignty and the need to establish a system of government. Although Sieyes had tried to resolve that tension through the principle of representation, no solution had been found to prevent political leadership from usurping the people's sovereign authority. Was Burke then right in predicting that the attempt to establish a political regime on a set of abstract principles divorced from social and political realities could lead only to violence and dictatorship?[65] Was the Terror an inevitable stage in the transition from the old feudal order of servitude to a modern regime based on equal liberty? Was a phase of violent dictatorship necessary in order to make a new people receptive to the precepts of true liberty? Is this what Rousseau had in mind when he said that the people may have 'to be forced to be free'? These questions, which continue to provoke intense controversy, set the context for assessing the juristic foundation of the Jacobin dictatorship.

Emergency had permitted the Jacobins to retain power without having gained popular support.[66] But it would not be accurate to say that during the Terror they simply suspended the law. Their objective was to supplant the principles of political right. Drawing on the authority of the 'solemn declaration' of 1789 with its reference to 'the natural, unalienable, and sacred rights of man', they went about instituting a new type of governing regime founded on *natural* right.

The main architect of this framework for natural jurisprudence was Louis Antoine de Saint-Just, who maintained that 'since there is no society if it is not founded on nature, the state cannot recognize laws other than those of nature'. Law, he

---

[63] See B Mirkine-Guetzévitch, 'Le gouvernement parlementaire sous la Convention' in J Barthélemy and B Mirkine-Guetzévitch (eds), *Le droit public de la Révolution* Cahiers de la Révolution 6 (Paris: Sirey, 1937), 45–91 (arguing that a new regime of government was established during the Terror founded on the idea of the Committee of Public Safety as the prototype of a system of cabinet government).

[64] S de Luca, 'Benjamin Constant and the Terror' in H Rosenblatt (ed.), *The Cambridge Companion to Constant* (Cambridge: Cambridge University Press, 2009), 92–114, at 93.

[65] Burke, *Reflections*, above n.45. See further Ch.4, IV–V. Note also Joseph de Maistre, who argued that the Terror was the punishment inflicted on France for abandoning Christianity: J de Maistre 'Considerations on France' in J Lively (ed.), *The Works of Joseph de Maistre* (London: Allen & Unwin, 1965), 47–91.

[66] Under the 1793 Constitution, new elections had to be held which it was not obvious that the Montagnards/Jacobins would win.

proclaimed, is 'not the expression of will but of nature'.[67] Saint-Just questioned whether France even needed a formal constitution. The 1793 Constitution may have been suspended but the Declaration of Rights had not and this provided an eternal code which amounted to a true constitution. No further documentary authority was required. In a speech to the Convention in May 1793, Robespierre reaffirmed this contention: 'The Declaration of Rights is the Constitution of all peoples, all other laws being variable by nature, and subordinated to this one'.[68]

The Jacobins thus replaced a formal set of rules promulgated by will with a set of principles expressing 'right reason'. One consequence of the claim to 'right reason' was that their ruling authority did not need legitimation by an expression of the people's will through elections and plebiscites. Ruling authority was legitimated by its adherence to the principles of liberty and equality inscribed in natural right. Nature and not the general will was the originating source of legal and political authority. The goal, explained Robespierre, is 'the reign of that eternal justice whose laws are engraved, not on marble or stone, but in the hearts of all men'.[69] And citizens were to be guided towards these principles of 'eternal justice' through the propagation of his cult of the Supreme Being.[70]

In these respects, the Jacobins were hardly faithful followers of Rousseau. Rousseau never claimed that political order rested on natural law: he invoked the social contract, the basic political pact, as a device to transform a world of natural inequality into a civil order of political equality. The civil order established by this pact is dictated by the sovereign people as an expression of the general will, not by a vanguard who consults their own hearts and minds to reveal the dictates of natural right.[71] The natural jurisprudence proclaimed by the Jacobins maintained that 'laws are the natural relations between things' and they are 'neither relative relations nor the effect of the general will'.[72] Rousseau, Saint-Just felt obliged to explain, 'says that the laws are not able to express the general will and concludes by invoking the necessity of a legislator'. But a legislator, Saint-Just contended, 'can only express nature and not the general will'.[73] The Jacobins, in short, were sceptical about the value of assertions of popular sovereignty. They had discovered the foundation of law: it was neither in the general will nor in a common will, but in the precepts of natural right.

The implications became clear in the trial of Louis XVI. Constitutional law decreed that the King was inviolable, but this provision was set aside in favour of a

[67] L-A de Saint-Just, 'De la nature, de l'état civil, de la cité ou les règles de l'indépendance, du gouvernement' [1791–1792] in Saint-Just, *Oeuvres complètes*, A Kupiec ed. (Paris: Gallimard, 2004), 1041–84, at 1079.

[68] May 10, 1793 (Robespierre, *Oeuvres*, vol.9, 507): cited in D Edelstein, *The Terror of Natural Right: Republicanism, the Cult of Nature and the French Revolution* (Chicago: University of Chicago Press, 2009), 190.

[69] Robespierre, *Textes choisis*, vol iii, 112; cited in W Doyle, *The Oxford History of the French Revolution* (Oxford: Oxford University Press, 2nd edn. 2002), 272.

[70] Ibid. 276–7.

[71] Note, however, that Sieyes had left open the possibility of falling back on natural law as a source higher than national sovereignty. After stating that the nation 'exists prior to everything' (above text at n.53) he states: 'Prior to the nation and above the nation there is only natural law'.

[72] Saint-Just, 'De la nature', above n.67, 1067.   [73] Ibid.

discourse of natural right. The Jacobins maintained that since the King had presided over a regime that had destroyed order and put France back into a state of nature, he could be tried as a criminal against humanity.[74] And although the King's subsequent conviction and execution could have been treated as an exception to the ordinary course of the law, this did not happen. The Terror became a state of affairs in which the exception was normalized.[75] In the following year, the law of 22 Prairial made anyone in principle liable for execution and, as the category of outlaw (*hors-la-loi*) was re-interpreted as 'enemy of the people' (*ennemi du genre humain*), offenders could lawfully be executed without trial.[76]

The Jacobins used the concept of natural right to bolster the legitimacy of laws underpinning the Terror. In effect, right triumphed over law. There are, proclaimed Saint-Just, 'too many laws, and too few civil institutions' and 'where there are too many laws the people are enslaved'.[77] Laws were replaced by a kind of cult, an abstract concept of natural right providing a cloak for violent repression.

VII. The Constitutional Question

The rule of natural right came to an abrupt end with the ousting of Robespierre on 9 Thermidor 1794. Realizing at last that a more oppressive government than that of absolute monarchy was possible, the Thermidorians sought to halt the Revolution and re-align the institutions of government with the principles of 1789. Their key task now was to provide the Republic with a stable constitution. Previous attempts had failed and their main proponents, most notably Condorcet, had perished.[78] The

---

[74] M Walzer (ed.), *Regicide and Revolution: Speeches at the trial of Louis XVI* (Cambridge: Cambridge University Press, 1974), 68. Robespierre had earlier been an opponent of capital punishment, just as Saint-Just had been a proponent of constitutional monarchy: see Saint-Just, 'L'Esprit de la Révolution et de la constitution de France' in *Oeuvres complètes*, above n.67, 362–471, at 389–93. Cf. Saint-Just, 'Discours sur le jugement de Louis XVI prononcé à la Convention nationale le 13 novembre 1792', above, n.67, 475–84.

[75] C Lefort, 'The Revolutionary Terror' in his *Democracy and Political Theory*, above n.6, 59–88, at 64: 'The basic argument seems clear: the Convention and the nation are one; the Convention's decisions are sovereign, and are made in accordance with the will of the people; the Committees and the Convention are one, because they are merely its emanation. Similarly, the organs of natural justice derive their authority from the Convention, and it follows that any suspicions directed against the Committees and their justice are also directed against the Convention itself, that suspicion of any kind is intended to destroy the Convention by divorcing itself from its own organs. In short, everything is deduced from the principle that the people, the Convention, the Committees and justice are one and the same; the legitimacy and pertinence of the decisions that have been taken therefore cannot be questioned.'

[76] Doyle, above n.69, 275. The hors-la-loi decree had initially been directed primarily against the Vendée insurgents but following Danton's motion all counter-revolutionaries were declared hors-la-loi. The execution of 'counter-revolutionaries', under the orders of military commissions, accounted for 78 per cent of deaths in the Terror: Edelstein, above n.68, 19.

[77] Saint-Just, 'Institutions républicaines' in *Oeuvres*, above n.67, 1085–147, at 1135–6.

[78] Condorcet was the only *philosophe* who performed an active role in the Revolution and the only one to espouse republicanism for France. He had advocated the establishment of a republic on the principle of universal suffrage, was critical of the property qualification in the 1791 Constitution but his key work, on the Girondine constitution of 1793, was rejected by the Jacobins because of its federalism and weak executive power. The Jacobins then took this over, perverted his project, and this became the still-born 1793 Constitution. Condorcet fell from favour because of his association with the Girondine

question remained: how could a supreme principle of popular sovereignty be reconciled with the protection of basic rights? Their deliberations resulted in the Constitution of Year III (1795), which established a two-chamber system and a weak executive indirectly elected by the legislative assembly. The problem was that the Convention, fearing counter-revolutionary movements, sought to preserve itself through re-election and co-optation but in doing so it 'destroyed what had been at the very heart of its plan – a Republic founded on law'.[79] That constitution lasted until Napoleon's coup of 18 Brumaire (9 November 1799).

Into this febrile atmosphere stepped Benjamin Constant, who had arrived in Paris from his native Switzerland in 1795. Constant, the quintessential Thermidorian jurist, devoted his considerable intellectual energies to the question of how the Republic might draw a line under its revolutionary origins and establish its constitutional authority. He produced the most innovative work on *droit politique* of the period. Constant welcomed the Revolution as marking the end of the old feudal order,[80] but criticized the manner of its unfolding. The Terror, he argued, enacted a parody of liberty: far from purifying citizens to render them ready for 'true' political liberty, it made them insecure and fearful.[81] It could lead the people only to slavishness or insurrection, both of which subverted political authority. A primary source of this evil had been the revolutionary devotion to a purely abstract conception of right. 'There is no despotism in the world, however inept its plans and oppressive its measures', he noted, 'which does not know how to plead some abstract purpose of a plausible and desirable kind.'[82]

Constant was a liberal by conviction but, more precisely, he was a political jurist.[83] Situating himself in the tradition of Montesquieu and Rousseau,[84] he built

---

constitution but also because he objected to the trial of the King by the Convention; he voted to find the King guilty but refused to vote for the death penalty. Arrested in April 1794, he died in prison before the guillotine was able to do its work. Condorcet's constitutional ideas, founded on universal suffrage, representative democracy, and protection of civil rights remain a model of a modern liberal democratic constitution. See D Williams, *Condorcet and Modernity* (Cambridge: Cambridge University Press, 2007), Chs 6–8. The other constitutionalist of note was Sieyes who, when asked what he did during the Terror, commented: 'I survived'.

[79] F Furet, *The French Revolution, 1770–1814*, A Nevill trans. (Oxford: Blackwell, 1992), 166.

[80] B Constant, 'Principles of Politics applied to all Representative Governments' [1815] in his *Political Writings*, B. Fontana trans. (Cambridge: Cambridge University Press, 1988), 169–305, at 173: 'Twenty-three years ago [1792] they [the European powers] . . . attacked us because we wanted our own government, because we had liberated the peasant from the tithe, the protestant from intolerance, thought from censorship, the citizen from arbitrary detention and exile, the plebeian from the insults of the privileged'.

[81] B Constant, *Principles of Politics Applicable to all Governments* [1810], D O'Keeffe trans., E Hoffman ed. (Indianapolis: Liberty Fund, 2003), at 20: 'It was in the name of freedom that we got prisons, scaffolds, and endless multiplied persecution'. [The Fontana edition is a translation of the only edition published in Constant's lifetime. The Hoffman edition, being less of a manual of applied politics, expresses his political principles in their most extended form.]

[82] Constant, *Principles* [1810], 59.

[83] The most subtle liberal account is: S Holmes, *Benjamin Constant and the Making of Modern Liberalism* (New Haven: Yale University Press, 1984). Holmes notes: 'The influence of this *politique* tradition [deriving from Bodin and Montaigne] on Constant's thinking was decisive' (at 9).

[84] Constant, *Principles* [1810], above n.81, 20: 'Research relating to the constitutional organization of government having been, since *The Social Contract* and *The Spirit of the Laws*, the favourite speculative

his argument from the elementary concepts of war and peace, state and sovereignty. He recognized that war, which is 'in man's nature', could help to shape certain fine human faculties, including 'heroic devotion', the formation of 'sublime friendships', and the forging of a 'national spirit of the people'.[85] If the birth of states is traced to their origins, this warlike characteristic—the criterion of friend-enemy—offered a perfectly serviceable account of their formation. But he also recognized that the modern world was the age of commerce and 'the more the commercial tendency prevails, the weaker must the tendency to war become'.[86] Following Montesquieu, Constant argued that in the modern era, war loses 'its charm as well as its utility'.[87]

Constant maintained that all governments, whether despotic or liberal, have a repressive and coercive aspect. Without a monopoly on the use of force, governments do not have the authority to ensure that citizens obey and that order is maintained. The critical distinction between liberal and despotic government is not the absence or presence of coercion; it is the existence of institutional arrangements that accord with the customs of a people. The revolutionaries' great failure was that they tried to 'build their edifice' by 'grinding and reducing to the dust the [inherited] materials that they were to employ'. This removed a 'natural source of patriotism', which they then sought to replace by 'a factitious passion for an abstract being, a general idea stripped of all that can engage the imagination and speak to the memory'.[88] Only by strengthening institutional arrangements which command the respect of the people could authority be acquired and political power generated. Constant, like Bodin and Montesquieu, advocated institution-building as the key principle of political right.[89]

Constant's great achievement was to have synthesized the principles of Montesquieu and Rousseau.[90] His *Principes de politique*, founding the political on the concepts of state and sovereignty, provides an authoritative statement of *droit*

---

focus of the most enlightened of our writers in France, is now very decidedly out of favour today. I am not examining here at all whether this disfavour is justified; but it is certainly quite understandable. In a few years we have tried some five or six constitutions and found ourselves the worse for it. No argument can prevail against such an experience.'

[85] B Constant, 'The Spirit of Conquest and Usurpation and their Relation to European Civilization' in his *Political Writings*, B Fontana trans. (Cambridge: Cambridge University Press, 1988), 43–167, at 51.

[86] Constant, ibid. 53.

[87] Constant, ibid. 55. See Montesquieu, above n.22, esp. Bks 20–24. Constant studied at Edinburgh University in 1783–1785, when scholars of the Scottish Enlightenment under Montesquieu's influence were developing their 'four stages thesis'. See reports of Adam Smith's lectures at Glasgow during the 1760s: A Smith, *Lectures on Jurisprudence*, RL Meek, DD Raphael, and PG Stein eds (Oxford: Oxford University Press, 1978), i.27 (p.14); RL Meek, *Social Science and the Ignoble Savage* (Cambridge: Cambridge University Press, 1976).

[88] Constant, 'Conquest', above n.85, 74. [89] Bodin, text at n16; Montesquieu text at n.33.

[90] T Todorov, *A Passion for Democracy: Benjamin Constant* (London: Algora, 1999), 35; H Rosenblatt, 'Why Constant? A Critical Overview of the Constant Revival' (2004) 1 *Modern Intellectual History* 439–53, at 444: 'Constant's thought was certainly more concerned with advancing democracy than it was with containing it. There is, in fact, little ambivalence about democracy in Constant. He admired Rousseau, was a consistent advocate of popular sovereignty, and looked very favorably upon what he hailed as the "march of equality" throughout history. Constant did not worry so much about the so-called "excesses" of democracy as he did about political hypocrisy—the abuse of words and concepts by despots with the aim of masking self-serving and oppressive regimes.'

politique for the modern world. From Rousseau he derives the principle that a regime acquires its legitimacy from popular sovereignty: monarchical regimes could be established by popular will, but they are commonly the product of force rather than right.[91] From Montesquieu he derives the principle that the ruling power acquires its authority not only from its legitimating source as an expression of popular will, but also from the manner in which power is exercised.[92] Modern governments must not only claim a democratic mandate but also act through accepted constitutional forms.

Many errors of the Revolution, Constant believed, could be traced to Rousseau's teaching,[93] though the Jacobins had often misinterpreted him. They had failed in particular to appreciate the importance of maintaining the clear distinction between sovereignty and government which Rousseau had adopted from Bodin. Instead, they instituted a regime of political liberty suffused with allusions to the republican virtues of ancient Greece and Rome which even Rousseau had recognized was inappropriate for modern nation-states. Under Rousseau's influence, the Jacobins had also conflated two different concepts of liberty, the ancient and the modern.[94] Modern liberty, founded on individual subjective right, protected a zone of privacy, independence, and protection from the exercise of arbitrary power. It was a concept unknown to the ancient world. The ancient idea of liberty, by contrast, expressed collective independence from rule by foreigners and required the active participation of citizens in collective self-government. This could only be achieved in small, culturally homogeneous city-states that promoted a politics of virtue founded on a martial spirit.[95] It was also invariably a slaveholding, warriors' republic of male citizens, which upheld a form of liberty incompatible with general equality. For some to be free, others had to be slaves.

Constant accepted the contemporary value of both concepts but advocated the need for balance. The prevalence of the modern conception, he suggested, was just as distortive as the dominance of the ancient; the atrophy of the political could be as dangerous as a total politicization of society. The Jacobin error stemmed from their adherence to an ancient idea of liberty in an emerging modern world founded on equality and the abhorrence of slavery. Liberty in the modern world of the political had to recognize the distinctions between public and private, political and social, participation and independence. Political liberty presupposes civil liberty and modern constitutional ordering involves an interlocking arrangement in which these two distinct forms of freedom reinforce one another.

---

[91] *Principles* [1810], above n.81, 22.

[92] *Principles* [1810], above n.81, 38: 'The legitimacy of government depends on its purpose as well as upon its source. When the government is extended to purposes outside its competence, it becomes illegitimate'.

[93] *Principles of Politics* [1815], 177: '...his *Social Contract*, so often invoked in favour of liberty, [made] the most formidable support for all kinds of despotism'.

[94] B Constant, 'The Freedom of the Ancients Compared with that of the Moderns' [1819] in his *Political Writings*, above n.80, 307–28.

[95] S Holmes, 'The Liberty to Denounce: Ancient and Modern' in Rosenblatt (ed.), above n.64, 47–69, at 52: 'The 'brutally violent, competitive and dangerous world outside each city's walls goes a long way to explaining the kind of liberty cherished by inhabitants of ancient republics'.

The serious limitation in Rousseau's concept of political right highlighted by Constant is that it did not have a sufficiently robust theory of government. Sovereignty might have been transferred from the King to the people but under Rousseau's influence revolutionary leaders failed to establish a stable system of government. Constant argued that a system of government relying entirely on the will of the people through election will struggle to maintain its authority. Authority could be enhanced only by establishing institutional arrangements with the same degree of permanence and independence as kingship. His objective, then, was to discover the principles of modern constitutional ordering that could meet these tests.

The modern political world founds itself on the division between public and private. Differentiation between state and society is created by the distinct sphere of civil society but this does not diminish the domain of the political; rather, the autonomy of the political and the autonomy of the social presuppose each other. In an assessment of Constant's achievements, Marcel Gauchet notes that 'it is misleading to speak as if there was a certain sum of power and authority to be divided, so that increase on one side leads to decrease on other'.[96] Modernity leads to a growth in both social and political power, with each drawing on the other in a reflexive process. The democratic impetus releases social power at the same time as it extends the nature, scale and range of governmental power. In modern regimes, hierarchical ordering, a characteristic of regal authority, diminishes, but 'the political' continues 'to serve as society's symbolic underpinning, the source of its collective identity and cohesiveness'.[97] This 'symbolic underpinning' is found in the constitutional form of modern states. But this constitution is arranged on the principle of complex organization rather than command and obedience.

This was Constant's insight. In order to maintain its authority and legitimacy, modern governments must fulfil the crucial function of representing society. Their primary goal was not the promotion of virtue but the maintenance of peace and for this an impartial rule structure—a constitutional arrangement of considerable institutional complexity—is required.[98] He acknowledged the principle of legislative supremacy—'it is representative assemblies alone that can infuse life into the political body'[99]—but also emphasized the importance of maintaining a division of powers. This is not to limit the power of government, as classical liberals demand. It is to build the power and authority of government by enhancing its capacity for collective action. A constitution is 'more than an instrument for protecting citizens from misuses of state power: it creates a mechanism for public learning and governmental self-correction'.[100]

Constant here touches on the central issue of how a constitution establishes its authority. He recognizes that the political power generated through a constitution contains an element that is not derived from delegation and mandate. In this respect,

[96] M Gauchet, 'Liberalism's Lucid Illusion' in Rosenblatt (ed.), above n.64, 23–46, at 34.
[97] Gauchet, ibid. 36.
[98] *Principles* [1810], above n.81, 418: 'The ancients, having less need of individual freedom than we, attached the highest importance to laws about social mores. We give a comparable importance to constitutional mechanisms.'
[99] *Principles* [1815], 197.   [100] Holmes, above n.83, 144.

'the political order is in some respects prior to the will of citizens'.[101] This is what political jurists had in mind when they conceived 'the state' as an omnipotent and impersonal power.[102] In other words, a constitution's authority is established only when its autonomy is recognized. Constant underscores this point by invoking the need to establish a 'neutral' or 'preservative' power.[103] Such power maintains the principle of unity in government: its purpose is 'to defend government against division among the governing and to defend the governed against oppression by the government'.[104] For this an authority independent of both the people and the executive is needed.[105] This is the constitution's monarchical element.[106] But it does not express a form of government; it merely operates 'as a cog in the constitutional division of functions'.[107] Its function is to ensure that society and government operate in harmony.[108]

Constant's objective was to demonstrate the central importance of the constitution in the construction of modern political authority. Constitutions are more than mere declarations of principles. 'All the constitutions which have been given to France guaranteed the liberty of the individual', he noted, 'and yet, under the rule of these constitutions, it had been constantly violated'.[109] In order to establish their authority, they must be in accordance with the social mores of their subjects.[110] Constant presents a profound analysis of the constitution's role in the concept of political right.

[101] Gauchet, above n.96, 41.

[102] See Loughlin, FPL, Ch.7. For its significance in the French tradition see: A Guéry, 'The State' in P Nora (ed.), *Rethinking France: Les Lieux de Mémoire, Vol. 1*, M Trouille trans. (Chicago: University of Chicago Press, 2001), Ch.1.

[103] See B Constant, *Fragments d'un ouvrage abandonné sur la possibilité d'une constitution républicaine dans un grand pays*, H Grange ed. (Paris: Aubier, 1991), Book 8: 'D'un pouvoir neuter ou préservateur, necessaire dans toutes les constitutions'.

[104] Constant. ibid. 387: 'Le but du pouvoir préservateur est de défendre le gouvernement de la division des gouvernants, et de défendre les gouvernés de l'oppression du gouvernement.'

[105] Constant, ibid. 375: 'Il faudrait en consequence créer un pouvoir dont l'intérêt fût distinct à la fois et de celui du pouvoir législatif et de celui du pouvoir exécutif'. [It would consequently be necessary to create a power whose interest would at the same time be distinct from both the legislative and the executive power.]

[106] Constant noted that this neutral power incorporates a monarchical dimension with two elements: the executive, with positive prerogatives, and the royal, which is based on illusions derived from religion and tradition (action and representation). Constitutional monarchy's strength is that it involved a separation not into three branches but five: royal power, executive, power that represents permanence (hereditary), power that represents opinion (elected), and judicial power. Royal power is neutral power: Constant, *Principles* [1815] ch 2, at 184–5.

[107] Holmes, above n.83, 145.

[108] 'This marks the beginning of an effort to explore the ultimate nature of power, its true raison d'être and authentic functions'. Gauchet, above n.96, 40.

[109] *Principles* [1815], 289.

[110] Constant, *Political Writings*, above n.80, 172: 'Constitutions are seldom made by the will of men. Time makes them. They are introduced gradually and in an almost imperceptible way. Yet there are circumstances in which it becomes indispensable to make a constitution. But then do only what is indispensable. Leave room for time and experience, so that these two reforming powers may direct your already constituted powers in the improvement of what has been done and the completion of what is still to be done.' See further Rosenblatt, above n.89, 444: 'one of the great innovations of French liberals like Constant was their sociological approach to both history and political theory. It was they who first emphasized socio-economic change and invented the concept of a social revolution.'

VIII. The Impact of Positivism and the Growth of Social Science

The philosophers of the Enlightenment maintained that reason and experience were the sole sources of authority. Relying heavily on the power of reason, their revolutionary disciples had destroyed the old political order without successfully fashioning a new one. The solution, some argued, must be to start from a different premise and anchor political ideas in experiential reality. Most prominent was Henri, Comte de Saint-Simon, who blamed the failure of the Revolution squarely on lawyers and their abstract theories. Metaphysical doctrines had led to the Terror and an unworkable form of government. Modern political leaders must be guided by scientific principles. 'The philosophy of the eighteenth century was critical and revolutionary', Saint-Simon noted, whereas that of the nineteenth century will have to be 'inventive and constructive'.[111] Political authority is acquired not through abstract reasoning but through the material benefits government confers. Authority is generated through the supply of collective goods—defence, law and order, and physical and social infrastructure—that enhance the security, wellbeing, and happiness of subjects.

During the nineteenth century, the growth in technical knowledge about the functions of government produced a new search for the sources of its legitimacy. This was driven by pioneering scholars of the nascent social sciences. Innovators such as Saint-Simon, Comte, and Durkheim situated themselves in the Cartesian tradition defined as: 'providing a fixed and unvarying meaning to concepts; expressing truth in clear and distinct ideas; arguing with precision and elegance; moving from simple to complex forms; cultivating a sense of moral autonomy and intellectual audacity; and overcoming one's passions'.[112] They drew on the work of the *philosophes*, especially Montesquieu and Condorcet, in their attempts to trace the trajectory of human progress, but were critical of their methods. Science, not metaphysics, was needed.

There had already been elements of functionalism in revolutionary discourse. In the opening pages of *Qu'est ce que le Tiers État?*, Sieyes had adopted a modern classification, arguing that the nation consists not of three hierarchical feudal estates, but of four distinct classes: landed labour, industrialists, merchants, and professional and scientific occupations. In similar vein, Saint-Simon argued that by 1789 the feudal order was defunct and that the true revolutionary challenge was that of 'organizing the industrial and scientific system summoned by the level of civilization to replace it [the feudal order]'. The underlying problem was that revolutionary leaders had just transferred power from one set of hands to another, whereas the real challenge was to recognize the changing nature of power itself. Modern governments, Saint-Simon maintained, 'will no longer command men: their function will be limited

---

[111] Cited in J Jennings, *Revolution and Republic: A History of Political Thought in France since the Eighteenth Century* (Oxford: Oxford University Press, 2011), 347.
[112] S Hazareesingh, *How the French Think: An Affectionate Portrait of an Intellectual People* (London: Allen Lane, 2015), 33.

to ensuring that all useful work is not hindered'.[113] Command would be replaced by co-ordination.

It fell to Auguste Comte, Saint-Simon's faithful pupil, to put his ideas into methodical form. In his *Système de politique positive* of 1824, Comte presented a systematic exposition of the main branches of social inquiry. He argued that human knowledge passes through three developmental stages: the theological (or fictional), the metaphysical (or abstract), and the scientific (or positive). Only in the scientific era can we, through observation and inductive reason, discover the laws that govern phenomena. In so doing, the disorder and uncertainties of the Revolution would be resolved. The abstractions of metaphysics must be replaced by the science of social physics, when the government of men could be replaced by the administration of things. In this new type of order, the word 'right'—being a theological-metaphysical concept—must be 'excluded from the proper language of politics' to be replaced by the language of duty.[114]

Comte's innovation in establishing a 'social physics'—what he later called 'sociology'[115]—was advanced by Émile Durkheim, holder of the first chair of social science in France. Analysing the methodology of Rousseau and Montesquieu in his doctoral dissertation, Durkheim explained that, in seeking to discover the nature of law, Montesquieu had been 'obliged to investigate religion, morality and the family, with the result that he has actually written a treatise dealing with social phenomena as a whole'.[116] It was society rather than the state as the source of political unity that should now come under scrutiny. His pioneering studies of such phenomena as religion were not intended to reveal either the truth or falsity of religious belief but to examine the significance of religion as a bond holding society together.[117]

So what impact did this positivist, scientific turn have on the concept of *droit politique*? Nineteenth century industrialization and urbanization had eroded traditional social cohesion, including religion, and opened up deep divisions in society. To address them, governmental action on an unprecedented scale was needed. This raised profound questions about the function of the state, about political unity, and about the relationship between legality and legitimacy. These became the most contentious jurisprudential issues of the Third Republic. The orthodox response from both the professions and the academy to the growing influence of positivist ideas was to confine their discipline to the study of positive law. In doing so, the state came to be conceived as a merely functional institution whose legitimacy depended on the delivery of collective services. The abstract concept of the state no longer served any useful purpose and should be replaced by the concrete expression, 'government'.[118]

---

[113] Saint-Simon, *Oeuvres*, vol.2, 168: cited in Jennings, above n.111, 349.

[114] A Comte, *Discours sur l'ensemble du positivisme* (1848), 357: cited in Jennings, above n.111, 359.

[115] See A Comte, *Cours de philosophie positive* (Paris: Ballière, 2nd edn. 1864); A Comte, *Auguste Comte and Positivism: The Essential Writings*, G Lenzer ed. (New York: Harper, 1975), 254–5.

[116] É Durkheim, *Montesquieu and Rousseau as Forerunners of Sociology*, R Mannheim trans. (Ann Arbor: Michigan University Press, 1960), 2.

[117] É Durkheim, *The Elementary Forms of Religious Life* [1912], C Cosman trans. (Oxford: Oxford University Press, 2001).

[118] See, e.g., Henri Berthélemy, Professor of Administrative Law in the University of Paris, who wrote that he wanted to avoid, so far as possible, the use of the word 'state': 'par lequel, presque toujours,

A parallel line of argument led jurists to redefine the state as a political fact of little legal significance. This reached its apogee in the work of Raymond Carré de Malberg, who placed the state at the centre of inquiry but ignored the sources of power on which its authority was established. He converted the issue of the state's legitimacy from a juridical question into one of fact.[119] In place of *droit politique*—how does the adherence to principles of right enhance the authority of the state?—he presented a simple functional logic: can the state serve its purpose of maintaining order and protecting the nation?

The Third Republic's Constitution of 1875, which established the basic organizational arrangements of government but contained no declaration of rights, sought to bring closure to the revolutionary rhetoric of *droit politique*. In the views of leading legal positivist public lawyers like Esmein and Carré de Malberg, the 1789 Declaration of Rights had no legal status whatsoever.[120] Nevertheless, the question remained of how to express a sense of political unity. The *doctrinaires*—liberals such as Royer-Collard and Guizot who were highly influential in the first half of the nineteenth century—sought a resolution by incorporating the authority to express the general will entirely into the legislative power.[121] But with the rapid growth in the administrative tasks of government, this answer was unconvincing. The 1875 Constitution had 'passed over the subject of the administration in silence',[122] but it remained a major source of contention. The answer offered by Joseph Barthélemy was that, although the legislature enacted the laws (*lois*), the fundamental law (*droit*) could be articulated and enforced only by the executive. The role of the executive was 'to assure through spontaneous and continuous intervention the very life of the state'.[123] This question of how political unity could be maintained in the administrative state preoccupied two of the Third Republic's most innovative public lawyers: Léon Duguit and Maurice Hauriou.

Using the ideas Comte and Durkheim, Duguit presents a sociological positivist account of law which discards *droit politique* due to its metaphysical foundation. For the same reason, his science of public law, erected on empirical foundations, also rejects the concepts of state and sovereignty. The state cannot possess a will: what exists are the 'individual wills of those governing', a fact that cannot be avoided by

on veut designer les gouvernants'. H Berthélemy, *Libres entretiens de l'Union pour la Vérité*, 4th series (1907–1908): cited in HS Jones, *The French State in Question: Public law and political argument in the Third Republic* (Cambridge: Cambridge University Press, 1993), 44.

[119] R Carré de Malberg, *Contribution à la théorie générale de l'État, spécialement d'après les données fournies par le droit constitutionnel français*, 2 vols. (Paris: Sirey, 1920), vol. 1, 65–6: 'The birth of the state coincides with the establishment of its first constitution, written or not . . . . This original constitution is, like the very state to which it gives birth, only a pure fact, unaffected by all juridical qualifications: its establishment in effect does not derive from a juridical order anterior to this state.'

[120] A Esmein, *Eléments de droit constitutionnel français et comparé* (Paris: Sirey, 1921), vol 1, 559; Carré de Malberg, above n.119, vol.1, 579.

[121] A Craiutu, *Liberalism under Siege: The Political Thought of the French Doctrinaires* (Lanham, Md: Rowman & Littlefield, 2003).

[122] Jones, above n.118, 70.

[123] J Barthélemy, *Le role du pouvoir exécutif dans les républiques modernes* (Paris: Giard & Brière, 1906): cited in DW Bates, 'Political Unity and the Spirit of the Laws: Juridical Concepts of the State in the Late Third Republic' (2005) 28 *French Historical Studies* 69–101, at 74.

postulating a legal personality for the state.[124] Duguit also rejected the idea of there being a particular form of power—political power—generated through 'rightful authority'. Political power is simply a fact, vested in those who govern. Since this power can never in its origins be legitimate, it cannot yield a right to govern. Those in power govern legitimately only by conforming to what he calls 'the jural principle' (*la règle de droit*).[125]

Duguit's 'jural principle' or 'rule of law' derives from the principle of social solidarity. It is a collectivist reworking of the categorical imperative: 'Do nothing which can possibly infringe upon social interdependence... [and] do all that is within your power... to insure and increase social interdependence'.[126] This is an objective law, a fact established through scientific observation. It confers no rights: rulers have no right to command and individuals have no rights of liberty or property. The jural principle establishes a regime of duties: everyone subject to this objective law is required to promote social solidarity. One consequence is that public service supersedes the general will as the foundational concept.

Droit politique, founded on a system of subjective rights, is thus overthrown and replaced with a regime of objective law. *Droit politique* is merely a scholarly invention that confers legitimacy on the exercise of force. Following Saint-Simon, Duguit contends that the true basis of public law is not command but organization.[127]

Duguit's realist analysis did not go unchallenged. Some argued that in criticizing theories founded on abstract principles, he had himself used the abstractions of solidarity, service, and government.[128] His analysis was also challenged by Hauriou, who accepted that theories founded on subjective right were skewed, but argued that so too was Duguit's objective law.[129] Writing at the end of the nineteenth century, Hauriou maintained that the foundations of authority in France had still not been settled after the violent upheavals of 1789.[130] The Revolution had been driven by three main ideological themes. First, despite the rhetoric of liberty, it had in fact been driven by egalitarianism. Secondly, egalitarianism in the name of a mystical *demos* had resulted in the conflation of legislative will with the general will, creating an overbearing centralization of power. Thirdly, the revolutionary spirit had imbibed a Rationalist mentality marked by a profound distrust of customary ways.[131] These three revolutionary themes were the source of problems with which France was still living. They determined Hauriou's agenda for political reform,[132] and also shaped

---

[124] L Duguit, 'The Law and the State' (1917) 31 *Harvard Law Review* 1–185, at 162.

[125] Ibid. 163.   [126] Ibid. 178.

[127] L Duguit, *Law in the Modern State*, F and H Laski trans. (London: Allen & Unwin, 1921), 49.

[128] L Michoud, *La théorie de la personnalité morale et son application au droit français* (Paris: Librairie Générale de Droit et de Jurisprudence, 1906), Pt I, 44–53.

[129] M Hauriou, 'Les idées de M. Duguit' (1911) 7 *Recueil de législation de Toulouse* 1–40; id, 'The Two Realisms' [1912] in Broderick (ed.), *The French Institutionalists*, 45–51, below, at n.133.

[130] M Hauriou, *La science sociale traditionelle* (Paris: Larose, 1896), 192: 'Nous n'avons pas retrouvé notre équilibre depuis la violente refonte révolutionnaire de 1789'. Cited in CB Gray, *The Methodology of Maurice Hauriou* (Amsterdam: Rodopi, 2010), 3.

[131] Hauriou, above n.130, 20–5.

[132] Hauriou's most basic reform argument, expressed throughout his studies, is that the revolutionary pursuit of equality through centralization had destroyed the authority of those intermediate associations

his legal method. He was evidently opposed to the Jacobin's abstract and deviant conception of *droit politique*, but did he supplant the concept or just rework it?

Hauriou's most innovative contribution to jurisprudence is his institutional theory of law. This holds that institutions provide the juridical basis of state and society.[133] Rousseau had used the device of the social contract because the institutions of his time were corrupt, but in the process he confused force with power. Society, Hauriou asserts, is not founded on violence but on the power that builds its authority through gradual social acceptance. He acknowledges the importance of power as *potestas*, a central concept of political right. Contrary to the received legal positivist view that law makes institutions, Hauriou maintains that institutions make law.[134] In this respect, his theory follows on from Montesquieu's spirit of the laws. Adopting Montesquieu's argument that order founds itself on a balance of governmental powers, Hauriou argues that this is why 'governmental power is not just a simple force but a rightful power capable of creating law'.[135]

The juridical basis for Hauriou's institutionalism is less clear.[136] His institutional theory maintains that 'the foundation of institutions has a juridical character and that...the bases of juridical duration are juridical themselves'.[137] In institutions that are constituted bodies, such as states, trades unions, and other incorporated associations, 'organized power' is an expression of the 'directing idea' (*idée directrice*) of that body. These two concepts form the core of his theory. The directing idea is an ideal manifestation of the tasks to be realized by that body and the organized power of government exists in order to realize the directing idea. But Hauriou also recognizes that the directing ideas of an institution often appear to be 'moral or intellectual' rather than 'properly juridical'.[138] He argues, nevertheless, that these ideas acquire a juridical status as 'higher principles of law', examples of which are the declarations of rights produced during the American and French revolutions.[139] These higher principles, illustrations of what he calls 'superlegality', are expressions of a 'constituent power' which keeps the laws and formal constitution in tune with the evolving character of the directing idea.[140]

Despite its ambiguities and complexities, Hauriou's theory is evidently a species of *droit politique*. He notes that corporate bodies such as the state 'sustain...themselves by their power'.[141] He recognizes that maintaining balance across governing institutions builds authority and presents the 'directing idea' as an institutional variant of Rousseau's general will. He also accepts that 'every positive law or order of the government is conformed to right order of some kind until it is proven contradictory to

---

that operated between citizens and central government and which provided the bedrock of order and equilibrium in the state.

[133] M Hauriou, 'The Theory of the Institution and the Foundation: A Study in Social Vitalism' in A Broderick (ed.), *The French Institutionalists: Maurice Hauriou, Georges Renard, Joseph T. Delos* (Cambridge, MA: Harvard University Press, 1970), 93–124, at 93 [trans. of 'La théorie de l'institution et de la fondation' (1925) 4 *Cahiers de la nouvelle journée* 2–45].

[134] Ibid. 123.   [135] Ibid. 105.   [136] See further Ch.6, III below.
[137] Hauriou, above n. 133, 99.   [138] Hauriou, 114.   [139] Hauriou, 115.
[140] Hauriou, 120.   [141] 'Theory of the Institution', above n.133, 122.

"the rule of law" which is another kind of law'.[142] Hauriou argues that Duguit's error was to have relied too much on the principle of objective law. This is limiting because it does not contain a 'subjective seed': a constituent power.[143] The objective element, he contends, subsists not in a juridical rule but in the institution with its directing idea and organized power. This comparative assessment led Carl Schmitt to note with some asperity that the 'juristic positivism of Duguit is thoroughly of the metaphysical kind, and the alleged mystic Hauriou is "more real", more down-to-earth and in this sense by far "more positive" than a doctrinaire of principles and pure "scientific" positivism'.[144]

IX. Post-War Legacies

Hauriou and Duguit were jurists of the first rank. Each recognized the impact that the rapid growth of governmental powers was having on legal form but neither Hauriou's institutionalism nor Duguit's realism established a strong school of French jurisprudence in twentieth century. Instead the dominant tradition of French scholarship in public law has been built on the relatively orthodox acceptance of legal positivism. This preserves the purity of legal science by severing issues of history and politics from juristic inquiry. Public law scholarship was based on the concept of the state but in accordance with positivist orthodoxy the state was conceived to be a legal person whose authority was just a political fact. Some jurists have resisted this reductive manoeuvre,[145] adopting a concept of public law within the broad idea of *droit politique*.[146] But such works are not typical.

Droit politique was therefore in danger of disappearing from French thought. But during the last fifty years it has been revived from an unusual source. *Droit politique* has been rejuvenated by political theorists working in a Marxist, or post-Marxist, tradition. As the Fourth Republic morphed into the Fifth in 1958, many on the left expressed concern that the growth of presidential powers marked the end of

---

[142] Hauriou, 'Les Ideés de M. Duguit' above n.129, 14: 'toute loi positive ou tout ordre de gouvernement sont présumés conformes à espèce de droit jusqu'à ce qu'ils sont en contradiction avec "le règle de droit" qui est une espèce de droit'.

[143] Ibid. 123.

[144] C Schmitt, *On the Three Types of Juristic Thought* [1934], JW Bendersky trans (Westport, CT Praeger, 2004), 87.

[145] See, e.g., G Burdeau, *L'État* (Paris: Éditions du Seuil, 1970), 14: 'The state is an idea, not a tangible phenomenon; it is a product of thought. There is no land, no people, no body of mandatory rules. Certainly, all these sensitive data are not foreign to it, but it transcends them. Its existence does not belong to the tangible phenomenology; it is of the order of the spirit. The state is in the full sense of the word, an idea. Having no other conceptual reality it exists only because it is thought.' ['Il n'est ni territoire, ni population, ni corps de règles obligatoires. Certes, toutes ces données sensibles ne lui sont pas étrangères, mais il les transcende. Son existence n'appartient pas à la phenomenology tangible; elle est de l'ordre de l'esprit. L'État est, au sens pleine du terme, une idée. N'ayant d'autre réalité que conceptuelle il n'existe que parce qu'il est pensé.']

[146] See, e.g., O Beaud, *La Puissance de l'État* (Paris: Presses universitaires de France, 1994), presenting a historically-orientated account of the development of public law from Bodin to present day, organized on the themes of *souveraineté* and *le pouvoir constituant*. See also, O Beaud, *Théorie de la Fédération* (Paris: Presses universitaires de France: 2007).

republicanism. Consequently, when Furet proclaimed that 'the Revolution is over', he intended to signal an end to the 'unlimited promise of equality', to the Revolution as 'a matrix of universal history', and to the belief that representative democracy was only 'a historical stage of social organization that was destined to be superseded'.[147] After the events of 1968, however, the French revolutionary catechism was amended, and some strands of this revision led to a restoration of *droit politique*—in thought at least if not in practice.

This reappraisal should be placed in context. French pioneers of sociology saw the evolution of modernity as positive, material progress based on advancements in scientific knowledge. They had little to say about its darker side. They recognized that continuing material progress would lead to the growth of administrative power, but not that this expansion of bureaucracy might lead to a loss of individual autonomy and creativity. Tocqueville had issued a warning in the mid-nineteenth century. Questioning the assumption that equality and liberty were complementary (and therefore that *droit politique* involved a simple reconciliation), he predicted that equality of conditions, far from providing its foundation might actually threaten liberty.[148] He foresaw that the growth of democracy could lead to a new variety of 'tutelary power' quite different from the arbitrary power exercised by the old regime. It would be 'regular, provident and mild' as well as 'absolute and minute' and it would emerge not through the whims of rulers but because of the need for government to be seen to promote the happiness of its subjects.[149]

This darker side of modernity, which became more prominent in the radical thought of the postwar period, is illustrated in the work of Michel Foucault. Foucault argues that with the growth of the administrative state and the emergence of 'the social question' (what he calls 'the problem of population'), the activity of governing takes on an entirely new form. Like Duguit, he recognizes that governmental authority can no longer be explained within the juridical frame of sovereignty. But whereas Duguit reconceptualized public law positively as being founded on public service and the promotion of solidarity, Foucault emphasizes the negative aspects of a new science of governmental reason. This science, which he calls *gouvernmentalité*, shows governing as a method 'of employing tactics rather than laws' or of 'using laws themselves as tactics', thus displacing the modern representation of 'rightful authority' through the concepts of state, sovereignty and constitution.[150] *Droit politique*, Foucault suggests, is the anachronistic leftover from an earlier metaphysical period which, with the extension of what he calls 'bio-power' involving the regulation of population, becomes redundant.[151]

---

[147] Furet, 'The Revolution is over' in *Interpreting*, above n.44, 1–79, 5.

[148] A de Tocqueville, *Democracy in America* [1835], H Reeve trans., DJ Boorstin intro. (New York: Vintage Books, 1990).

[149] Tocqueville, ibid. vol.2 [1840], 318–19.

[150] See M Foucault, *Society must be defended: Lectures at the Collège de France, 1975–76*, D Macey trans. (London: Penguin, 2003).

[151] Cf. J Rancière, 'Who is the Subject of the Rights of Man?' in his *Dissensus: On Politics and Aesthetics*, S Corcoran trans. (London: Continuum, 2010) 62–75 (following Agamben, Rancière argues that rather than contrasting sovereign power and bio-power they have converged since sovereign power now operates in a permanent state of exception and can be equated with 'control of life').

Foucault's analysis has been highly influential in radical circles, but some of his post-Marxist contemporaries have reworked the concept of *droit politique* in order to realize its emancipatory potential.

X. Jacobinism Revived?

The French came late to Marxism and even then it was primarily an intellectual movement.[152] Louis Althusser, who had produced a 'scientific' account of Marxism of considerable philosophical abstraction, became a pivotal figure. Now split into various factions, many contemporary scholars who have revived Jacobin thought to offer novel reworkings of *droit politique* came under his influence. If Foucault's thesis on the emergence of *gouvernmentalité* were reinterpreted in Althusserian terms, it might be said that the discourse of *droit politique* had become an element of what Althusser called the 'ideological state apparatus'.[153] This is the supposition under-pinning the work of two of Althusser's quarrelsome offspring: Alain Badiou and Jacques Rancière.

Both reject the standard account of politics as 'the set of procedures whereby the aggregation and consent of collectivities is achieved, the organization of powers, the distribution of places and roles, and the systems for legitimating this distribution'.[154] Each maintains that this set of practices, whether conceived in the terms of Hauriou, Duguit, or Carré de Malberg, constitutes a rigid disciplinary apparatus. Politics, says Badiou, is not concerned with governing, it 'cannot be governed by the State', and it cannot have anything to do with opinion, even the common opinion manifest as democratic consent.[155] This is because politics is not at all concerned with the 'common will': it is specific, momentous and concerned only with truth.[156] For Badiou, the authentic domain of the political is that of 'freedom' and 'justice'. In a similar vein, Rancière argues that the correct name for the conventional exercise of politics in modern society is 'the police' *tout court*. Properly understood, politics (*la politique*) is antagonistic to the activity of policing. Politics is a term that should be re-served for challenges to the established regime in the name of justice and freedom, action which commonly results when the gulf between inequality and equality, or between 'empty freedom' and 'true freedom', arises in social consciousness.[157] Since Rancière's concept of 'the police' includes the 'system for legitimating this distribution', it is evident that most of the conceptions of *droit politique* we have been considering are incorporated within that disciplinary regime.

---

[152] Hazareesingh, above n.112, 194: 'Marxism...was a relatively unknown quantity in France before 1940'.

[153] L Althusser, *On the Reproduction of Capitalism: Ideology and Ideological State Apparatuses*, GM Goshgarian trans. (London: Verso, 2014).

[154] J Rancière, *Disagreement: Politics and Philosophy*, J Rose trans. (Minneapolis: University of Minnesota Press, 1999), 28.

[155] A Badiou, *Metapolitics*, J Barker trans. (London: Verso, 2005), 87.

[156] Ibid. Ch.1: 'Against "Political Philosophy"', 10–25.   [157] Ibid. 18–19.

Badiou and Rancière are speaking the authentic language of the Jacobin natural right: when reading their critiques, we hear Saint-Just echoing down the ages. This resonance is even more explicit in Miguel Abensour's *Democracy Against the State*.[158] Some of Abensour's analysis follows in the steps of Badiou and Rancière, but in place of their concepts of politics he posits 'insurgent democracy'. This 'is not a variant of conflictual democracy, but its exact opposite': whereas conflictual democracy operates 'within the State', insurgent democracy 'situates conflict in another space, outside the State, against it'.[159] The state must be forced 'to avow that "democracy is the enigma of all constitutions solved", to confess that whatever its form may be, its origin is the sovereignty of the people, the people as an acting power'.[160] Insurgent democracy is a way for politics to bring about 'a transformation of the power in potential to act in concert: it signifies the passage from power *over* human beings to power *with* and *between* human beings, the *between* being the place where the possibility of a common world is won'.[161]

With this radical conception of the constituent power of the people, Abensour contends that a fundamental conflict exists between *l'État de droit* and the true democratic institution of society. Liberty and equality can flourish only in a political movement that affirms 'the possibility of annihilating the division between governors and governed, or reducing it to almost nothing, inventing a public space and political space under the banner of isonomy'.[162] These principles cannot be realized through 'the rule of law'. The rule of law 'generates a new concentration of power, one that holds all forms of independence in contempt' and one that has in fact 'transformed itself into a new absolutism against democracy'.[163]

In common with Badiou and Rancière, Abensour sees the state as a machine that oppresses by transforming the power *between* humans into a power *over* them. Since 'democracy is not a political regime but an action characterised by the irruption of the demos or the people onto the political stage in their struggle against the grandees', the idea of a democratic state is oxymoronic.[164] With this claim, Abensour makes a direct connection with Jacobinism. The 'potential for compatibility between insurgent democracy and institution exists', he suggests, only 'so long as the constitutional act, the fundamental norm, recognizes the people's right to insurrection, as did the Constitution of 1793'.[165] And he argues explicitly that we should 'follow the trail that Saint-Just blazed in *Institutions républicaines*, i.e. of opposing institutions and laws, with institutions being granted primacy while laws are mistrusted'. The concept of institution invoked here bears little similarity to Hauriou's: it may be the foundation of both government and law, but for Abensour it expresses 'the essence of the [ideal] republic'.[166]

Scholars such as Abensour, Badiou, and Rancière directly oppose those who claim that 'the Revolution is over' by seeking to restore the power of Jacobin thought. They

---

[158] M Abensour, *Democracy Against the State: Marx and the Machiavellian Moment*, M Blechman and M Breaugh trans. (Cambridge: Polity, 2011).
[159] Ibid. xl., Foreword to the 2nd French edn.   [160] Ibid. 94.   [161] Ibid. 96–7.
[162] Ibid. 96.   [163] Ibid. 97, 98.   [164] Ibid. xxv. Introduction to Italian edn.
[165] Ibid.   [166] Ibid. xxvii.

reject the idea of law as a set of rules promulgated by a common will in favour of Saint-Just's conception of 'right reason' founded on 'true freedom' and 'real equality'. *L'État de droit* is set in opposition to Robespierre's 'reign of that eternal justice whose laws are engraved . . . in the hearts of all men'. Their arguments respond to the criticism that Jacobinism promotes 'universal natural right' over 'political right' with a radical re-interpretation of *droit politique* as a set of principles of liberty and equality that must operate in the material world. But the logic of their argument suggests that politics is that which disrupts any order of police: politics becomes a purely oppositional activity. This is a form of anarchy which, beyond utopian abstraction, contains no guidance on how a world might be built. And while it remains so, it provides no adequate basis for political jurisprudence.

XI. *Droit Politique* as Symbolic Order

Neo-Jacobinism has not gone unchallenged. Étienne Balibar, another of Althusser's intellectual children, moves away from structural Marxism to provide a bridge between 'natural jurisprudence' and 'political jurisprudence', between the Saint-Justs and the Constants *de nos jours*. Balibar suggests how 'a critical reading of Marx and Marxist theory . . . could be combined with other interpretations of the tradition of political philosophy (Spinoza, Rousseau, Kant, Fichte) and above all with contributions to contemporary debates about universalism, racism, nationalism, and citizenship – more generally, what I called a "politics of the Rights of Man"'.[167] Recognizing the autonomy of the political underpinned by a concept of sovereignty,[168] and accepting that politics is 'a determinate practice, not the utopia of an efficient administration of things, nor the eschatological hope of converting humanity to the paths of justice',[169] Balibar places the ideas of Rancière and Foucault in a more conventional dialectical frame of (respectively) emancipation and transformation, to which he adds a third concept—civility.[170]

In fact, there is little Marxism in Balibar's political writing. He suggests that just as Marx had urged radicals 'to turn away from the "apparent scene" of politics structured by discourses and ideas/ideals, and unveil the "real scene" of economic processes', this pattern should be inverted so that '"material" processes are themselves . . . determined by the processes of the imaginary'.[171] This is so, because 'all

---

[167] É Balibar, *Politics and the Other Scene* (London: Verso, 2002), viii.

[168] Ibid. Ch.1 ('Three Concepts of Politics: Emancipation, Transformation, Civility'). See also É Balibar, *Spinoza and Politics*, P Snowden trans. (London: Verso, 1998).

[169] *Politics and the Other Scene*, above n.167, 11.

[170] Ibid. Ch.1, 5–8 (Rancière), 8–21 (Foucault). Balibar later writes of Rancière: 'we should . . . distinguish ourselves from him (or incorporate his radically egalitarian intentions into a more dialectical framework) by pointing out that the anti-political (which he, playing skillfully with etymology, calls by the name "police") is not a reality that is foreign to the political (and therefore to democracy) but a counter-tendency that is internal to it, and from which the political is constantly seeking to disassociate and differentiate itself.' É Balibar, *Citizenship*, T Scott-Railton trans. (Cambridge: Polity, 2015), 122–3.

[171] *Politics and the Other Scene*, above n.167, xiii.

forces which interact in the economico-political realm are also collective groupings, and consequently possess an (ambivalent) imaginary identity'.[172] Since Balibar calls the imaginary 'the infrastructure of the infrastructure',[173] we might wonder— especially given his views on the role of institutions in maintaining civility[174]—how far removed he is from Hauriou's conception of the state as 'the institution of institutions'. But it is the pivotal importance he attaches to the principle of 'equaliberty' (*égaliberté*) that demonstrates his allegiance to the Enlightenment conception of *droit politique*.[175] He uses this neologism to mean 'the unity (or reciprocity) of the concepts of liberty and equality', which are 'two sides of the same "constituent power"'.[176] Expressing the continuous dialectic 'of insurrection and constitution', or of the 'co-occurrence of inclusions and exclusions',[177] equaliberty simply repackages Rousseau's concept of the general will.

When Balibar links his argument on citizenship to Claude Lefort's thesis on the need for democracy to continuously reinvent itself,[178] he directs us to a body of work that explicitly recognizes the contemporary importance of the concept of *droit politique*. Together with his collaborators, Marcel Gauchet and Pierre Rosanvallon, Lefort worked with Furet at the *École des Hautes Études en Sciences Sociales* (EHESS) to demonstrate the continuing significance of the political in contemporary society. Praising the Revolution as the moment when modern democracy was invented, they maintain that the overriding political problem ever since has been to determine the Revolution's continuing significance. For Lefort, the democratic achievement of the Revolution was to have opened up a 'space of power' previously occupied by the King. To maintain fidelity to that achievement, he argues, this symbolic space must be forever kept empty. The error of the Jacobins was to have claimed that 'the people' occupied that place of power, thereby converting the symbolic into the actual and destroying the space of the political.[179]

Using the abstract philosophical language of phenomenology, Lefort gives a sophisticated rendering of the continuing relevance of *droit politique*. He argues that the political is not a distinct sphere within society; it refers to 'the principles that generate society' and the way in which an entire society maintains order and unity.[180] This is acquired through a series of symbolic representations, such as the nation, the state, and the constitution. For Lefort, political power is symbolic power that

---

[172] Ibid.   [173] Ibid.   [174] Ibid. 29–30.

[175] See É Balibar, '"Rights of Man" and "Rights of the Citizen": The Modern Dialectic of Equality and Freedom' in his *Masses, Classes, Ideas: Studies in Politics and Philosophy before and after Marx* (London: Routledge, 1993), ch 2; Balibar, *Citizenship*, above n.170.

[176] Balibar, *Citizenship*, ibid. 31.   [177] Ibid. 55, 117.

[178] Ibid. 18, 124. See C Lefort, *L'invention démocratique: Les limits de la domination totalitaire* (Paris: Fayard, 1981) [for English translations of some of the essays from this work see: Lefort, *The Political Forms of Modern Society* (Boston, Mass: MIT Press, 1986), Chs 7–10].

[179] C Lefort, 'Interpreting Revolution within the French Revolution' in his *Democracy and Political Theory* above n.6, 89–114, at 107: 'Revolutionary ideology is constituted by the insane assertion of the unity, or indeed the identity, of the people. The legitimacy, the truth and the creativity of history is assumed to come together in the people.' See also n.75 above.

[180] C Lefort, 'The Permanence of the Theological-Political?' in his *Democracy and Political Theory*, above n.6, 213–55, at 217.

maintains the authority of this distinctive worldview. It does this by maintaining
political unity in the face of social diversity, implying 'a reference to a place from
which it can be seen, read and named'.[181] This is what he calls 'the *place of power*',[182]
the point of orientation from which representations of the 'common good' or 'the
public interest' are made. In democracies, that 'place' is the state, which 'remains the
agency by virtue of which society apprehends itself in its unity and relates to itself in
time and space'.[183] Yet the state is a purely symbolic entity: it may shape understanding and confer meaning on a set of political relations,[184] but as a symbol of unity it
remains 'an *empty place*' that 'cannot be occupied'.[185] The state is a regulative idea, a
scheme of intelligibility. Modern democracy's defining characteristic is the existence
of a 'gap between the symbolic and the real' in which a 'notion of a power which no
one... can seize' is able to do its work.[186]

Lefort's conception of *droit politique* is now clear. In modern democracies, the
symbolic order of the political is structured through such 'generative principles' as
popular sovereignty, equality, and rights. It is because of their abstract character,
together with the loss of 'the ultimate markers of certainty' within democracies,[187]
that these principles of 'political right' fulfil the role of maintaining unity while
containing social tensions. Human rights for example 'reduce right to a basis which,
despite its name, is without shape' and 'eludes all power which could claim to take
hold of it'. Since rights are the subject of continuous contestation, then 'from the
moment when the rights of man are posited as the ultimate reference, established
right is open to question' and 'where right is in question, society – that is, the established order – is in question'.[188]

Similarly, political equality does not entail material equality and the fact that the
latter can never be realized is not evidence of the former's hypocrisy. A society
founded on political equality can no longer confer special status by virtue of the
circumstances of one's birth. Political equality may be a symbolic ideal, but material
inequality becomes visible only within its purview. The principles of *droit politique*
may be symbolic ideals of ambiguous meaning, but they enable citizens to maintain
a system of authority at the same time as continuing to question the authority of
established institutions.

What are the implications of this conception of *droit politique* for political order
in modern France? Gauchet and Rosanvallon question many of the assumptions
underpinning the legacy of a Jacobin political culture that erases the authority of

---

[181] Ibid. 225.   [182] Ibid.
[183] Lefort, 'The Question of Democracy' in his *Democracy and Political Theory*, above n.6, 9–20 at 17.
[184] Lefort, 'The Permanence of the Theological-Political?', above n.180, 218–19: 'We can further
specify this notion of shaping [*mise en forme*] by pointing out that it implies both the notion of giving
meaning [*mise en sens*] to social relations and that of staging them [*mise en scéne*]. Alternatively, we can
say that the advent of a society capable of organizing social relations can come about only if it can institute the conditions of their intelligibility, and only if it can use a multiplicity of signs to arrive at a
quasi-representation of itself.'
[185] Lefort, 'The Question of Democracy' above n.183, 17.
[186] Lefort, 'The Permanence of the Theological-Political', above n.180, 228.   [187] Ibid.
[188] Lefort, 'Politics and Human Rights' in his *The Political Forms of Modern Society* (Boston, MA:
MIT Press, 1986), 239–72, at 258.

institutions mediating between the citizens and the state, that sees symbolic order as masking the rule of particular interests, and treats disagreement as a threat to the unity of the people.[189] Aware of the threats posed by bureaucratization, they do not assume that the administrative state must be one of servitude. They recognize the decline of the grand narratives of sovereignty, equality, and the unitary conception of democracy, but seek to reconstruct the meaning of those concepts today.[190]

The EHESS scholars work within a frame of *droit politique* that follows in the tradition of Montesquieu, Constant, and Hauriou. Lefort, their intellectual leader, takes from Montesquieu the conception of 'political right' as a symbolic order expressing 'the necessary relations arising from the nature of things'. From Constant, he recognizes the vital role of government in representing society. And from Hauriou he develops a concept of rights analogous to that of 'superlegality' which keep the constituted order in harmony with the evolving character of the 'directing idea'. Their work demonstrates that although *droit politique* no longer informs the organizational framework within which French public lawyers work, the concept is still an active force in French public life.

XII. Conclusion

Writing in the mid-nineteenth century, Henry Maine noted that 'the part played by jurists in French history, and the sphere of jural conceptions in French thought, has always been remarkably large' and that 'the theory of Natural Law' has been 'the source of almost all the special ideas as to law, politics, and society which France during the last hundred years has been the instrument of diffusing over the western world'.[191] If 'natural law theory' can be reformulated as *droit politique*, then Maine highlights my two central themes. From Bodin through Montesquieu and on to the lawyers in the vanguard of the Revolution, jurists have played a major role in articulating the principles on which the modern French republic is founded. Under the rubric of *droit politique*, these principles might seem distinctively French but they have also underpinned the efforts of jurists across the world seeking the logic of modern constitutional ordering.

Yet since Maine wrote, the position of French jurists in public life has altered. In the course of trading natural law for legal positivism, their role has changed. Since the mid-nineteenth century, French public lawyers mainly worked within a legal positivist philosophy that saw the state as a legal person and presupposed the authority

---

[189] See, e.g., P Rosanvallon, *Le Peuple introuvable: Histoire de la rèpresentation démocratique en France* (Paris: Gallimard 1998); id., *Le Modèle politique français: La Société civile contre le jacobinisme de 1789 à nos jours* (Paris: Éditions du Seuil, 2004); M Gauchet, *La Démocratie contre elle-même* (Paris: Gallimard, 2002).

[190] See, especially, P Rosanvallon, *Counter-Democracy: Politics in an Age of Distrust*, A Goldhammer trans. (Cambridge: Cambridge University Press, 2008); id., *Democratic Legitimacy: Impartiality, Reflexivity, Proximity*, A Goldhammer trans. (Princeton: Princeton University Press, 2011); id., *The Society of Equals*, A Goldhammer trans. (Cambridge, MA: Harvard University Press, 2013).

[191] HS Maine, *Ancient Law: Its Connection with the Early History of Society and its Relation to Modern Ideas* [1861] (London: Murray, 10th edn.1919), 70.

of the state as a fact. So although French lawyers have retained their status as technicians of the working code of the modern French state, they are no longer interested in how the authority of the state is established and maintained. A century ago, Duguit and Hauriou in their different ways reformulated the basis for public law in the light of modern social, economic and political developments, but today the thinking that inspired their work languishes on the margins of their discipline.

There is still intense reflection on the nature of the modern republic and the conditions of its flourishing. But although it is expressed in the jural form of *droit politique*, it has become the language of philosophers rather than lawyers and this is regrettable. The French philosophical style is distinctive: 'abstract in design, systematic in its form and radical in its goals', it is strong on critique and generates a 'utopian way of thinking about politics [that] has been one of France's enduring contributions to modern political thought—and undoubtedly its most controversial'.[192] Yet the great strength of the tradition of *droit politique* has been its ability to hold in tension the relationship between norm and fact, legal and political, and between abstract and concrete. Political philosophers have advanced this discourse in recent years. It is unfortunate that public lawyers, with all their practical knowledge of the difficulties of making an actuality of equal liberty,[193] have so little contribution to make.

---

[192] Hazareesingh, above n.112, 106.

[193] Consider, as one illustration of the gap between the abstract principle and its institutionalized achievements, the issue of equality between the sexes: see JW Scott, *Parité: Sexual Equality and the Crisis of French Universalism* (Chicago: University of Chicago Press, 2005).

6

Law as Institution

I. Introduction

The five decades stretching from the 1880s through to the 1920s constitute a rich period in the history of European legal thought. The dynamic forces of industrialization and urbanization had loosened many traditional communal bonds, generating new forms of functional interdependencies. But towards the end of the century the destructive creativeness of laissez-faire capitalism was giving way to a new stage of organized capitalism. The need for more extensive state regulation over economic and social activity gained acceptance and West European states began to assume a different institutional shape. These developments unsettled traditional categories of legal thought.

Under the prevailing tenets of classical liberalism, improved well-being had been a matter of individual responsibility with governmental intervention mainly confined to the prevention of harm. But during this transitional period, political movements emerged that challenged these assumptions with alternative conceptions of the relationship between individual and state. These movements gradually had an impact on public policy, leading to basic reforms in the state's governing arrangements. The various changes in socio-economic organization, in state form, and in social philosophy also had a profound impact on legal thought. The period is commonly regarded as a pinnacle in the development of positivist legal science. But what makes it an especially rich period in the history of jurisprudence is that the moment of legal positivist hegemony was also one in which many of its underpinning assumptions were subverted by innovative jurists who drew radical implications about the nature of law in the world that was unfolding.

Institutionalism, the claim that law is neither norm nor command but institution, is one expression of the innovative jurisprudence of the period. The objective of this chapter is to explain the importance of institutional jurisprudence by examining its historical context and offering some reflections on its continuing significance. It will be argued that institutionalism, in part because of the lack of English translations of its leading exponents, has been unduly neglected in Anglo-American jurisprudence, that it constitutes a distinct strand of political jurisprudence, and that institutional theories continue to offer insight into contemporary juristic controversies.

Political Jurisprudence. Martin Loughlin. © M Loughlin 2017.
Published 2017 by Oxford University Press.

II. Intellectual context

Rapid advances in scientific and technological knowledge during the nineteenth century had a profound influence on social thought, which moved towards a recognition that in the social context truth must be validated through experience and testing. This shift was most clearly marked in the work of the French positivist scholars, Henri de Saint-Simon and Auguste Comte. Arguing that social thought must be shaped by scientific principles, they maintained that human knowledge moves through three developmental stages—the theological, the metaphysical, and the scientific—and that in the nineteenth century the scientific was beginning to emerge. Earlier metaphysical modes of thinking had thus become anachronistic and needed to be replaced by 'social physics', what Comte called 'sociology'.[1]

Legal scholars are invariably followers rather than innovators, and it was not long before the scientific re-orientation of social philosophy began to permeate jurisprudential thought. Saint-Simon and Comte had argued that the theological foundations of classical natural law and the metaphysical abstractions of natural right must be overcome in order to discover, by observation and inductive reason, the laws governing all social phenomena. A manifestation of their influence in jurisprudence was the emergence and eventual dominance of legal positivism.

Following Comte's lead, legal positivists devised a science of law based on empirical investigation into the nature of positive laws. Their investigations rested on three basic contentions. The first was that laws are simply commands of the sovereign within a state. Secondly they claimed that this sovereign is not some transcendental being but simply a special category of legal person identifiable through sociological observation as the person whose commands are habitually obeyed and who does not obey any other. And thirdly, it was maintained that subjects obey these laws not from some metaphysical sense of duty, but from fear of sanctions inflicted by the sovereign.

With the adoption of the claims of legal positivists, the scholarly study of law was transformed. The role of the professor of law, it was asserted, was neither to venerate nor to criticize the law: it was to expound. The professor's primary duty was to provide a rational explanation of the structure and logical relations of the laws of the state. Through this positive analytical method legal scholars were able to maintain law's status within the field of scientific inquiry as a discrete category of human knowledge.

But some jurists recognized that this autonomy was acquired at the cost of narrowing the subject's disciplinary boundaries, thereby altering its character. Law could no longer be seen as a cultural artefact offering insight into a society's evolution and its collective values; within these narrower confines it became merely a kind of technical knowledge, a technique by which the modern state could carry out its various tasks.

---

[1] See A Comte, *Cours de philosophie positive* (Paris: Ballière, 2nd edn. 1864); G Lenzer (ed.), *Auguste Comte and Positivism: The Essential Writings* (New York: Harper, 1975), 254–5. See further, Ch.5, VIII above.

As the school of legal positivism increased its sway during the latter half of the nineteenth century, its hegemony was challenged by a set of jurisprudential theories that drew different conclusions from scientific principles. These alternative modes of legal thought shared a deep scepticism that the individual could be extracted from history and culture and reconstituted as an isolated datum of social or legal analysis. In place of the Newtonian physics on which legal positivism seemed to rest its scientific claims, they drew their jurisprudential ideas from Darwinian biology. Law, they maintained, is not a data set to be analysed but an organic arrangement whose structure continuously adapts to its social and political environment. Rejecting the atomistic basis of legal positivism, these jurists asserted the critical importance of *experience*, that is, of acquiring a practical understanding derived from living within a specific social milieu.[2] Since society is an organism and individual life has an inherently social character, it follows that experience must precede any formal distinction between subject and object.

From this perspective, the aim of the human sciences is not that of gaining objective knowledge but of acquiring understanding; in William James' language, the human sciences are 'tender' rather than 'tough' disciplines.[3] Insight into a field such as law is acquired through a hermeneutical exercise in which a certain level of understanding of the subject is attained through a detailed study of its parts and further understanding of the parts is assimilated through a provisional grasp of the nature of the whole. Such a circular exercise seeks 'to understand life in its own terms'.[4] Life and experience, Wilhelm Dilthey explains, 'contain the framework which we find in the forms, principles, and categories of thought'.[5] This vitalist approach, founded on 'lived experience' (*Erlebnis*), deploys a historical method and remains sceptical of the value of abstract conceptual thinking.[6]

This approach suggests that the study of law involves a continuous search for meaning. Our understanding of law evolves as we acquire a worldview (*Weltanschauung*), a provisional sense of how things hang together. Legal knowledge is not gained by the mind joining together discrete bits of data like particular rules; knowledge is gained only through experience. Only then are we able to acquire real understanding of the nature of legal relations.

This hermeneutical method underpins many of the more sociologically-orientated jurisprudential ideas of the time. It exerted a particular influence on jurists who developed the institutional theories of the period. They accepted Comte's basic account of human development but rejected what Dilthey called his 'crude naturalistic

---

[2] As one contemporary jurist famously put it: 'The life of the law has not been logic; it has been experience. The felt necessities of the time, the prevalent moral and political theories, intuitions of public policy, avowed or unconscious, even the prejudices which judges share with their fellow-men, have had a good deal more to do than the syllogism in determining the rules by which men should be governed.' OW Holmes, Jr, *The Common Law* (London: Macmillan, 1887), 1.

[3] W James, *Pragmatism and Other Essays* [1907] (New York: Washington Square Press, 1963), Lct.1.

[4] W Dilthey, *Introduction to the Human Sciences: An Attempt to Lay a Foundation for the Study of Society and History* [1883], RJ Batanzos trans. (London: Harvester Wheatsheaf, 1988), 12.

[5] Ibid.

[6] This vitalist approach is one which Dilthey shared with many other philosophers of his generation, including Bergson, Nietzsche, Schopenhauer, and Simmel.

metaphysics', that is, his attempt to present a sociology based on the natural rather than the human sciences.[7] In their various ways, institutional theorists sought to manage rather than overcome the tensions between monism and pluralism, idealism and materialism, rationalism and empiricism.[8] Institutional theorists emphasized the necessity of relating text to context, norms to life.

III. Hauriou's Institutional Theory

The earliest exponent of institutional theory was the French legal scholar, Maurice Hauriou (1856–1929). Appointed to a chair in administative law at the University of Toulouse in 1888, he stayed there for the rest of his career, producing a series of leading treatises on public law which secured him pre-eminent status as a legal scholar.[9] By the beginning of the twentieth century, he had also acquired an international reputation as one of France's leading legal philosophers. Hauriou's distinctive philosophy of law came from thinking systematically about the implications of the recent growth in public law for general jurisprudence, a line of thought culminating in his 'theory of the institution'. He produced various studies from the 1890s onwards[10] but only in 1925 did he publish a comprehensive statement of institutional theory.

Hauriou's institutional theory entailed a shift from conceptual to phenomenal thinking, from formalism to realism. With respect to the nature of legal order, he disagreed both with legal positivists, who treated the sovereign as the source of law, and with contemporary sociologically-orientated jurists such as Léon Duguit, who, following Comte and Durkheim, founded law on social fact. For Hauriou, normative order could be derived neither from the sovereign nor from social fact; it derived from an amorphous metaphysical source that was able to incorporate the dynamic aspects of social life into its framework of understanding.

In his mature statement of the theory, Hauriou maintained that institutions constitute the juridical basis of state and society.[11] States and societies are founded not on violence but on a power which derives its authority from its gradual social acceptance by their subjects. Critical to this process is the formation of institutions, which,

---

[7] Dilthey, above n.4, 140.

[8] On the affinities in western thought see JT Kloppenberg, *Uncertain Victory: Social Democracy and Progressivism in European and American Thought, 1870–1920* (New York: Oxford University Press, 1986).

[9] M Hauriou, *Précis de droit administratif* (Paris: Larose et Forcel, 1892); id., *Principes de droit publique* (Paris: Larose et Tenin, 1910); id., *Précis de droit constitutionnel* (Paris: Sirey, 1923).

[10] See, e.g., M Hauriou, *La science sociale traditionelle* (Paris: Larose, 1896). The 6th edition of his administrative law treatise, published in 1907, first introduced the idea that institutions had superseded sovereignty in performing the key role in the foundation of the modern state: see M Hauriou, *Précis de droit administratif et de droit public* (Paris: Larose et Tenin, 6th edn. 1907), viii–ix, Ch.1.

[11] M Hauriou, 'The Theory of the Institution and the Foundation: A Study in Social Vitalism' in A. Broderick (ed.), *The French Institutionalists: Maurice Hauriou, Georges Renard, Joseph T. Delos* (Cambridge, MA: Harvard University Press, 1970), 93–124 [translation of 'La théorie de l'institution et de la fondation' (1925) 4 *Cahiers de la nouvelle journée* 2–45]. Its sub-title displays the influence of the Bergson's philosophy (see n.6 above).

having 'duration, continuity and reality', are the true repositories of a society's creative power.[12] Contrary to legal positivist theories, Hauriou claimed that it is not law that creates institutions, but institutions that make law.[13] Legal rules are secondary phenomena. Lawyers often mistake the legal rule for action, but in reality the legal rule is an element of reaction. This is because rules generally limit the powers of individuals and institutions,[14] whereas it is individuals and institutions that constitute the creative forces in society.

Hauriou defines the institution as 'an idea of a work or enterprise that is realized and endures juridically in a social milieu'.[15] In order for this idea to be realized 'a power is organized that equips it with organs'.[16] With respect to the institution of the state, an order is established that generates its authority by achieving a balance of governmental powers. This balance means that 'governmental power is not just a simple force but a rightful power capable of creating law'.[17] This concept of the institution is seen most explicitly in formally-established corporate bodies, but it extends beyond this to embrace all types of associations that are 'manifestations of communion' among the group members.[18] These institutions 'are born, live, and die juridically'.[19]

In constituted bodies, such as states, trades unions, and other incorporated associations, there is an 'organized power' which is an expression of its 'directing idea' (*idée directrice*). These two concepts—'directing idea' and 'organized power'—are the core elements of Hauriou's theory. The directing idea is an ideal manifestation of the tasks to be realized by that body. He is careful to explain that this is not the same as its function. 'The idea of the state', he says, 'far transcends the notion of the functions of the state'.[20] Its function is only that which has already been realized, whereas the directing idea contains an as yet undetermined element. The second core concept is that 'the idea of the state has at its service an autonomous power of government that is imposed on the citizens themselves and in which they only participate'.[21] This organized power of government, which must conform to the principles of representation and separation of powers, exists in order to realize the directing idea. Governors may at times distort the task, but 'surely and progressively' they end up by 'submitting to its service'.[22] Constitutional mechanisms certainly assist but they 'would have been useless if they had not been supported by a public spirit imbued with the idea of the state'.[23] This point expresses the hegemony of the directing idea over the organized power.

Hauriou then asks: 'what laws of the state... precisely express the idea of the state?'[24] Since most legal rules impose limits, 'the highest forms under which the directing ideas of an institution tends to express itself subjectively are not properly juridical': they are primarily 'moral or intellectual'.[25] Nevertheless, they are capable of becoming juridical. They achieve this status as 'higher principles of law'.[26] Examples

---

[12] Ibid. 93.   [13] Ibid. 97, 123.
[14] Ibid. 98: 'Juridical rules are transactional limits imposed upon the claims of individual and institutional powers'.
[15] Ibid. 99.   [16] Ibid.   [17] Ibid. 105.   [18] Ibid. 100.   [19] Ibid. 100.
[20] Ibid. 102.   [21] Ibid. 104.   [22] Ibid. 106.   [23] Ibid.   [24] Ibid. 114.
[25] Ibid. 114.   [26] Ibid. 114.

of these 'higher principles' include the declarations of rights produced during the American and French revolutions and which 'express the heart of the idea of the modern state'.[27] These higher principles, which are illustrative of a modern phenomenon of 'superlegality', are expressions of a 'constituent power' which keeps the laws and formal constitution in tune with the evolving character of the directing idea.[28]

Hauriou's pioneering work on institutional theory has been interpreted in a variety of ways. In France, it has been regarded by some jurists as a modern re-interpretation of Thomist social thought.[29] But Hauriou himself did not accept this, maintaining that his was a sociological positivist method and claiming to be a faithful disciple of Comte.[30] Other assessments of his work accept that self-appraisal.[31] Irrespective of these ambiguities, his work is of the first importance in providing the intellectual groundwork of an institutional theory. But although he led the way, Hauriou did not develop a general institutional theory of law. For this, we turn to the Italian scholar, Santi Romano, whose work 'ran parallel' with Hauriou's.[32]

IV. Romano's Institutional Theory of Law

Romano presents a systematic account of legal order from the perspective of institutional theory. Whatever doubts exist about the orientation of Hauriou's theory, Romano's work is a radical empirical account of legal order with no traces of Thomism or natural law.[33] For this reason, a leading Italian political philosopher has claimed that his work is 'the version [of institutional theory] that has most widely influenced contemporary legal and political thought'.[34]

Having developed its themes over the previous decade, in 1917 Santi Romano published *The Legal Order*.[35] That both he and Hauriou were professors of public

---

[27] Ibid. 115.   [28] Ibid. 120.

[29] This is mainly because the next generation of institutional scholars, especially George Renard and Joseph Delos, gave institutional theory a distinctively Thomist interpretation. See G Renard, *La théorie de l'institution: essai de l'ontologie juridique* (Paris: Sirey, 1930); JT Delos, 'La théorie de l'institution: la solution réaliste du problème de la personnalité morale et le droit à fondement objectif' (1931) 1 *Archives de philosophie du droit et de sociologie juridique* 97–153. For excerpts of their work see Broderick (ed.), above n.11, 163–213 (Renard) and 222–65 (Delos). See also O Beaud, 'Hauriou et le droit naturelle' (1989) 8 *Revue d'histoire des facultés de droit* 123–38.

[30] M Hauriou, 'Le fondement de l'autorité publique' (1916) 33 *Revue de droit publique* 20–5: 'J'étais positiviste à la seconde pouvoir, à la façon d'Auguste Comte …' ['I was a positivist to the second power, in the style of Comte…'.] Cited in CB Gray, *The Methodology of Maurice Hauriou* (Amsterdam: Rodopi, 2010), 9.

[31] See, e.g., WI Jennings, 'The Institutional Theory' in Jennings (ed.), *Modern Theories of Law* (London: Oxford University Press, 1933), 68–85, at 69: 'I do not believe that Hauriou consciously adopted any Thomistic philosophy when he began to formulate the institutional theory'.

[32] M Hauriou, *Précis de droit constitutionnel*, above n.9, 75: 'Un effort parallel le très remarquable est fait en Italie pour organiser la théorie de l'institution. Je citerai Santi Romano, *L'ordinamento giuridico*, 1917.'

[33] J Stone, *Social Dimensions of Law and Justice* (London: Stevens, 1966), Ch.11.

[34] A Passerin d'Entrèves, *The Notion of the State: An Introduction to Political Theory* (Oxford: Clarendon Press, 1967), 127.

[35] Romano initially divided the work into two parts that were published in two separate issues of the journal *Annali delle Università Toscana* in 1917 and 1918. The two were then published together in book

law is significant;[36] both reflected on the rapid development of public law in its various forms (constitutional law, administrative law, municipal law, labour law, international law, etc.) before working through its implications for modern jurisprudence. Also like Hauriou, instead of imposing a clear hierarchical normative frame on his material in order to maintain the integrity of the 'legal system', Romano squarely faced the challenge presented by the emergence of special bodies of administrative law, recognizing in particular the dynamic role played by powers—rather than norms—in this development. *The Legal Order* represents the maturation of his thought in which Romano gives a concise and rigorous account of the implications for general jurisprudence.

The book is divided into two parts. The first is devoted to the phenomenon of legal order, but as he states at the beginning of Part II: 'From the concept of a legal order which I have offered [in Part I], we can deduce the corollary that there are as many legal orders as institutions' (§ 25). In the second part he therefore examines the issues raised by the plurality of normative orders. How the two parts relate has been the subject of debate but before considering the book's significance I summarize its salient features.

Romano explains that contemporary jurists assume that the essence of law is located in the norm, thereby defining law as normative order. In so doing they overlook certain antecedent features of law with the result that many legal problems remain 'obscure or unresolved' (§ 2). One reason for this oversight is their disregard for modern realities, especially the fact that public law has now become so dominant. Private law is 'conditional' on public law (which 'constitutes its root and trunk, and is necessary to its safeguard'), yet legal theories are still presented in the image of private law (§ 2). A comprehensive definition, he argues, must take into account all parts of the law.

Romano's first contention is that a legal order is not just a set of norms; it is a unity unto itself. Although jurists pay lip-service to this idea, often referring to the legal order as a 'living whole' or as expressing the 'general will', this claim should not be seen as a metaphorical abstraction. Rather, the legal order is 'a concrete and effective unity' that must be differentiated from the distinct normative elements that comprise it (§ 3). Just as 'we cannot have a precise idea of the various limbs of the human being or of the wheels of a given machine unless we know in advance what a human being or that machine is', so too 'we cannot have an adequate concept of norms that are embodied in a legal order unless we provide in advance the unitary concept of it' (§ 3). Norms, Romano explains, are merely secondary phenomena which 'appertain to the essential traits of law almost by reflex' (§ 5). Consequently, a definition of law is not to be found in the norm but in 'that which informs it and gives it a certain shape' (§ 6). Law is 'the very entity that establishes that norm' (§ 7). It is, in essence, 'the impersonality of the power that elaborates and establishes the rule' (§ 7).

form as: S Romano, *L'ordinamento giuridico* (Pisa: Mariotti, 1918). The first English translation appeared in 2017: S Romano, *The Legal Order*, M Croce trans. (London: Routledge 2017).

[36] Romano was appointed to his first chair at Modena in 1906 and in 1908 at Pisa. In 1901 he had already published *Principi di diritto amministrativo italiano* (Milan: Società editrice libraria, 1901).

One great advantage of Romano's definition is that it incorporates contemporary phenomena into the idea of legal order. Jurists who define law as a set of norms frequently find it difficult to include certain measures, especially of an administrative nature, within their concept of law because they are not sufficiently abstract or general. They therefore either exclude from their definition such directives or they extend the meaning of the norm such that it strains common understanding. Similarly, normativists have difficulty incorporating the role of the sanction into their definitions of law. Some define law as a set of norms that include derivative rights of coercion, but Romano suggests that the sanction cannot be expressed as a norm: 'if one only concentrates on norms, one ends up denying that sanction is a feature of law' (§ 8). Far from 'being complementary or ancillary to the norms', sanctions 'form the base on which norms are constructed' (§ 8). The sanction is more fundamental than the norm, again suggesting that law is not a normative but a concrete-order.

By exposing the limitations of normative legal positivism Romano bring us to his core thesis, which rests on two basic claims. First, he maintains that law forms an *order* rather than a *system* and that the latter, which suggests a high degree of abstract integration, is one of the main causes of inaccuracy in its definition (§ 9). Secondly, this legal order is formed in a social context as a concrete unity. Law is ordered existence and before it can be expressed as norm it is a type of *organization*. These two claims constitute the foundation of his thesis that the concept which gives expression to any notion of legal order is that of institution (§ 10).

Some jurists use the idea of institution as a synonym for corporate legal personality. This, Romano argues, is mistaken: it would mean the concept of institution being absorbed into the idea of normative order, and he is adamant that institution is an expression of concrete-order. He recognizes the similarity of his thesis to Hauriou's broad concept of institution, noting in particular Hauriou's use of the concept as a juristic rather than a political or sociological entity. But he disagrees with Hauriou's account for three reasons: he rejects his claims that the concept of institution stands for a social organization that has reached a certain level of development, that an institution must have a constitutional and representative structure, and that law is a product of the institution. Romano suggests in particular that Hauriou 'was carried away with the idea of modelling his institutions on the broadest among them, that is, the state' (§ 11). Romano's criticisms are clues to the nature and breadth of his ambition. The institution, he emphasizes, is not an object and, treated as a unity, 'the concept of institution and the concept of law ... are absolutely identical' (§ 11).

For Romano, the most important characteristic of an institution is that it has 'a firm and permanent unity' even as its membership, orientation, and norms change over time (§ 12). Consequently, all social bodies are institutions, even if they have only relative autonomy. But he emphasizes that the institution 'is the prime, original and essential manifestation of law' and it 'exists and can be defined as such only inasmuch as it is created and preserved by the law' (§ 13). The corollary also holds: law is 'that which animates and holds together the various elements' that comprise the institution and which 'determines, fixes and preserves the structure of immaterial entities'(§ 15). Law and institution are not 'two phenomena standing in a given relation to one another, ... it is the same phenomenon' (§ 15).

In the rest of Part I, Romano explains some implications of his institutional thesis. First, it resolves the problem that many jurists find in the relationship between state and law, that is, whether one is anterior to the other. If a state exists, there has to be a legal order so whether the state is a legal or an ethical entity makes little sense: it is like asking whether 'the human being is a living or a moral being' (§ 15). Similarly, state power is not 'a *de facto* power, a pre-legal attribute of the state itself' because the power of the state 'can never be extra- or pre-legal, but emerges with it and its order, which it always disciplines and regulates' (§ 21). Secondly, constitutional law is not a set of norms that regulate relationships within the state: rather, it 'encompasses the state in itself and for itself, in its elements, structure, [and] functions' (§ 24). Finally, Romano addresses the vexed question of whether or not international law is law. For him, the answer depends solely on the status of the international legal order as an institution, so that, for example, the question of whether the international community is a legal person is irrelevant. And the conclusion he arrives at is that, just as state law comes into being with the state, 'so does international law come into being with the community of states, which necessarily presupposes a legal order that constitutes and regulates it' (§ 17). International law is 'the immanent order of the community of states' and it is 'to be found in the institution to which this very community gives form' (§ 17).

Romano concludes Part I by emphasizing that the institution 'is not a rational requirement, an abstract principle, an ideal *quid*; it is a real, effective entity'. But this entity is to be examined 'not from the point of view of the material forces that produce and sustain it, nor in relation to the environment where it develops and lives as a phenomenon intertwined with others, nor with regard to cause-effect relationships that affect it, and therefore, not sociologically, but in itself and for itself, inasmuch as it results from a legal order' (§ 24). This does not mean that norms are irrelevant; it is simply that 'norms that can be found in a particular positive law are nothing but elements of a broader, more complex order' (§ 24). Lawyers who focus on formal legal relationships often adopt a subjective conception of law, but legal order itself is institution and because it has 'an effective, concrete and objective existence' it constitutes 'objective law' (§ 18).

In Part II, Romano examines a range of practical issues arising from his institutional theory. These mainly come from his argument about the plurality of legal orders, that there are as many legal orders as there are institutions. He notes that each state is 'an order completely distinct from the other states' and that the international community forms a distinct institution, though one which 'presupposes the various state orders' (§ 25). This is commonplace, but there are also legal orders which do not derive from state law. One needs think only of the law of the Church, 'which could hardly be considered as part of state law' (§§ 26, 29). 'In spiritual and disciplinary matters', he explains, 'the Church enjoys a normative power that certainly does not derive from the state' and the state, albeit within certain limits, recognizes the effects that the ecclesiastical order attributes to its own laws (§ 42). But there are many other similar institutions and it is only with the growth of the modern state that the illusion has been nurtured of a unified legal order. In fact, says Romano, 'the state is nothing other than a species of the genus "law"' (§ 26). Even though many entities that earlier were independent of the state have now become subsumed under its authority, 'the idea that the state system has become the only system in the legal world is to be most decidedly rejected' (§ 27).

Romano then directly confronts those who deny the proposition that there are as many legal orders as there are institutions. He gives short shrift to those who object on the grounds that it might mean giving criminal or immoral organizations status as legal orders. This ethical argument can only be defended if one assumes 'the necessary and absolute dependence of positive law on morality', issues to which the jurist must be 'utterly indifferent' (§ 30). He finally examines the significance of the various types of institutions, distinguishing between original and derivative institutions and those that are intermediate, and between those with particular, therefore limited ends and those pursuing general, therefore potentially limitless ends (§ 33).

Romano concludes by returning to the role of the state. With respect to complex entities 'such as the state, but certainly not only the state', a distinction should be made between their several institutions—such as the legislative body, governmental departments, other public agencies, and so on—and the more general institution of the state. Based on this he distinguishes between general powers, founded on the order of the state considered as a whole, and special powers, founded upon the order of a state institution considered in itself. This, he concludes, might form the basis of a new theory 'of public law relationships and . . . the division of powers' (§ 48).

V. Institutionalism's Uncertain Legacy

The institutional theory of law emerges from a specific intellectual milieu. It flourishes in the late-nineteenth and early-twentieth centuries, shaped by the changes ushered in by modernity. It was an empirical orientation aligned to a progressive political outlook which not only embraced the coming of democracy—the institutionalization of political and civil equality—but also believed that continuing progress depended not on revolutionary action but on incremental reform. Hauriou and Romano distrust conceptualist legal thinking and present an account of law as a positive phenomenon in the modern world. But we see also a collectivist orientation in the way they highlight, and seek to integrate, an evolving sphere of administrative action within the legal order. Perhaps the most distinctive feature of institutional theory, however, is the hermeneutical method they adopt in conceiving of a legal order not as some abstract principle, but as an entity found in life itself.

The institutionalists found common cause in the organic, pluralist conception of society that was shared not only with Duguit in France, but also with Gierke and Preuss in Germany, Ehrlich in Austria, Dewey and James in the US, and Green, Bosanquet, Figgis, Cole, and Laski in Britain. But it is Romano's singular achievement to have turned this general pluralist outlook into a systematic theory of law. Some have suggested that the relationship between the two parts of *The Legal Order* is ambiguous: is this a thesis on the plurality of legal orders in society or on the modern form of law as a concrete-order? But close reading reveals this was for him a non-issue; he elaborates both themes equally and treats them as complementary.

He was not unaware of the general problem; in a celebrated lecture in 1909 he attributed the crisis of the modern state to the growth in power of sectional interest groups with which the state was obliged to negotiate. He recognized that the challenge for the idea of the state as the 'institution of institutions' was to somehow transcend these interests to realize the common good.[37] He did not indicate clearly how the state might achieve that ambition, but it is evident that the Romano of *The Legal Order* regards this as a political rather than a legal issue, and therefore not relevant to the juridical nature of his task in the latter work.

This political aspect cannot, however, be entirely avoided. If law is 'a concrete and effective unity' (§ 3) which constitutes an expression of impersonal power (§ 7), then, even though the state is simply a species of the genus 'law' (§ 26), the question of maintaining its efficacy to 'discipline and regulate' its field (§ 21) is a pressing juridical—and not solely political—question. It may not be a critical issue for jurisprudential inquiry into the nature of the genus, but it is one for the predominant species of this genus: the legal order of the modern state. This is a pressing question for political jurisprudence. How the state relates to other institutional orders also confounded the political pluralists of the period. Their difficulties are vividly exemplified in the intellectual trajectory of Harold Laski, whose early pluralist studies sought to displace the state from its pivotal position,[38] but who later felt obliged to abandon this stance, moving on to a variant of Marxism that required a revolutionary shift rather than gradual reform.[39]

There is an answer to the question of how the state relates to other institutions, but it should first be noted that the seeds sown by the institutional theories before the First World War found the interwar period infertile ground. Responses to the crisis of the state that Romano had so clearly identified in 1909 became much more radical, illustrated most dramatically in the political movements of fascism and communism. In these circumstances, Romano—in common with Laski, though for different reasons—was required to downplay the pluralist aspects of his theory. This was because, after the establishment of fascism in Italy in 1925, pluralism was no longer considered an acceptable philosophy. This was compounded personally for him when in 1928 he joined the Fascist Party and accepted Mussolini's offer of appointment as President of the Italian Administrative Court.

During the interwar period the most prominent German advocate of institutionalism was Carl Schmitt who in 1933 had joined the Nazi Party. Schmitt maintained that all legal theories emphasize one of three foundational elements of law: norm, decision, or concrete-order.[40] Although he had vigorously promoted a decisionist

---

[37] S Romano, 'Lo stato moderno e la sua crisi' (1910) *Rivisita di diritto pubblico* 87. A French translation is available as: S Romano, 'L'État moderne et sa crise' (2014) 14 *Jus Politicum*: [http://juspoliticum.com/article/L-Etat-moderne-et-sa-crise-968.html].

[38] HJ Laski, *Studies in the Problem of Sovereignty* (New Haven: Yale University Press, 1917); id., *Authority in the Modern State* (New Haven: Yale University Press, 1919); id., *The Foundations of Sovereignty and other essays* (New York: Harcourt Brace, 1921).

[39] HJ Laski, *The State in Theory and Practice* (London: George Allen and Unwin, 1935); id., *Law and Justice in Soviet Russia* (London: Hogarth Press, 1935).

[40] See further Ch.7, V below.

theory during the 1920s, in 1934 he moved towards an institutionalist approach, a reorientation for which the influences of Hauriou and Romano were explicitly acknowledged.[41] Nevertheless, Schmitt also underplayed the pluralist dimensions of Romano's work, which is not surprising since his aim was to promote the idea of the state as the 'institution of institutions' and to subject the plurality of normative ordering to the ultimate authority of the state.[42] Only by establishing a stable institutional structure founded on the primacy of the state, he argued, could political unity be maintained. And for Schmitt, this led to the disastrous argument that such unity requires the formation of an ethnically homogeneous people at one with a leadership imbued with the 'concrete, substantive thinking of the National-Socialist Movement'.[43]

Institutionalism was slow to revive following its neglect and misrepresentation in the turbulent interwar period. When it was restored in European legal thought, it took the form of the so-called 'neo-institutionalism' of Ota Weinberger and Neil MacCormick. This was announced in their joint work of 1986, *An Institutional Theory of Law: New Approaches to Legal Positivism*.[44] But this work has precious little in common with the institutional theories of Hauriou and Romano and contains no reference to their work at all.[45] Neo-institutionalism does not engage with the philosophical basis of institutional theory as an expression of lived experience; rather, it reinforces a clear division between is and ought, converts institutions into 'social facts', and confuses institutions and legal institutions.[46] It is as an attempt by orthodox legal positivism to colonize the field of institutionalism.

---

[41] C Schmitt, *On the Three Types of Juristic Thought* [1934], JW Bendersky trans. (Westport, CT: Praeger, 2004), esp. 56–7 (on Romano), 86–8 (on Hauriou and Romano). In the Preface to the 2nd edn. of *Political Theology* in 1933, Schmitt noted that he had arrived at institutionalism as a result of studying Hauriou's work: C Schmitt, *Political Theology: Four Chapters on the Concept of Sovereignty*, G. Schwab trans. (Chicago: University of Chicago Press, 2005), 2–3.

[42] Schmitt, *Three Types*, above n.41, 88: 'the state itself is no longer a norm or a system of norms, nor a pure sovereign decision, but the institution of institutions, in whose order numerous other, in themselves autonomous, institutions find their protection and their order'. For analysis see: M Croce and A Salvatore, *The Legal Theory of Carl Schmitt* (Abingdon: Routledge, 2013), Ch.7.

[43] C Schmitt, *State, Movement, People: The Triadic Structure of Political Unity* [1933], S Draghici trans. (Corvallis, Oregon: Plutarch Press, 2001), 47.

[44] O Weinberger and N MacCormick, *An Institutional Theory of Law: New Approaches to Legal Positivism* (Dordrecht: Reidel, 1986).

[45] O Weinberger's subsequent work, *Law, Institution and Legal Politics: Fundamental Problems of Legal Theory and Social Philosophy* (Dordrecht: Kluwer, 1991) does make some reference, but he explains that the new work is best described as 'institutional legal positivism' and emphasizes that 'our conception is not based on the sociological theory of institutions, nor is it in terms of the history of ideas an offspring of Hauriou's theory of law'. MacCormick's mature statement of the theory again makes no reference to Hauriou or Romano: N MacCormick, *Institutions of Law: An Essay in Legal Theory* (Oxford: Oxford University Press, 2007).

[46] Even a disciple of neo-institutionalism, one who believes that there has been a 'steady exhaustion' of the institutional theories of Hauriou and Romano and that we are 'indebted to the work of Neil MacCormick and Ota Weinberger for reopening discussion of institutionalism in the context of the theory of law', recognizes that a 'confusion of terms [between "institution" and "legal institution"] is … present in the neo-institutionalist authors': M La Torre, *Law as Institution* (Dordrecht: Springer, 2010), 98, 104.

VI. Institutional Theory as a Type of Political Jurisprudence

Institutionalism is sceptical both of the rationalist's conceptualism and the empiricist's 'social facts': it rests on the belief that social life is intrinsically relational and that its meaning is embedded in a specific culture conveyed through 'concrete-order' thinking. If we are to accept, as has been claimed, that there has been a 'steady exhaustion' of the 'driving force' of institutional theory,[47] it seems to reveal more about the rationalist and instrumentalist proclivities of legal thinking than about the realities of the regimes under which we live. But is this true?

Contemporary resonances are not easily recognized but they exist. Consider by way of example Robert Cover's highly-influential study '*Nomos* and Narrative'.[48] In this paper, Cover argues that law is 'not merely a system of rules to be observed, but a world in which we live':[49] the rules and institutions of law are merely second-order phenomena forming only a small part of the normative world of the *nomos*. This *nomos* 'is as much "our world" as is the physical universe' and 'our apprehension of the structure of the normative world is no less fundamental than our apprehension of the structure of the physical world'.[50] *Nomos* signifies a form of civilization. It generates 'paradigms for dedication, acquiescence, contradiction and resistance' and is held together 'by the force of interpretive commitments' which are mediated by narrative schemes—languages and myths—that 'build relations between the normative and the material universe, between the constraints of reality and the demands of an ethic' and which 'integrate . . . the "is" and the "ought"'.[51] What Cover here calls a *nomos* is precisely the concept of institution that Hauriou and Romano had elaborated in considerable detail six decades earlier.[52]

Like the early institutionalists, Cover maintains that although *nomos* emerges through a collective process, the order it creates is not primarily attributable to a

---

[47] Ibid.

[48] RM Cover, 'Foreword: *Nomos* and Narrative' (1983–4) 97 *Harvard Law Rev.* 4–68. According to Google Scholar citations, this article has been cited over 3,000 times (3,267 at November 2016). It appears at number 16 in the 'most-cited law review articles of all-time': see FR Schapiro and M Pearse, 'The Most-Cited Law Review Articles of All Time' (2012) 110 *Michigan Law Rev.*1483–520. Note that an additional resonance can be found in the work of Cover's Yale colleague, Paul Kahn. In a recent book, Kahn asks: 'When the Supreme Court declares a law unconstitutional, what exactly is the course of legitimacy for that judgment?' He recognizes that it is not a judgment 'as to the justice of the legislation' and that the text of the Constitution does not provide an adequate answer. 'While the Court likes to appeal to the rule of law to legitimate its exceptional role', he concludes, 'political theology suggests that we look in a different direction: to the Court's capacity to speak in the voice of the popular sovereign': P Kahn, *Political Theology: Four New Chapters on the Concept of Sovereignty* (New York: Columbia University Press, 2011), 9. Political theology might indeed suggest that, but Kahn could have given an equally powerful answer in the language of Hauriou's concept of 'superlegality': above p.114.

[49] Cover, above n.48, 5.   [50] Cover, 5.   [51] Cover, 6, 7, 9, 10.

[52] This is made even more explicit in Schmitt's post-war work: see C Schmitt, *The Nomos of the Earth in the International Law of the Jus Publicum Europaeum* [1950], GL Ulmen trans. (New York: Telos Press Publishing, 2003). For analysis see: M Loughlin, 'Nomos' in D Dyzenhaus and T Poole (eds), *Law, Liberty and State: Oakeshott, Hayek and Schmitt on the Rule of Law* (Cambridge: Cambridge University Press, 2015), Ch.4.

'state'.[53] Like them he recognizes that *nomos* is a 'jurisgenerative'—that is, a 'world-creating'—phenomenon. Since a multiplicity of worlds—that is, institutions or legal orders—exist and are 'subject to no formal hierarchical ordering', there is 'a radical dichotomy between the social organization of law as power and the organization of law as meaning'.[54] Like the early institutionalists, he recognizes the normative power of the factual, such that utopian movements with no social traction 'may be movements, but they are no longer movements of the law'.[55] When Cover states that the problem for the judiciary (of a state) arises because of the proliferation of legal meaning and that its rulings are 'jurispathic',[56] he echoes Hauriou's claim that the legal rule is a product not of action but of reaction. When he states that 'each "community of interpretation" that has achieved "law" has its own *nomos*',[57] he is restating Romano's claim about the plurality of legal orders. When he says that 'for every constitution there is an epic' to be understood through 'the narratives that give it meaning',[58] he is giving voice to Hauriou's observation that the highest forms of expressing the 'directing idea' are the 'higher principles' of 'superlegality'. Cover may never have read their work and may have believed in the originality of his thesis, but he writes entirely within the frame of Hauriou and Romano's institutionalism.

But there is one major point of disagreement between Cover and Romano, and that is over scholarly method. Romano uses a rigorous empirical method to specify the character of the modern phenomenon of law. He accepts that the law of the state is simply 'a species of the genus "law"' and maintains a strict agnosticism over the relationship between the state's law and other legal orders in society. Cover, by contrast, presents a radical ideological argument: that the modern state assumes an entirely bureaucratic—what he calls 'jurispathic'—form. Judges 'are people of violence' who 'characteristically do not create law, but kill it'[59] and he concludes that 'we ought to stop circumscribing the *nomos*; we ought to invite new worlds'.[60] This is not only radically pluralist and ultimately anarchic, it is also incoherent.[61] If his position is that officials of the state's legal order occupy a jurispathic office then, as Hauriou and Romano clearly grasped, logically this claim is not unique to the institution of the state: it can apply to all organized normative orders. And if, as Cover implies, no agency can legitimately perform a mediatory or regulatory role with respect to the plurality of legal orders, then how—except by force—are conflicts between these orders to be resolved?

---

[53] Cover, above n.48, 11.   [54] Ibid. 11–12, 17, 18.   [55] Ibid. 39.
[56] Ibid. 40.   [57] Ibid. 42.   [58] Ibid. 4–5.
[59] Ibid. 53. This argument is reinforced in his article 'Violence and the Word' (1985–6) 95 *Yale Law J.* 1601–29, the thesis of which is that: 'Legal interpretation [sc. acts of the state's judiciary] takes place in a field of pain and death. This is true in several senses. Legal interpretive acts signal and occasion the imposition of violence upon others: A judge articulates her understanding of a text, and as a result, somebody loses his freedom, his property, his children, even his life. Interpretations in law also constitute justifications for violence which has already occurred or which is about to occur. When interpreters have finished their work, they frequently leave behind victims whose lives have been torn apart by these organized, social practices of violence. Neither legal interpretation nor the violence it occasions may be properly understood apart from one another.' (at 1629).
[60] Cover, above n. 48, 68.
[61] Cover himself glimpses the incoherence of his argument by equivocating on the violence of the judicial office and stating that 'judges are also people of peace' who 'assert a regulative function that permits a life of law rather than violence' (Cover, above n. 48, 53). Quite where this leaves his thesis is anyone's guess.

Cover's argument once again exposes the weakness of the ideologically-driven pluralist claim. But it also confronts us with the need to specify the role of the state in institutional theory. Hauriou and Romano isolated and identified the key point that states are founded not on violence but on power. Whatever violence was involved in the foundation of the state, the authority of the norm is a function of the power that any order is able to generate. But neither writer fully explains the significance of this claim. They accept that orders build authority by virtue of acceptance of their subjects, but they do not examine what is special about political power.

The answer, I suggest, is in the distinction between two concepts of power: *potestas*, the power generated by being-in-common and experienced as 'power to', and *potentia*, the ability to achieve intended effects, and experienced as 'power over'. Institutions evolve and maintain their world-building capacity only through the dialectical interplay of *potestas* and *potentia*.[62] *Potestas* is the power created by drawing people together in a common undertaking. Its source is often traceable to the founding moment when a multitude begins to conceive itself as a collective singular, a 'we', a movement, a people. Although that foundation is invariably shrouded in myth and legend, the institution generally builds its power through the augmentation of these founding myths. *Potestas* is a type of imaginative power that produces a symbolic representation of the group existing in common association. Cover recognizes this when he refers to the role of 'narrative'. But he does not recognize that it is only by the generation of *potestas* that officers of an institution can use their *potentia* ('power over') to control and regulate conflict, to maintain order, and to promote the collective aims of the institution. Institution-building, world-building, legal-order creation—these involve a ceaseless dialectic of *potestas* and *potentia*, that is, between the juris-generative and the juris-pathic.

An institution's power in the world rests primarily on the scale of its membership, the resources at its disposal, and, crucially, on the bonds of allegiance of the membership to the collective aims of that institution. If we widen Romano's empirical method of observing the working of institutions in the world, we can find a plurality of institutions (or *nomoi*, or legal orders), examine their interaction, and draw conclusions about their relative authority in society. Some ideological pluralists today believe that because a multiplicity of orders exist in the world they must be worthy of equal respect or have equal authority.[63] But this is a normativist fallacy, one that denies the most basic of Romano's claims about the nature of institutions as concrete-orders. Institutions range in aim and scale from those formed for limited purposes to religious bodies that believe they hold the key to the meaning of life. But as social life is presently constituted, it is idle to deny that, notwithstanding the growing influence of international and transnational institutions, the rise of religious movements with worldly aims, and the weakening of ties of nationality, the legal orders of nation-states still constitute the primary form of institutional world-building in contemporary life.

---

[62] See Loughlin, FPL, esp. Ch.6.
[63] See M Loughlin, 'Constitutional Pluralism: An Oxymoron?' (2014) 3 *Global Constitutionalism* 9–30.

7

Politonomy

I. Introduction

It seemed strange to Carl Schmitt that the new scholarly discipline that emerged at the end of the eighteenth century became known as 'national economy' or 'political economy'. How odd, he suggested, that with the extension of the concept of *nomos* from the household to the polity, the term retained its linguistic relation to the household. It was called eco-nomy when logically it should have been labelled politonomy.[1] As he would have been aware, there were particular reasons for this usage. It was a consequence of the extension of Cameralist methods of managing the prince's household resources to the task of establishment and maintenance of the 'well-ordered commonwealth'.[2] Schmitt was nevertheless making an astute observation and one that now has heightened significance.

Recent work claims that this eighteenth century development was critical to the formation of modern government.[3] Michel Foucault argues that the transition was 'from an art of government to a political science', a change 'from a regime dominated by structures of sovereignty to one ruled by techniques of government'.[4] But he also claims that, far from sovereignty dissipating with the emergence of political economy, the question of sovereignty has renewed relevance. That question involves 'an attempt to see what juridical and institutional form, what foundation in the law, could be given to the sovereignty that characterizes a state'.[5] This is the specifically juristic question with which Schmitt was concerned. It is also the key issue behind a more precise conception of politonomy.

---

[1] C Schmitt, '*Nomos-Nahme*-Name' [1957] in his *Nomos of the Earth in the International Law of the Jus Publicum Europaeum*, GL Ulmen trans. (New York: Telos Press, 2006), 336–50 at 339.

[2] See M Raeff, *The Well-Ordered Police State: Social and Institutional Change through Law in the Germanies and Russia, 1600–1800* (New Haven: Yale University Press, 1983); P Bourdieu, 'From the King's House to the Reason of State: A Model of the Genesis of the Bureaucratic Field' (2004) 11 *Constellations* 16–36; K Tribe, 'Cameralism and the sciences of the state' in M Goldie and R Wokler (eds), *The Cambridge History of Eighteenth-Century Political Thought* (Cambridge: Cambridge University Press, 2006), 525–46; Loughlin, FPL, Ch.14.

[3] M Foucault, 'Governmentality' in *Essential Works of Foucault 1954–1984, vol. 3. Power* (London: Penguin, 1978), 201–22; M Mann, *The Sources of Social Power, Volume 2: The Rise of Classes and Nation-States* (Cambridge; Cambridge University Press, 1993); PS Gorski, *The Disciplinary Revolution: Calvinism and the Rise of the State in Early Modern Europe* (Chicago: University of Chicago Press 2003); G Agamben, *The Kingdom and the Glory: For a Theological Genealogy of Economy and Government*, trans. L Chiesa (Stanford: Stanford University Press 2011).

[4] Foucault, ibid. 217–8.   [5] Foucault, ibid. 218.

Political Jurisprudence. Martin Loughlin. © M Loughlin 2017.
Published 2017 by Oxford University Press.

Politonomy does not just refer to the governmental management of the state's resources. It is a broader science that specifies the 'law' by which the political presents itself as a domain of reality. Schmitt is known today as the quintessential theorist of the 'autonomy of the political'.[6] Yet he also maintained that his entire scholarly contribution was that of a jurist examining the constitution of modern political authority. In this respect he joins a long line of political jurists who conceived public law broadly as 'an assemblage of rules, principles, canons, maxims, customs, usages, and manners that condition and sustain the activity of governing'.[7] These jurists were engaging in the elaboration of public law as political jurisprudence.

Schmitt situated himself within this lineage, even claiming to be its 'last conscious representative', 'its last teacher and researcher in an existential sense'.[8] This is significant because the main aim of the political jurists was to specify the 'law of the political', in other words to engage in elaborating politonomy. Schmitt recognized that a 'word bound to *nomos* is measured by *nomos* and subject to it', as is illustrated by the words astronomy and gastronomy.[9] His various studies, from an explanation of the autonomy of the political,[10] through an analysis of sovereignty,[11] legality,[12] and constitutional order[13] to his account of the order of ordering,[14] make an important contribution to the discipline of politonomy.

In this chapter I begin by situating Schmitt as a jurist and especially as a *Staatsrechtler*, one who occupied a position within the distinctively German juristic tradition of state theory. I consider whether Schmitt acknowledged a basic law of the political and conclude that his position is ambivalent, an ambivalence that came from his distrust of the scientific significance of general concepts. To the extent that he acknowledged any 'law of the political', I suggest it is implicit in his embrace of institutionalism in the 1930s and later in his account of *nomos* as the basic law of appropriation, division and production.

II. Schmitt the Jurist

On several occasions Schmitt commented that everything he published was a scholarly contribution to jurisprudence, in particular to two fields of legal scholarship: constitutional law and international law. These fields were the most directly exposed

---

[6] See E Bolsinger, *The Autonomy of the Political: Carl Schmitt's and Lenin's Political Realism* (Westport, CT: Greenwood Press, 2001).

[7] Loughlin, IPL, 30.

[8] C Schmitt, *Ex Captivitate Salus: Erfahrungen der Zeit 1945–47* (Cologne: Greven, 1950), 75.

[9] Schmitt, '*Nomos-Nahme*-Name', above n.1, 338.

[10] C Schmitt, *The Concept of the Political* [1932], G Schwab trans. (Chicago: University of Chicago Press, 2007) (*CP*).

[11] C Schmitt, *Political Theology: Four Chapters on the Concept of Sovereignty* [1922], G Schwab trans. (Chicago: University of Chicago Press, 2005) (*PT*).

[12] C Schmitt, *Legality and Legitimacy* [1932], J Seitzer trans. (Durham, NC: Duke University Press, 2004).

[13] C Schmitt, *Constitutional Theory* [1928], J Seitzer trans. (Durham, NC: Duke University Press 2008) (*CT*)

[14] C Schmitt, *The* Nomos *of the Earth in the International Law of the* Jus Publicum Europaeum [1950], GL Ulmen trans. (New York: Telos Press, 2006) (*NE*).

to 'danger from "the political"'.[15] He argued that the dominant legal philosophies of positivism and normativism that had emerged in the late-nineteenth century were designed as attempts to avoid this problem. Positivist public lawyers sought to exclude politics by the simple trick of presupposing the authority of the constitution as the 'fundamental law' of the subject. And, as its name suggests, normativism stands for the belief that law is an autonomous discipline constructed and bounded by its own norms or laws.[16] Schmitt's point was that there was a prevailing tendency of lawyers to redefine the boundaries of their field so as to exclude its political dimensions. This leads to a skewed understanding of the nature of their discipline.

Rejecting the normativist claim about law's autonomous character, Schmitt contended that the modern concept of law is in fact derivative of the political. Positive law comes from political power and the modern jurist cannot avoid this fact. The most a jurist can do 'is mitigate the danger [of exposure to the political] either by settling into remote neighbouring areas, disguising himself as a historian or a philosopher, or by carrying to extreme perfection the art of caution and camouflage'.[17] Schmitt refused this retreat. His work sought to examine the nature of public law from a perspective that asserts the primacy of the political.

Schmitt is sometimes regarded as an occasional writer,[18] at his most incisive when adopting a polemical argument. But when his work is assessed as a contribution to political jurisprudence, he is revealed to be a more systematic thinker. With extensive knowledge of the historical and comparative aspects of the discipline, Schmitt's writing rigorously addresses the foundational questions in public law, displaying an acute awareness of the main points of tension.

This explains some, though not all, of the confusion and controversy surrounding his work. In later life he wrote that 'I have always spoken and written as a lawyer and, accordingly, only to lawyers and for lawyers'. It was his particular misfortune, he contended, 'that the lawyers of my time had become technical managers of positive law, profoundly uninformed and uneducated, at best Goetheans and neutralized humanitarians'.[19] He predicted that political and social theorists who had followed the lead of the lawyers' criticisms 'would stumble with every word and every

---

[15]   C Schmitt, *Ex Captivitate Salus*, above n.8, 55.

[16]   See, e.g., H Kelsen, *Introduction to the Problems of Legal Theory*, BL Paulson and SL Paulson trans. of first edn. [1934] of *Reine Rechtslehre* (Oxford: Clarendon Press, 1992), 1: legal science must be 'purified of all political ideology' and of 'every element of the natural sciences'.

[17]   Schmitt, *Ex Captivitate Salus*, above n.8, 55.

[18]   K Löwith, 'The Occasional Decisionism of Carl Schmitt' in his *Martin Heidegger and European Nihilism*, R Wolin ed. (New York: Columbia University Press, 1995), 137–59.

[19]   C Schmitt, *Glossarium: Aufzeichnungen der Jahre 1947–1951* (Berlin: Duncker & Humblot, 1991), 17. Some sense of what he means by the term 'Goetheans' is grasped from his comment in *NE*, above n.14, at 70 (n.10): 'The German language today is largely one of theologians – the language of Luther's bible translation – as well as a language of craftsmen and technicians (as Leibniz observed). In contrast to French, it is not a language of jurists or of moralists. German gives a heightened, even sublime significance to the word *Gesetz*. Poets and philosophers love the word, which acquired a sacred tone and a numinous power through Luther's bible translation. Even Goethe's *Urworte orphisch* is nourished by this source: *Nach dem Gesetz, nach dem du angetreten* [According to the law by which you began]'. On the humanitarians see: C Schmitt, 'The Age of Neutralizations and Depoliticizations' [1929] in his *CP*, above n.10, 80–96.

formulation and tear me apart like a desert fox'.[20] There is a considerable degree of self-serving pathos in those words. Yet his core point remains. Seen as a contribution to social or political theory, Schmitt's work will be misunderstood. It is the work of a jurist seeking to grasp the nexus between the legal and the political for the purpose of explaining the nature of modern public law.

This point takes us only so far. If law is not an autonomous discipline and if the legal is derived from the political, then the scientific inquiry is simply pushed back a stage. The question becomes: how is the autonomy of the political to be explained? This is the deeper question that arises from Schmitt's politonomy: how does his account of the political provide a basis for understanding 'the law of the political'?

III. State Theory

Schmitt's scholarship is situated within the German tradition of *Staatslehre*. During the eighteenth and nineteenth centuries, this 'doctrine of the state' was a single discipline embracing political theory, sociology, and law and offering a scientific account of the modern institution of the state.[21] Schmitt acknowledged the importance of this tradition but maintained that since the establishment of the German Reich in the 1870s there had been a progressive 'decline of consciousness in the field of state theory'.[22] This he attributed to the growing influence of legal positivism. Under the sway of positivist public lawyers such as Gerber and Laband, a new conceptualization of the subject held that all questions of history and politics must be expelled from juristic consideration. The state was refashioned as a purely legal institution equipped with a special type of corporate personality; it was deemed to be an institution created by, and regulated in accordance with, the operations of positive public law.[23] Schmitt contended that under the influence of these ideas, by 1914 the great tradition of state theory developed over the previous two or three hundred years had been lost.[24] There could be no systematic and scientific account of public law if it began by postulating the authority of the positivist conception of the state.

For Schmitt, the institution of the state emerged from intense political struggle. 'The state that came into being in the seventeenth century and prevailed on the continent of Europe', he explained, 'differs from all earlier kinds of political units'.[25] Understood as an 'organized political entity, internally peaceful, territorially enclosed,

[20] Schmitt, *Glossarium*, 17.

[21] See J Kersten, *Georg Jellinek und die klassische Staatslehre* (Tübingen: Mohr Siebeck 2000).

[22] C Schmitt, *Hugo Preuss: Sein Staatsbegriff und seine Stellung in der deutschen Staatslehre* (Tübingen: Mohr, 1930), 14; Eng trans. 'Hugo Preuss: His Concept of the State and his Position in German State Theory' (2017) 38 *History of Political Thought* 345–70, at 359.

[23] CF von Gerber, *Grundzüge eines Systems des deutschen Staatsrechts* (Leipzig: Tauchnitz, 1865); P Laband, *Das Staatsrecht des deutschen Reiches* (Tübingen: Laupp, 4 vols, 1876–82); M Stolleis, *Public Law in Germany, 1800–1914* (New York: Berghahn Books, 2001), Ch.8.

[24] Schmitt, *Hugo Preuss*, above n.22, 6 (Eng. 351–2).

[25] *CP*, 34. His account of the state is explained in more detail in his 'Staat als ein konkreter, an eine geschichtliche Epoche gebundener Begriff' [1941] in C Schmitt, *Verfassungsrechtliche Aufsätze aus den Jahren 1924–1954* (Berlin: Duncker & Humblot, 1958), 375–85.

and impenetrable to aliens', he recognized that its creation was an historic achievement.[26] But its authority could not be taken for granted. In the context of the specific crisis of the Weimar Republic in which conditions of internal peace had not been established, an account of that regime's system of public law could not assume the authority of the state. A scientific account of public law had to be constructed from more basic elements of political understanding.

For this reason Schmitt proclaimed that the 'concept of the state presupposes the concept of the political'.[27] In the political circumstances of the Weimar Republic, it was evident that the logic of friend/enemy—Schmitt's criterion of the political—not only manifested itself externally, that is with respect to inter-state conflicts, but had also emerged as a feature of the internal dynamics of the political unit. In such circumstances, a scientific account of public law could not assume the authority of either the constitution or the state. A foundational account must first offer an explanation of the relationship between the legal and the political.

The account Schmitt presented was arguably as systematic and radical as that of Thomas Hobbes. Hobbes had given us an image of life in the state of nature, a 'war of all against all', as the platform for a rational solution to the problem of order. Conscious of the conditions of life in a state of nature, where insecurity reigns and force and fraud are the cardinal virtues, we see the necessity, as a matter of self-preservation, of trading our natural liberties for the protections offered by an absolute sovereign.[28] For Hobbes, the bargain is between living free in a world of interminable conflict and living in peaceful conditions under the protection of a sovereign authority. In Hobbes' estimation, this bargain constitutes the fundamental law of the political.

But Hobbes' stark contrast between life in a state of nature and life under civil order reveals this as a formal legal exercise. If the concept of the political is derived from the distinction between friend and enemy, then the transition Hobbes envisages from the state of nature, in which everyone is a potential enemy, to the civil state, in which all are bound to the sovereign's rule, is a transition that negates—or externalizes—politics. Hobbes has given us a purely juristic concept of the state, in which the sovereign-subject relationship is entirely formal. Since all honour and all power is vested in the office of the sovereign, Hobbes evidently saw no place for political struggle within the state. Hobbes' theory is a juridical account that is antipolitical in character.[29]

For Schmitt, Hobbes' contrast between war (in a state of nature) and peace (in the state) is formal, abstract, and general. If political jurists are to acquire scientific knowledge of the institution of the state they must acknowledge the existential conditions under which the authority of the state is established and maintained. Schmitt contended that in reality the state can assure 'total peace within ... its territory' and

---

[26] *CP*, 47.   [27] *CP*, 19.

[28] T Hobbes, *Leviathan*, R Tuck ed. (Cambridge: Cambridge University Press, 1996), Ch.13. See further Ch.2 above.

[29] See L Strauss, 'Notes on *The Concept of the Political*' in *CP*, 97–122 at 108(n 2): 'In truth Hobbes is *the* antipolitical thinker (political understood in Schmitt's sense)'.

establish itself as 'the decisive political entity' through a historic struggle involving violence and domination.[30] Only then could a 'normal situation', which is 'the pre-requisite for legal norms to be valid', be established.[31] Since conflicts continue to exist even in a well-ordered state, 'this requirement for internal peace compels it [the state] in critical situations to decide also upon the domestic enemy'.[32] It is for this reason that the sovereign power of decision must be retained to ensure the preservation of a constitutional state.[33] Sovereign, Schmitt declared, is 'he who decides on the exception'.[34]

Schmitt saw these political necessities as being of profound juristic significance. Any attempt to hide them behind abstract concept would lead to a distortion of the nature of public law. He recognized that within any well-ordered state, law has 'its own relatively independent domain'.[35] But although positive law might occupy an independent domain, it loses that autonomy the closer it intrudes on political matters. This is because political conflicts 'can neither be decided by a previously determined general norm nor by the judgment of a disinterested and therefore neutral third party'.[36] Only politically engaged parties can settle an extreme case of conflict. If there is a threat to political existence then, even in a constitutional state, 'the battle must then be waged outside the constitution and the law'.[37] This is because 'unity and order lies in the political existence of the state, not in statutes, rules, and just any instrument containing norms'.[38] For Schmitt, the most fundamental concept behind the modern understanding of law is neither the constitution nor the state: it is the concept of the political.

IV. The Law of the Political

In *Political Theology*, Schmitt observes that 'all law is situational law'.[39] Given that he also contends that the concept of the political grounds the modern concept of law, then whatever 'the law of the political' means, it is not a reference to positive law. This notion must belong within the broader tradition of public law as political jurisprudence.

From this perspective, the concept of the 'law of the political' refers to those laws, rules, conditions which determine and sustain the autonomy of the political. As has been indicated, public law in its broader conception is concerned with rules, principles, canons, maxims, etc. that sustain the activity of governing. They can be divided into two main parts: constitutive rules and regulative rules. The former are those that establish a conceptual understanding of the political, while the latter are those which sustain the power of this way of acting in the world. For Bodin, acknowledged by

---

[30] *CP*, 46. [31] *CP*, 46 [32] *CP*, 46 [33] *CP*, 47. [34] *PT*, 5.
[35] *CP*, 66.
[36] *CP*, 27. This forms the core of his argument that a court cannot act as ultimate guardian of the constitution: C Schmitt, *Der Hüter der Verfassung* (Tübingen: Mohr, 1931) L Vinx (ed.), *The Guardian of the Constitution: Hans Kelsen and Carl Schmitt on the Limits of Constitutional Law* (Cambridge: Cambridge University Press, 2015), Chs 2 and 3.
[37] *CP*, 47 [38] *CP*, 65 [39] *PT*, 13.

Schmitt as having given us 'the first depiction of modern public law',[40] constitutive rules are those that elaborate his concept of sovereignty, while regulative rules are those that express the principle that restraints on power generate power.[41] But does Schmitt acknowledge the existence of any such basic rules that constitute 'the political'?

Schmitt argued that the political acquires its specificity in contrast to other 'relatively independent endeavours of human thought and action, particularly the moral, aesthetic and economic'.[42] The essential criterion of the political is the friend-enemy distinction, two aspects of which should be emphasized. The first is that the friend-enemy distinction is not metaphor; it has an existential meaning. Secondly, the political does not have a substance; it is not located in some discrete sector of social life called 'the political sphere' but is capable of manifesting itself in any aspect of group existence. The autonomous character of the political is thus founded on two basic conditions. First, conflicts emerge which divide humans according to the criterion of friend-enemy and, secondly, this criterion is a consequence of a particular 'intensity of an association or dissociation of human beings'.[43]

In Schmitt's analysis, conflicts can arise in any social situation for a variety of unpredictable reasons—theological, economic, ethnic, or cultural. Consequently, it is difficult to see how any form of predictability, let alone normative rationality, can apply to this dimension of human experience. This suggests that Schmitt treats friend-enemy conflicts simply as an existential condition on which no further intellectual energy need be expended. But it might be noted that for Schmitt the friend-enemy criterion has a distinctive meaning: it is both a collective and public matter. That is, it should not be understood 'in a private-individualistic sense as a psychological expression of private emotions and tendencies'.[44] The enemy 'is solely the public enemy... The enemy is *hostis*, not *inimicus*....'[45] The enemy is neither competitor nor private adversary: 'the enemy is solely the public enemy, because everything that has a relationship to such a collectivity of men, particularly to a whole nation, becomes public by virtue of such a relationship'.[46] Elaborating, he explained that 'an organized political entity'—that is, a state—must 'decide for itself the friend-enemy distinction'.[47]

Schmitt's account is ambiguous, but it does indicate two things. It suggests that the political pertains only to a *group* and this group has a *public* identity. The concept of the political must therefore enable us to identify a group as a group, as an 'organized political entity'. It is also constituted by factors that distinguish between public and private concerns. These features suggest the formation of an institution.[48] If the constituent nature of this institution could be specified, then his conception of the law of the political might become clear. But this is not straightforward, mainly because he doubts both the capacity of general concepts to govern conduct and the value of undertaking general methodological inquiries.[49] Nonetheless, what is clear

---

[40] *CT*, 101.   [41] See Ch.1, III above.   [42] *CP*, 25–6.   [43] *CP*, 38.
[44] *CP*, 28.   [45] *CP*, 28.   [46] *CP*, 28.   [47] *CP*, 29–30.
[48] JR Searle, 'What is an Institution?' (2005) 1 *J. of Institutional Economics* 1–22.
[49] J Müller, 'Carl Schmitt's Method: Between Ideology, Demonology and Myth' (1999) 4 *J. of Political Ideologies* 61–85, at 63.

is that Schmitt sees the friend-enemy distinction as the essential criterion of the *concept* of the political.

Schmitt's nominalism leads him to claim that political and legal concepts acquire meaning only in their specific historical context. Concept formation is an immanent process arising from an actual political situation. 'All political concepts, images and terms', he argues, 'have a polemical meaning'. By this he means that they 'are focused on a specific conflict and are bound to a concrete situation whose ultimate consequence (which manifests itself in war or revolution) is a friend-enemy grouping'.[50] As he explains in *The Concept of the Political*: 'Words such as state, republic, society, class, as well as sovereignty, constitutional state, absolutism, dictatorship, economic planning, neutral or total state, and so on, are incomprehensible if one does not know exactly who is to be affected, combated, refuted, or negated by such a term'.[51] Devoid of reference to such antagonisms, concepts become meaningless abstractions. 'The critical moment in the history of a concept', he suggests, 'is the moment in which its adversary is forgotten'.[52]

Schmitt maintains that a concept's meaning is determined by the existence of a concrete antithesis. Since abstract concepts do not carry an independent authority, generalizations are deceptive. Concepts must either somehow be 'found' in a concrete reality or are tools to be used as weapons in the struggle for power. In most cases, 'the exigencies of ideological combat and a strategic politics of concepts (*Begriffspolitik*) tended to override Schmitt's *Wissenschaftlichkeit*'.[53] Schmitt's method must of necessity extend to the concept of the political itself. If there is a 'law of the political', it cannot be founded on the appeal of some concept, whether of sovereignty, universal right, or the elaboration of the 'general will'. This suggests that Schmitt held to the crude realist notion that 'might makes right', which is all there is to say about the 'law of the political'.

Such a conclusion might be resisted because in other writings Schmitt adopted a more nuanced position. In these he rejects the claim that concepts are merely the products of an extant political reality. He recognizes that political struggles are invariably fought out through general ideas but points out that these conceptual struggles are not entirely derivative. That is, they 'are not merely "ideological" delusions serving only propaganda purposes'. Rather, they are 'only a case in point of the simple truth that all human activity bears a certain intellectual (*geistigen*) character'. Even in the context of political struggle, he acknowledges that there 'has never in human history been an absence of such justifications and principles of legitimation'.[54] Concepts, he seems to be saying, are drawn into conflictual struggle and used as weapons in those struggles, but they are not purely the product of these struggles.

---

[50] *CP*, 30.   [51] *CP*, 30–1.

[52] Schmitt, *Hugo Preuss*, above n.22, 17 (Eng. 362). See also, C Schmitt, 'Reich-Staat-Bund' [1933] in his *Positionen und Begriffe im Kampf mit Weimar-Genf-Versailles, 1923–1939* (Berlin: Duncker & Humblot 1988), 191; id., *Der Hüter der Verfassung* (Tübingen: Mohr 1931), 128.

[53] Müller, above n.49, 62.

[54] C Schmitt, 'Völkerrechtliche Formen des modernen Imperialismus' [1932] in his *Positionen und Begriffe*, above n.52, 162–80, at 163.

Rather, these power conflicts need to be legitimated through concepts at the level of political and constitutional theory.[55]

Since Schmitt is not consistent on this basic point, it is difficult to assess his contribution to politonomy. He says both that 'the content of world history...has always been a struggle for words and concepts'[56] and that the 'struggle over concepts is not a dispute about empty words but a war of enormous reality and presence'.[57] But he also claims that the key point is 'who interprets, defines and applies them'. Contrary to many political jurists, he asserts that '*Caesar dominus et supra grammaticam*. The emperor is also ruler over grammar'.[58] If 'grammar' is a metaphorical expression of the law of the political, then Schmitt is saying that the sovereign determines not just the exception but also the political itself.

Schmitt's position on the significance of concepts in understanding the phenomenon of the political can be situated within the German school of *Begriffsgeschichte*. This body of work is exemplified in the writings of Reinhart Koselleck who maintains that, whatever else it might be, a concept 'bundles up the variety of historical experience together with a collection of theoretical and practical references into a relation that is given and can be experienced *only* through the concept'.[59] Koselleck acknowledges that social and political concepts do not simply 'define given states of affairs'; they aim to shape a state of affairs and thus to 'reach into the future'.[60] In this respect, 'a concept must remain ambiguous in order to be a concept', because a political concept is of necessity 'the concentrate of several substantial meanings'.[61] The claim that political concepts are contestable and have become the medium through which political struggles are fought fits Schmitt's argument. It also suggests that there is a conceptual frame through which the political is engaged.[62]

The ambiguity in Schmitt's position casts a shadow over his contribution to politonomy, an ambiguity some believe he exploited.[63] From a juristic perspective, this ambiguity may have been part of his uncertainty about whether there exist two different concepts of power in the domain of the political. Here power not only

---

[55] Bolsinger, above n.6, 37–40.   [56] Schmitt, 'Reich – Staat – Bund', above n.52, 191.

[57] Ibid. 198.

[58] Schmitt, 'Imperialismus', above n.54, at 179. Cf. I Kant, 'An Answer to the Question: "What is Enlightenment?"' [1784] in his *Political Writings*, HB Nisbet trans., H Reiss ed.(Cambridge: Cambridge University Press, 2nd edn. 1991), 54–60, at 58. See also Loughlin, FPL, 178–80.

[59] R Koselleck, '*Begriffsgeschichte* and Social History' in his *Futures Past: On the Semantics of Historical Time*, K Tribe trans. (New York: Columbia University Press, 2004), 75–92, at 85 (emphasis supplied).

[60] Ibid. 80.   [61] Ibid 85.

[62] This view of the nature and role of political concepts is now more widely accepted. Quentin Skinner has recently acknowledged that in believing that concepts 'not only alter over time, but are incapable of providing us with anything other than a series of changing perspectives on the world in which we live and have our being' we are following in a tradition that stems from Nietzsche and Weber (in whose company Schmitt would have felt at home). Skinner joins with Koselleck in maintaining that 'we need to treat our normative concepts less as statements about the world than as tools and weapons of ideological debate'. In pursuing this line of argument about concepts, Skinner relies on Foucault's Nietzschean argument that 'the history which bears and determines us has the form of a war'. Q Skinner, 'Retrospect: Studying Rhetoric and Conceptual Change' in his *Visions of Politics. Vol.1: Regarding Method* (Cambridge: Cambridge University Press, 2002), 175–87, at 176–7. Skinner's reference is to: M Foucault, *Power/Knowledge* (Brighton: Harvester, 1980), 114.

[63] See, e.g., Müller, above n.49.

signifies supremacy over the material means of rule (*potentia*) but also the capacity to build unity through the establishment of authority (*potestas*).[64] Schmitt speaks mainly of the former aspect of power, on which he maintains a realist position. But occasionally, as in an early work in which he suggested that 'to the political belongs the idea, because there is no politics without authority and no authority without an ethos of belief',[65] he alludes to the idea of power as *potestas*. And when he invokes the idea of power as *potestas*, he has to acknowledge the power-shaping capacity of concepts.

V. Institutionalism

To advance this inquiry, Schmitt's concept of law must be directly addressed. As we have seen, he regarded all concepts of law as being historically situated. During the 1920s, his primary task was a critique of the ahistorical abstractions of legal norma- tivism. His thesis was that normativist jurists distort understanding of the true na- ture of law by severing the norms of legal ordering from the facts of political existence.[66] Schmitt, by contrast, promoted a type of legal decisionism. Law being the product of will, the existence of a sovereign act of will can never be removed from the sphere of legal thought. In furthering this argument, he showed how normativist jurists, interested only in the normal situation, cannot account for exceptional cir- cumstances. Even if the norm is destroyed in exceptional circumstances, the excep- tion is still of juristic significance: 'both elements, the norm as well as the decision, remain within the framework of the juristic'.[67]

In his Preface to the second edition of *Political Theology* in 1933, Schmitt begins to modify this argument. He distinguishes 'not two but *three* types of legal thinking; in addition to the normativist and the decisionist types there is the institutional one'.[68] 'Whereas the pure normativist thinks in terms of impersonal rules, and the decisionist implements the good law of the correctly recognized political situation by means of a personal decision', Schmitt explains that 'institutional legal thinking unfolds in institutions and organizations that transcend the personal sphere'.[69] Schmitt's advocacy of institutionalism was intended to grasp 'the stable content in- herent in every great political movement'.[70] What might this content be? And could this element provide the key to Schmitt's politonomy?

Schmitt's institutional argument is most clearly presented in his 1934 book, *On the Three Types of Juristic Thought*.[71] Here he explains that all legal theories comprise three basic elements: norm, decision, and concrete-order formation. Legal theories are categorized according to the emphasis they place on each of these elements. The

---

[64] Loughlin, FPL, 164–77.

[65] C Schmitt, *Roman Catholicism and Political Form* [1923], GL Ulmen trans. (Westport, CT: Greenwood, 1996), 17.

[66] *PT*, Ch.2.   [67] *PT*, 12–13.   [68] *PT*, 2.   [69] *PT*, 3.   [70] *PT*, 3.

[71] C Schmitt, *On the Three Types of Juristic Thought* [1934], JW Bendersky trans. (Westport, CT: Praeger, 2004) (*TT*)

type of political regime envisaged in these theories is invariably linked to the pre-dominance given to one or other of these elements. 'Every form of political life', he maintains, 'stands in direct, mutual relationship with the specific mode of thought and argumentation of legal life'.[72] Schmitt again criticizes normativism, but he turns against the decisionism he advocated in *Political Theology*, arguing instead for a type of institutionalism he calls 'concrete-order' thinking.[73]

Normativists promote a purely conceptualistic understanding of law, law as a set of rules. The arguments of decisionists, by contrast, are reduced ultimately to factual analysis. Institutionalism, or concrete-order thinking, is Schmitt's attempt to finesse the distinction between normativity and facticity.[74] Rules and decisions are integral parts of legal order, but they are only formulations of concrete-order. Law as norm does not yield sound jurisprudence because a norm 'cannot apply, administer, or enforce itself'[75] and decisionism is unsustainable because a legal decision never emerges from a normative vacuum.[76] Legal order is an expression of the underlying concrete-order. Rules and decisions achieve regularity by reliance on 'concepts of what, in itself, is normal, the normal type and the normal situation'.[77] Schmitt is arguing that political unity depends on a stable institutional structure. There is a 'concrete-order' that determines legal norms and guides the exercise of legal decision-making. But how is a stable institutional structure established and maintained?

With this question in mind, we turn to Chapter 13 of his *Constitutional Theory*. There Schmitt analyses the nature of the *Rechtsstaat* in what by now will be a familiar trajectory. To invoke the idea of 'the rule of law' is 'an empty manner of speaking if it does not receive its actual sense through a certain opposition'.[78] For Schmitt, the *Rechtsstaat* is a legislative state, one in which the authoritative expression of will takes the form of legislation and the legislature is itself bound by this law. This makes sense, he explains, only when a statute is expressed in the form of a general norm. Law is not to be understood as *voluntas*, will or decision, but as *ratio*, norms or rules. The problem with this claim, he continues, is that within any actually-existing con-stitutional order, the *Rechtsstaat* concept of law must be situated alongside an alter-native concept of law, what he calls a 'political concept' of law. This political concept is a juristic concept, both of which are essential elements in modern constitutional thought.

By a 'political concept of law', Schmitt means a concept of law that 'results from the political form of existence of the state' arising 'out of the concrete manner of the formation of the organisation of rule'.[79] In the *Rechtsstaat* concept, law is a norm—a rule of a general character. In the political concept, law is the expression of a concrete will taking the form of a command and conceived as an act of sovereign will. The *Rechtsstaat*, he argues, seeks to suppress this political concept and establish

---

[72] *TT*, 45.

[73] Although Schmitt acknowledged his indebtedness to the work of Hauriou' (*PT*, 2–3), in *Three Types* he seems to have recognized that, with the establishment of the Nazi regime, it would be politic to call this 'concrete-order thought' so as to avoid any association with neo-Thomism exhibited in Hauriou's work: see Bendersky's note in *Three Types* at 112 (n.59). On Hauriou, see Ch.6, III above.

[74] *TT*, 53.   [75] *TT*, 51.   [76] *TT*, 62.   [77] *TT*, 54.   [78] *CT*, 181.

[79] *CT*, 187.

a 'sovereignty of law'. This however is a vain hope since, without a political expression of law as will, the *Rechtsstaat* formulation cannot exist.

Schmitt's analysis in *Constitutional Theory* emphasizes the dependence of norm on will. But in the light of his later argument about concrete-order thinking, it is clear that law-as-norm and law-as-will both depend on institutional ordering. He alluded to this point in this chapter of *Constitutional Theory* when stating that those who promote the concept of law as norm find themselves in a contradictory position because 'that which is directly lacking is the nomos'.[80] In 1950 in *The* Nomos *of the Earth*, he offers a systematic account of this crucial concept.

VI. Nomos

Schmitt's objective in *The* Nomos *of the Earth* is to specify the original legal-constitutional meaning of *nomos* 'in its energy and majesty'[81] to show that jurists who translate *nomos* simply as law or custom do not get to the root of the matter. His explanantion of the true meaning of *nomos* is intended to reveal how the concept of law is founded in 'concrete-order thinking'.

The Greek noun *nomos* derives from the Greek verb *nemein* and, in common acceptance, *nemein* has three main meanings: these are (in German) *nehmen* (to appropriate), *teilen* (to divide), and *weiden* (to pasture). In its first meaning it signifies a taking, especially the appropriation of land. Land-appropriation is the basic story of every settled people: 'not only logically, but also historically, land-appropriation precedes the order that follows from it'. *Nomos* thus signifies the constitution of 'the original spatial order, the source of all further concrete-order and all further law'. The constitutive process of land-acquisition 'is found at the beginning of the history of every settled people, every commonwealth, every empire'.[82] Schmitt contends that 'all subsequent law and everything promulgated and enacted thereafter as decrees and commands are *nourished*... by this source'.[83]

Nomos is an *ordo ordinans*, an order of ordering, the constitutive act of establishing a spatially-determined regime. In the beginning, order was not established on the basis of consent, or on some universal principle or basic norm but on a simple land-grab. It was after the violence of that initial appropriation and division that 'some degree of calculability and security' was achieved and *nomos* emerged as the expression of order.[84] This order evolves; it is not fully formed at its foundation, though it is still 'nourished' by this source. *Nomos*, he implies, holds the key to politonomy: *nomos* is an expression of the basic law of the political.

For Schmitt, the law of the political is revealed through the way in which appropriation, division, and production give rise to the substantive order of a political unity. This defines the relationship between *nomos*, state, and constitution. The state is 'the concrete, collective condition of political unity';[85] in modernity, it becomes

---

[80] *CT*, 184.   [81] *NE*, 67.   [82] *NE*, 48.   [83] *NE*, 48.   [84] *NE*, 341.
[85] *CT*, 60.

the 'master ordering concept' of this political unity.[86] It is clear that Schmitt's concept of constitution in its absolute sense differs profoundly from the modern notion of constitutional law. For Schmitt the order that emerges within the state arises from 'a pre-established, unified will',[87] and therefore the state 'does not *have* a constitution'; rather, 'the state *is* constitution'. In this sense, the state/constitution is 'an actually present condition, a *status* of unity and order'.[88] The basic law of the state finds its authoritative expression not in enacted legal norms but in 'the political existence of the state'.[89] The state as political unity, the constitution as the status of unity and order and *nomos* as the order of a concrete spatial unity are, to all intents and purposes, synonyms.

Schmitt recognizes that, like *nomos*, state and constitution continue to evolve. The state expresses 'the principle of the *dynamic emergence* of political unity, of the process of constantly renewed *formation* and *emergence* of this *unity* from a fundamental or ultimately effective *power* and *energy*'.[90] And he accepts that the 'continuity of a constitution is manifest as long as the regress to this primary appropriation is recognizable and recognized'.[91] If state symbolizes unity and constitution is the form of that unity, then *nomos* shapes the form of that unity. *Nomos* is 'the full immediacy of a legal power not mediated by laws; it is a constitutive historical event – an act of *legitimacy*, whereby the legality of a mere law first is made meaningful'.[92] It is the law of the political.

Schmitt's institutionalism brings his legal thought much closer to Hegel's legal and political philosophy, in which 'the state is a "form (*Gestalt*), which is the complete realization of the spirit in being (*Dasein*)"; an "individual totality", a *Reich* of objective reason and morality'.[93] This type of state, Schmitt emphasizes, is not an 'order of a calculable and enforceable legal functionalism' (that is, the product of decisionism) and nor is it a 'norm of norms' (normativism). The state 'is the concrete order of orders, the institution of institutions'.[94] This is not Hegel's state in which the universal is willed; it more closely approximates his concept of *Notstaat*, the state based on necessity, an expression of the form within civil society 'wherein the livelihood, happiness, and legal status of one man is interwoven with the livelihood, happiness, and rights of all'.[95]

Schmitt's politonomy is founded on the concept of *nomos*. In *The* Nomos *of the Earth* his most basic claim is that law is tied to space, to a defined territory that distinguishes insiders from outsiders. Without this boundary, there can be no

---

[86] C Schmitt, 'Staat als ein konkreter, an eine geschichtliche Epoche gebundener Begriff' [1941] in his *Verfassungsrechtliche Aufsätze aus den Jahren 1924–1954* (Berlin: Duncker & Humblot, 1958), 375–85, at 375: '*In diesem Zeitalter … ist der Staat der alles beherrschende Ordnungsbegriff der politischen Einheit*'. Cf. the claims of Clifford Geertz and Quentin Skinner. C Geertz, *Negara: The Theatre State in Nineteenth-Century Bali* (Princeton: Princeton University Press, 1980), 121: 'That master noun of modern political discourse, *state*'. Q Skinner, 'The State' in T Ball, J Farr, and RL Hanson (eds), *Political Innovation and Conceptual Change* (Cambridge: Cambridge University Press, 1989), 90–131, at 123: the state is 'the master noun of political argument'.
[87] *CT*, 65.   [88] *CT*, 60.   [89] *CT*, 65.   [90] *CT*, 61.   [91] *NE*, 326, n.6.
[92] *NE*, 73.   [93] *TT*, 78.   [94] *TT*, 78–9.
[95] GWF Hegel, *Philosophy of Right*, TM Knox trans. (Oxford: Oxford University Press, 1952), § 183.

domain of the political: *nomos*, then, is constitutive of the political. This space—this territory—is not merely geographical. It is also a legal and political concept which concerns 'the space between individuals in a group whose members are bound to, and at the same time separated and protected from, each other by all kinds of relationships, based on a common language, religion, a common history, customs and laws'.[96] The establishment of these relationships creates the space for political freedom, a freedom that is always spatially limited, always an achievement, and always ordered. *Nomos* gives expression to a concrete-order that was initiated by a taking and harnessed through institutionalization.

VII. Schmitt's Contribution to Politonomy

Schmitt is situated in a tradition of thought that sees the relationship between the legal and the political as a critical aspect of the constitution of modern political authority. Rather than postulating the autonomy of law, this tradition seeks to expose the fundamental laws of the political.

The nature of this discipline can be explained by situating it within western political thought. Much of political thought has evolved because, in the face of a common experience of regimes built on conflict, domination, and the threat of disorder, scholars have felt the lingering power of the idea of human community as an ordered and peaceable existence. One influential strand devotes itself to the task of overcoming that gulf. A line of thought started by the Stoics, embraced by medieval Christian scholars, and eventually secularized by Enlightenment thinkers claims that the laws of reason and the laws of nature operate in harmony. Reconciliation between them is achieved through a type of human association made possible through the power of reason. Initially expressing an overarching, divinely-sanctioned unity, in its post-theological phase this line of thought is presented as a set of principles of association that humans are impelled rationally to adopt and which they must strive to realize.

Politonomy opposes this powerful strand of political thought. Sceptical of the possibility of reconciliation through transcendence, it asserts the unbridgeable nature of this gulf.[97] The power of 'abstract universals' is acknowledged, but 'necessary conditions' cannot be ignored.[98] Politonomy appeals to reason but confronts human history. Presenting itself as a practical discourse orientated to norms, it always has regard to consequences. It seeks through phenomenological investigation to explain the immanent logic of political reason.

The first systematic exponent of this discipline was Jean Bodin who affirmed the sovereign authority of the system of political rule and built on this foundation with

---

[96] H Arendt, *Eichmann in Jerusalem: A Report on the Banality of Evil* (New York: Penguin Books, rev. edn. 1965), 262.

[97] I Hunter, *Rival Enlightenments: Civil and Metaphysical Philosophy in Early Modern Germany* (Cambridge: Cambridge University Press 2001).

[98] Hegel, above n.95, §§ 29–33; A Honneth *The Pathologies of Individual Freedom: Hegel's Social Theory* (Princeton: Princeton University Press, 2010), 15.

a set of rules to be followed if the prince was to maintain his state.[99] By bringing sovereignty, the *right* to rule, into alignment with the rules of civil prudence that maintain the *capacity* of rule, Bodin drew the template for politonomy. His formal claim of absolute authority (*potestas*) laid the foundation for a new field of political knowledge necessary to establish, maintain, and extend the powers of civil government (*potentia*).

Following this tradition, Schmitt advocates a type of political realism. Recognizing that Bodin 'stands at the beginning of the modern theory of the state'[100] and acknowledging that his work 'had a greater and more immediate impact than had any other book by a jurist in the history of law',[101] he maintains that Bodin's real achievement was overlooked. Bodin's innovation, according to Schmitt, rests not so much on his definition of sovereignty as 'the absolute and perpetual power of a republic' as on his recognition that the sovereign's defining characteristic is the ability in an emergency to overturn established laws. 'When the time, place and individual circumstances demand it', he notes, Bodin accepted that 'the sovereign can change and violate statutes'.[102] Rather than the world-building potential of Bodin's fusing of the constitutive and regulative rules of politonomy, Schmitt chooses to emphasize the decisionism behind the sovereign's power to determine an issue that 'cannot be settled normatively', to decide 'that which advances the public good'.[103]

Schmitt's reading of Bodin also signals his ambivalent relationship to Hobbes. Although praising Hobbes as 'a great and truly systematic political thinker',[104] he also acknowledges that Hobbes was 'a spiritual forefather of the bourgeois law-and-constitutional state that materialized in the nineteenth century'.[105] It is for this reason that, in contrast to the liberal leanings of such jurists as Bodin and Hobbes, Schmitt sought to resurrect the work of Joseph de Maistre and Juan Donoso Cortés.[106] He emphasized how 'with an energy that rose to an extreme between the two revolutions of 1789 and 1848', Maistre and Donoso Cortés, 'thrust the notion of the decision to the center of their thinking'.[107] Once again Schmitt's decisionism is all-important.

Schmitt's general orientation is highlighted by contrasting his thought with another great public lawyer, Montesquieu. Like Schmitt, Montesquieu believed that the law of the political is not discovered through normative inquiry but through the empirical study of the history of government. Only immersion in the various particulars of government he believed would reveal 'the principles on which they are founded'.[108] Montesquieu's aim was to identify the 'laws' that have shaped the formation of political regimes. This—'the work of twenty years'[109]—was an exercise in politonomy. But law could not be conceived as command; the 'law of the political',

---

[99] See Ch.1, III above.   [100] *PT*, 8.   [101] *NE*, 127.   [102] *CT*, 101.
[103] *CT*, 101.   [104] *CP*, 64.
[105] C Schmitt, *The Leviathan in the State Theory of Thomas Hobbes: Meaning and Failure of a Political Symbol* [1938], G Schwab trans. (Chicago: University of Chicago Press 2008), 67.
[106] *PT*, Ch.4.   [107] *PT*, 53.
[108] Montesquieu, *The Spirit of the Laws*, A Cohler, B Miller, and H Stone trans. and eds (Cambridge: Cambridge University Press, 1989), xliii.
[109] Ibid.

he realized, was an expression 'of the necessary relations deriving from the nature of things'.[110]

Through meticulous investigation into the history of government, Montesquieu distinguishes between the objects of his studies—the laws and practices of regimes—and his findings: the laws that determine their form. He distinguishes in effect between 'political laws', the positive laws that regulate government in particular regimes, and politonomy, the law of the political. The latter, he suggests, is directed towards causes rather than motives, and the main determining causes are climate and geography, customs and commerce, population and religion. Even though individuals might be unconscious of such factors, they invariably determine the type of regime that is established. Montesquieu maintains that the critical issue is consonance of nature and principle. Each type of government, whether democracy, aristocracy, monarchy, or despotism, has both its nature, 'that which makes it what it is', and its driving principle, 'that which makes it act'.[111] The power of any regime, he concludes, is determined by the degree to which nature and principle—the constitutive and the regulative—are united.

Montesquieu's line of inquiry takes its cue from Bodin, an approach that historical sociologists have often adopted.[112] It is also a tradition in which Schmitt, especially with respect to the scheme of development in *The* Nomos *of the Earth*, can be situated. But this type of investigation provides only a partial account of politonomy; its strict empiricism reduces the political to observable data and a one-dimensional account of political power as *potentia*. This is the substance of Rousseau's objections. He recognizes the difficulty of conceiving political power purely in normative terms. In his *Discourse on Inequality*, for example, he notes that if we think of government as originating in a foundation, then the pact that might have been struck in the remote past was a deceptive and fraudulent device, drafted by the wealthy for the purpose of exploiting the poor.[113] But he also claims that Montesquieu had created a 'great and useless science' because he had not drilled down to 'the principles of political right', an exercise requiring the consideration of agency as well as of structure. Montesquieu had been 'content to discuss the positive right of established governments', which according to Rousseau is very different from uncovering the principles of political right.[114]

---

[110] Ibid. 3.   [111] Ibid. 21.

[112] See O Hintze, *Staat und Verfassung: Gesammelte Abhandlungen zur Allgemeinen Verfassungsgeschichte*, G Oestreich ed. (Göttingen: Vandenhoeck & Ruprecht, 3rd edn. 1970); id., *The Historical Essays of Otto Hintze*, F Gilbert ed. (New York: Oxford University Press, 1975); M Weber, *Economy and Society*, G Roth and C Wittich eds (Berkeley: University of California Press, 1978); id., *Political Writings*, P Lassman and R Spiers eds (Cambridge: Cambridge University Press, 1994). More recent studies include T Ertman, *Birth of the Leviathan: Building States and Regimes in Medieval and Early Modern Europe* (Cambridge: Cambridge University Press, 1997); M Mann, *The Sources of Social Power, 3 vols* (Cambridge: Cambridge University Press, 1986, 1993, 2012).

[113] J-J Rousseau, *Discourse on the Origin and Foundations of Inequality Among Men* [1755] in his *The Discourses and other early political writing*, V Gourevitch ed. (Cambridge: Cambridge University Press, 1997), vol. 1, 111–222.

[114] J-J Rousseau, *Emile, or On Education* [1762], Allan Bloom trans. (New York: Basic Books, 1979), 458. See further Ch.5, IV above.

Politonomy, then, is the discipline that requires conjoining constitutive with regulative laws to produce a dialectical interaction between power as *potestas* and power conceived as *potentia*. Schmitt staked his position within politonomy on the understanding of the political in existential rather than conceptual terms—that is, using the criterion of friend/enemy rather than that of autonomous sovereignty. He also saw power essentially as the capacity to decide (*potentia*) rather than as something generated by institutional forms of representation (*potestas*). In order to do this he suppresses aspects of the conceptual and the rightful, and in that respect doubts persist about the cogency of his theory. But by virtue of his insight Schmitt deserves recognition as one of the leading modern scholars of political jurisprudence.

This is a double-edged compliment. The fact that the most powerful twentieth century exponent of political jurisprudence made such a disastrous political judgment has been used by some scholars to reject, or at least to marginalize, the importance of an entire tradition of thought. Normativism is once again on the ascendant in legal thought, with the insights of political jurisprudence often ignored. By making Schmitt the exemplary figure of political jurisprudence, normativists try to ensure that his own vain boast of being the last representative of the tradition will in fact come to pass.

VIII. Conclusion

Carl Schmitt's primary scholarly contribution was that of a jurist. To understand its significance, his writing must be situated within a tradition of political jurisprudence. This line of thought has offered a compelling account of the constitution of political authority in circumstances in which a hierarchically-organized, religiously-constituted universe has been supplanted by a world differentiated into various domains of thought and action. Only in modernity do we see the emergence of discrete spheres of human activity operating according to their own criteria and necessities, including those of the scientific, the technical, the aesthetic, the legal, and the political. The founding assumption of the political jurists is that the modern form of law, that is, positive law, is the product of political power. They offer an account of the way in which the domain of the political is constituted so as to render that modern form of positive law authoritative and this we might call an exercise in politonomy.

Political jurists have constructed their various accounts on foundational concepts, most commonly those of the state and sovereignty. Schmitt used a realist method to subject those foundational elements to critical appraisal. Although his work was—and remains—controversial, it provides a singular insight into the relationship between law and politics. Whether we are trying to make sense of the recent extension in the constitutional jurisdiction of courts, or trying to balance conflicting claims of duties and rights with respect to the values of security and liberty, or determining the status of the 'sovereign' nation-state in a globalizing world, keeping a clear view of the relationship between the legal and the political remains of critical importance. Schmitt might not have resolved those issues to our satisfaction, but his distinctive contribution deserves to be taken seriously.

8

Reason of State/State of Reason

I. Introduction

Political jurists seek to explain not just the nature of political order but also its underlying mode of reasoning. They accept that the political is founded on an inclusionary-exclusionary distinction but recognize that Schmitt's binary division between friend and enemy is a rudimentary criterion.[1] The political establishes its autonomy by enhancing the hegemony of its singular worldview. This can only happen when political power is consolidated in institutional arrangements, reaching its apogee in the territorially organized nation-state. The driver of this process is political reason, strictly, political-legal reason and in this chapter I trace the way it has developed in modern thought.

The history of political-legal reasoning begins with the emergence in the Renaissance of a doctrine of 'reason of state'. Widely debated in European political circles between the late-sixteenth and early-eighteenth centuries, this doctrine remained contentious throughout. Michel Sennellart provides its most concise definition. Reason of state, he says, 'concerns the imperative in the name of which one is authorized, in the public interest, to break the law' and it has three determining conditions: 'the criterion of necessity, the justification of means by a higher end, the requirement of secrecy'.[2]

If reason of state encapsulates modern political reason then, as Sennellart's definition indicates, the relationship between legal reason and political reason is put in question. Ordinary legal reason is generated from the principles of equality before the law, of justice according to the prescribed law, and of the importance of rational argument in open court. It therefore appears to run directly counter to political reason. What then is the relationship between legal reason, reason of state, and the political-legal reason advocated by political jurists?

---

[1] C Schmitt, *The Concept of the Political* [1932], G. Schwab trans. (Chicago: University of Chicago Press, 1996). Cf. HJ Morgenthau, *The Concept of the Political* [1933], M. Vidal trans. (New York: Palgrave Macmillan, 2012); A Botwinick, 'Same/Other versus Friend/Enemy: Levinas contra Schmitt' in J Meierhenrich and O Simons (eds), *The Oxford Handbook of Carl Schmitt* (Oxford: Oxford University Press, 2016), Ch.12.

[2] M Senellart, *Machiavélisme et raison d'état, XIIe–XVIIIe siècle* (Paris: Presses universitaire de France, 1989), 5: 'La raison d'État, de nos jours, désigne l'imperatif au nom duquel le pouvoir s'autorise à transgresser le droit dans l'intérêt public. Trois conditions la déterminent: le critère de la nécessité, la justification des moyens par une fin supérieure, l'exigence du secret.'

Political Jurisprudence. Martin Loughlin. © M Loughlin 2017.
Published 2017 by Oxford University Press.

I propose to show, first, that a relatively precise doctrine of reason of state evolved during the period of early-modern state-building. This doctrine reasoned that the state asserts its identity as an autonomous institution by operating according to its own laws, logic, standards, and criteria. The doctrine expressed the fundamental law of political development of its time. Reason of state did not lack an ethical dimension, neither did it fail to respect the authority of the written law. It was controversial because it asserted the priority of collective over individual interest and held that what that entailed was for the ruling authority to determine. Ethical considerations were influential only in accordance with time, place, and circumstance.

I argue secondly that reason of state is not a universal doctrine. It is historically-situated.[3] The doctrine emerged at a critical moment in European political history and acquired more precise meaning according to the local policies it served. Such policies were for the ruler to determine, and they varied according to whether the struggle was against the law courts, the Empire, the Church, or foreign powers.[4] Reason of state might, for example, require the enforcement of religious orthodoxy or the promotion of religious tolerance, but that choice was determined by the requirements of rule. Furthermore, although the doctrine came to prominence at a moment of transition, with the establishment of the modern state it was gradually eclipsed.[5]

Reason of state has continued to exert an influence in the modern political world, but that influence is complicated by several factors. First, the doctrine was geared towards offering guidance to 'the ruler', but because the office of ruler is corporatized within the modern state and its various responsibilities dispersed across a range of agencies, the question of who is authorized to speak for 'the state' is ambiguous. Secondly, the modern state incorporates 'an unresolved tension between two irreconcilable dispositions'.[6] One of these, *societas*, is a law-governed disposition and the other, *universitas*, advances policies to further the *salus populi*. But with the

---

[3] PL Weinacht, 'Fünf Thesen zum Begriff der Staatsräson. Die Entdeckung der Staatsräson für die deutsche politische Theorie (1604)' in R Schnur (ed.), *Staatsräson: Studien zur Geschichte eines politischen Begriffs* (Berlin: Duncker & Humblot, 1975), 65–71, at 65: '*1 These: Staatsräson ist kein Universale, sondern ein geschichtlich-konkreter Begriff.*' [Reason of state is not a universal, but a historical-concrete concept.] See also YC Zarka (ed.), *Raison et Déraison d'État: Théoriciens et théories de la raison d'État aux XVI et XVII siècles* (Paris: Presses Universitaires de France, 1994), 1: 'L'ouvrage qu'on va lire concerne une dimension majeure de la pensée politique, mais aussi un phénomène historiquement singulier'. [The book we are to read concerns a major dimension of political thought, but also a historically singular phenomenon.] It is therefore an error to assert that 'reason of state is a relative constant, having been in continuous usage since Machiavelli's time': T Poole, *Reason of State: Law, Prerogative and Empire* (Cambridge: Cambridge University Press, 2015), 4.

[4] Weinacht, above n.3, 65: '*5. These: Die geschichtlich-konkrete Profilierung des Begriffs Staatsräson lässt sich entlang der zeittypischen Konflikt-Linien darstellen (Landesfürst versus Stände, Reich, Kirche, auswärtige Mächte).*' [The concrete-historical profiling of the concept can be represented on time-determined lines of conflict (prince v. administration, empire, church, foreign powers).]

[5] H Butterfield, 'Raison d'État: The Relations between Morality and Government' (Martin Wight Memorial Lecture, University of Sussex, 23 April 1975), 7, 12: 'I doubt whether the term politically survives in the twentieth century...It would be wisest for us to treat the term as a fossil, or an example of conscious archaism. Let us look upon it as a historical curiosity.... The term...becomes really important, particularly in Italy, in the later decades of the sixteenth century.... The main development of the concept of reason of state took place in seventeenth century France... [where] the idea of the state was still unachieved in reality, still not really grasped, for the most part, even in thought, even in theory.'

[6] M Oakeshott, 'On the Character of a Modern European State' in his *On Human Conduct* (Oxford: Clarendon Press, 1975), 185–326 at 200–1. See further, Ch.1,V above; M Loughlin, IPL, Ch.2; M Loughlin, FPL, Ch.6.

dramatic extension of the state's role as *universitas*, ruling 'policy' is institutionalized and the exception normalized. Thirdly, the modern state presents itself as a constitutional state which, especially under the influence of social contract thinking, conceives all governmental power to be exercised through established constitutional forms.[7] Once the constitution is established as 'fundamental law', whatever remains of reason of state discourse is subsumed under the idea of 'constitutional legality'. Finally, the modern constitutional state builds its power through the inculcation of belief in its rightful authority. This *potestas* or 'power to' is generated by governing according to law,[8] and if reason of state suggests that rulers must use their *potentia* or 'power over' that claim is not easily sustained under the conditions of contemporary constitutional government.

For these reasons, those elements of the doctrine that live on in contemporary practice no longer fall into a distinct category of reason of state. They have become a facet of the emergence of the modern 'state of reason'.

II. The Origins of Reason of State

In its most general sense, reason of state means simply the application of reason to the political challenge of governing. This idea has been with us for as long as there has been reflection on the activity of governing. It is conveyed in Cicero's concept of *ratio republicae* and is also present in the work of the medieval scholar, John of Salisbury, who employed such phrases as *utilitas rei publicae* and *ratio communis utilitatis*.[9] During the high Middle Ages, such principles of public utility and common good were commonly incorporated into the more general concept of *ratio status*.[10] But *ratio status* is not a synonym for the doctrine of reason of state. These principles at that time derived their meaning from belief in the existence of divinely-ordained values.[11] Also, since the medieval world had no clear sense of the state as a formally-established centralized institution equipped with a monopoly of coercive power, *status* was not equivalent to the modern concept of the state.[12]

---

[7] See, e.g., T Paine, 'Rights of Man' in his *Rights of Man, Common Sense and other Political Writings* [1791], M Philp ed. (Oxford: Oxford University Press, 1995), 83–331, at 123: 'A constitution contains...everything that relates to the compleat organization of a civil government, and the principles on which it shall act, and by which it shall be bound'.

[8] For discussion of the two types of power see Loughlin, FPL, 164–77; Ch 6,VI, Ch 7,IV, VII above. See further, M Loughlin, 'Political Jurisprudence' in (2016) 16 *Jus Politicum: Revue de droit politique* 15–32, at 24–7.

[9] MT Cicero, *De Respublica* [c.52 BC], CW Keyes trans. (London: Heinnemann, 1928); John of Salisbury, *Policraticus*, C. Nederman ed. (Cambridge: Cambridge University Press, 1990). On John of Salisbury, see M Senellart, above n.2, 19–31, 108; Loughlin, FPL 28–30.

[10] G Post, 'Ratio Publicae Utilitatis, Ratio Status and "Reason of State", 1100-1300' in his *Studies in Medieval Legal Thought: Public Law and the State, 1100–1322* (Princeton, NJ: Princeton University Press, 1964), Ch.5; MS Kempshall, *The Common Good in Late Medieval Political Thought* (Oxford: Oxford University Press, 1999); G Sfez, *Les doctrines de la raison d'état* (Paris: Armand Colin 2000), 10–16.

[11] See, e.g., W Ullmann, *Principles of Government and Politics in the Middle Ages* (London: Methuen, 1961), Introduction.

[12] A Osiander, *Before the State: Systemic Political Change in the West from the Greeks to the French Revolution* (Oxford: Oxford University Press, 2007), Ch.1.

Affinities between *ratio status* and the early-modern doctrine derive from the King's dual role as protector of the political order and dispenser of justice. The tensions inherent in the King's responsibility to maintain order and uphold justice were exposed in moments of crisis. When urgent action was required, jurists recognized that to maintain public safety the King might act contrary to law without having acted unjustly. Justifying this, medieval legal scholars drew on such Roman law maxims as *salus populi suprema lex esto* (the safety of the people is the highest law), *necessitas legem non habet* (necessity has no law), and *princeps legibus solutus* (the sovereign is free from the laws).

Such maxims might be read as authorizing the arbitrary actions of a tyrant. But this was not the case in the jurisdictions in which they were invoked, not least because they had to operate within a body of sophisticated medieval jurisprudence. They might be invoked to justify, say, the requisitioning of property needed to prosecute a defensive war,[13] but the claim that the King was not bound by the law never absolved him of responsibility to act for the public good. These maxims acquired more contentious meanings with the social, economic, and technological changes associated with modernization. Such changes led to a more autonomous conception of politics and once politics emerged as a set of practices differentiated from law and theology, maxims that seemed to authorize discretionary action in the name of 'safety' and 'necessity' could more easily be used to justify expediency.

Describing this transition, Maurizio Viroli has shown how in the late-sixteenth century classical and republican traditions of political thinking in Italy were gradually replaced by new ideas that could fall under the heading of 'reason of state'.[14] As structural changes in political order undermined the authority of medieval practices of 'mixed constitutionalism', scholars orientated their inquiries away from questions about the origins and legitimacy of government and towards effective methods with which rulers might maintain and enhance the power of their state. Instead of focusing on constitutional forms, these new studies addressed the art of governing.

This approach, illustrated by the works of Machiavelli and Guicciardini, derived scientific conclusions from studying statecraft. Reason of state emerges as a product of this new scholarly method. The first book explicitly dedicated to the study of this novel concept, Giovanni Botero's *Della ragion di stato*, demonstrates this reorientation in political thinking.[15] But although he never actually used the term, it was Machiavelli who was the first to clearly explain what reason of state entailed.[16]

Believing that we acquire true nobility only in the realm of the political, Machiavelli maintained that upholding the authority of political community is the

---

[13] Pierre Dubois, the court jurist of Philip the Fair (1285–1314), is supposed to have coined the phrase 'the king is emperor in his realm' with the intention of justifying the King's authority to requisition property when needed to defend the realm: A Guéry, 'The State: The Tool of the Common Good' in P Nora (ed.), *Rethinking France: Les Lieux de Mémoire, Vol. 1*, M Trouille trans. (Chicago: University of Chicago Press, 2001), 1–52, at 17.

[14] M Viroli, *From politics to reason of state: the acquisition and transformation of a language of politics, 1250–1650* (Cambridge: Cambridge University Press, 1993).

[15] G Botero, *The Reason of State* [1589], PJ and DP Waley trans. (London: Routlege & Kegan Paul, 1956).

[16] But for an argument that cautions against treating Machiavelli as the precursor of a modern doctrine see: C Vasoli, 'Machiavel inventeur de la raison d'État?' in Zarka (ed.), above n.3, Ch.2 (43–66).

most important political goal. To achieve this, the people must be willing to sacrifice themselves for the sake of the *patria*. This special quality, which he called *virtù*, was needed for people to overcome life's necessities. He declared that whenever 'the safety of one's country wholly depends on the decision to be taken, no attention should be paid either to justice or injustice, kindness or cruelty, or to its being praise-worthy or ignominious'.[17] This is a powerful statement of reason of state. But it does not constitute a modern definition, partly because Machiavelli did not have a clear conception of the state as an autonomous entity.[18] In addition, steeped as he was in classical thought which held *patria* as the highest value, he was unable to take ac-count of the tension that exists in modern thought between moral and political conduct. Machiavelli never felt the need to justify the use of immoral means to maintain the state.

What *is* modern in Machiavelli's writing is its dynamic principle of political ac-tion. This is what gives birth to the concept of 'policy', a term denoting the strategic knowledge vested in the ruler which provides the basis for determining his 'reason of state'. Policy is solely a matter for the ruler and when systematically deployed by him the distinction between efficacy and tyranny is blurred. Machiavelli himself did not promote a crude version of a ruler's reasons of state,[19] but in the turbulent con-ditions of late-sixteenth century Europe, overshadowed by a series of intense civil and religious wars, 'Machiavellianism' flourished as it became the ideological expres-sion of rulers' willingness to use immoral means for strategic advantage.

Botero's work acquires its significance when set against the emergence of the phe-nomenon of Machiavellianism. A former Jesuit who had acted as secretary to the future Cardinal Borromeo, Botero wrote for rulers who believed in the importance of maintaining the state's religious foundation. His prime concern was to halt the unravelling of traditional Christendom, to which end he sought to impress upon rulers the value of the new doctrine of reason of state. By the time his *Della ragion di stato* was published in 1589, reason of state was already the subject of intense discus-sion in the courts of Europe. Botero's intervention was aimed at harnessing this novel doctrine to the cause of Counter-Reformation state-building.

Defining the state as 'a stable rule over a people' and reason of state as 'knowledge of the means by which such a dominion may be founded, preserved and extended',[20] Botero neutrally and dispassionately presents methods of augmenting the power of the state. He conveys the impression that this involves a repackaging of the older advice to princes, but there is a limit; once reason of state is tarnished by the barbarous methods of Machiavellianism it must be condemned.

---

[17] N Machiavelli, *The Discourses*, LJ Walker trans., B Crick ed. (Harmondsworth: Penguin, 1983), III.41. See further Loughlin, IPL, 37–42.

[18] JH Hexter, *The Vision of Politics on the Eve of the Reformation: More, Machiavelli, and Seysssel* (London: Allen Lane, 1973), 170: 'one thing that *lo stato* never means in *Il Principe* is the state conceived as a political body transcending the individuals who compose it'.

[19] Machiavelli, *Discourses*, above n.17, III.5 (recognizing that rulers 'lose their state the moment they begin to break the laws and to disregard the ancient traditions and customs under which men have long lived').

[20] Botero, above n.15, 3. Botero, however, equivocates on whether the term includes the foundation of a state 'for Reason of State assumes a ruler and a State (the one as artificer, the other as his material) whereas they are not assumed – indeed they are preceded – by foundation' (3).

Although Botero's book contained few original ideas it proved a runaway success.[21] His message is that, especially in a time of wars of religion, 'policy' and 'reason of state' are essential techniques for a ruler trying to maintain a true Christian state. He opposed the separation of politics from religion advocated by Bodin and the French *politique* jurists,[22] believing that the toleration of false faiths would undermine a ruler's authority. Botero's doctrine, remarked Friedrich Meinecke, 'resembles a very richly decorated Jesuit church, in a style evolved from the Renaissance'.[23] But despite such flourishes, his work does provide intimations of the modern doctrine. Significantly he treats prudence (*prudenza*) not as a virtue but as a type of political knowledge and therefore as a technique of governing. He also incorporates economic knowledge—issues of population, commerce, and agriculture—into the range of matters relevant to the maintenance of the state.[24]

The sixteenth-century works of Machiavelli and Botero erected the framework within which the doctrine of reason of state could grow. Botero's influential treatise is entirely conventional in the way it presents the arts of war and peace and the reign of justice as the two main branches of the doctrine. His innovation is in seeing reason of state as a special kind of political knowledge and this prepares the way for its evolution into a more general science of governing. But his work also indicates that by the late-sixteenth century Machiavelli had already been converted from a writer into a slogan. Thereafter, scholars could refer to the Florentine's innovative teachings only if simultaneously denouncing the evils of 'Machiavellianism'.

III. The Doctrine of Reason of State

Introduced in Italy in the mid-sixteenth century, by the early-seventeenth century reason of state had become the most widely debated topic in European political circles.[25] The emergence of the modern idea of the state had signalled the terminal

[21] In Botero's lifetime his book went through ten Italian editions, six editions in Spanish translation, four in Latin, and one in French: Introduction to Botero, above n.15, ix.

[22] On Bodin's idea of reason of state, a term he never uses, see F Meinecke, *Machiavellism: The Doctrine of Raison d'État and Its Place in Modern History*, D Scott trans. (New Haven: Yale University Press, 1957), 56–64. See further, H Quaritsch, 'Staatsraison in Bodins *République*' in Schnur (ed.), 43–63. Quaritsch argues that Machiavelli and Bodin raised the awareness of power and domination to a new level and that the ambivalence of Bodin's position on the doctrine of reason of state was the consequence of his interest, as a jurist, not only in the techniques of governing but also in the constitution of government.

[23] Meinecke, above n.22, 67.

[24] See Senellart, above n.2, 71–83. See further Guéry, above n.13, who notes that Botero was the first to see the link between reason of state and mercantilism, and argues: 'Mercantilism is a theory that puts the acquisition of wealth at the level of the state, its means, and powers. It cannot therefore be separated from ideas associated with reason of state. From this perspective, the power of the state and well-being of the king's subjects were no longer viewed as opposed, as Machiavelli asserted, but as inextricably linked. As a discourse of reason of state, mercantilism saw economic life in terms of state power, which is why it must also link to public good' (at 29).

[25] In 1860, J Ferrari reported that he had discovered 424 Italian writers advocating reason of state or, as he put it, who 'boldly taught the art of guiding kings, cheating the people, flattering leaders, crushing rebels, governing events' [Bientôt 424 écrivains enseignèrent hardiment l'art de mener les rois, de surprendre les peoples, de flatter les chefs, d'écraser les rebelles, de dominer les événements]. But he had

decline in authority of the medieval idea of a mixed constitution and reason of state was a specific response to the ensuing intellectual crisis. It provided a new science of governing for the emerging world of nation-states.

This new world was primarily the result of the formation in the early-modern period of merchant empires. Having imposed fiscal and material burdens that their medieval constitutions were unable to bear, the imperial ventures of such states as Spain, Portugal, England, the Netherlands, and France generated intense pressures to centralize governing arrangements.[26] The modern state was forged in the crucible of these imperial ventures. As other nations followed suit, whether by internal reforms or by overthrowing an imperial power, a process was set in train that would lead to a system of nation-states.

But the doctrine was as yet far from clear. Reason of state was so widely debated because it had become a vogue term indicating that changes were afoot in the art of governing. But it had become a catchword in search of a concept. Did 'reason' connote reflection, motive, justification, knowledge, method, or rationale? Did 'state' refer to a condition, a standing, an estate, a regime, or a commonwealth?[27] Reason of state discourse flourished through maxims and aphorisms rather than the specification of precise doctrinal knowledge.[28] Formulations such as the Duc de Rohan's 'princes rule the people, and interests rule princes' may have been concise,[29] but all too often such formulations of reason of state became a placeholder for a set of contestable issues about the appropriate relationship between the means and the ends of governing. These may have been pressing issues in all regimes, but only within a specific historical context could the expression acquire more precise meaning.[30]

Take, for example, the reception of reason of state in Spain. Here Jesuit scholars mounted a vehement attack on the Machiavellianism of the French *politiques*, this 'most abominable sect ever invented by Satan' which had sought 'to set reason of state apart from the law of God'.[31] But rather than reject the term, they were determined

also found 470 scholars opposed to this 'occult science' which had been 'killed by modern publicity' ['une science occulte, tuée par la publicité moderne']: J. Ferrari, *Histoire de la raison d'état* (Paris: Michel Lévy Frères, 1860), at vi, x.

[26] JD Tracy (ed.), *The Rise of Merchant Empires: Long-Distance Trade in the Early Modern World 1350–1750* (Cambridge; Cambridge University Press, 1993), esp.1–14; M van Creveld, *The Rise and Decline of the State* (Cambridge: Cambridge University Press, 1999); M Mann, *The Sources of Social Power, Volume 1: A History from the Beginning to 1760 AD* (Cambridge: Cambridge University Press, 1986). See Loughlin, FPL, Ch.9.I.

[27] For discussion see H Höpfl, 'Orthodoxy and Reason of State' (2002) 23 *History of Political Thought* 211–37, 217–18; Meinecke, above n.22, 119–24.

[28] Consider, e.g., the prevalence of the metaphor of the lion and the fox: see M Stolleis, 'Löwe und Fuchs: Eine politische Maxime im Frühabsolutismus' in his *Staat und Staatsräson in der frühen Neuzeit* (Frankfurt aM: Suhrkamp, 1990), 21–36.

[29] Henri, duc de Rohan, *De l'Interest des Princes et Estats de la Chrestienté* (Paris, 1639), 1: 'Les Princes commandent aux peuples, et l'interest commande aux Princes'. Cited in JHM Salmon, 'Rohan and Interest of State' in R Schnur (ed.), *Staatsräson: Studien zur Geschichte eines politischen Begriffs* (Berlin: Duncker & Humblot, 1975), 121–40, at 121.

[30] Sfez, above n.10, 188: 'Il n'existe pas de concept unifié de la raison d'État'. (No unified concept of reason of state exists.)

[31] P de Rivadeneira, *Tratado de la religion y virtudes que debe tener el principe Cristiano* (1595); cited in JA Fernández-Santamaria, 'Reason of State and Statecraft in Spain (1595–1640)' (1980) 41 *J. of the History of Ideas* 355–79, at 357.

to give it a meaning consonant with their own interests. Led by Pedro de Rivadeneira, former secretary to Loyola, the Jesuits argued that although Machiavellianism is treacherous and false, there is another conception of reason of state that is certain and true; the false 'creates religion out of the state', whereas the true 'makes the state out of religion'.[32] Far from disapproving of the term, the defenders of Catholic moral orthodoxy complained only that reason of state had been corrupted at the hands of 'political atheists' who 'put their republic in the place of God'.[33]

The Spanish Jesuits did not seek to refute the doctrine but to domesticate it. They presented their argument in three phases. First, by demonstrating that Machiavelli sought to turn religion into a political instrument and his followers, the *politiques*, modify this only by freeing the state from ethical restrictions through their promotion of religious toleration. Secondly, by showing that the error of Machiavellianism is that it violates the basic political truth that the state cannot survive without true religion. Thirdly, they formulated their own reason of state founded on the reconciliation of political action with the laws of God.[34] Recognizing the power of the doctrine, they set about harnessing it for their own purposes.

This tactic met with opposition in Spanish jurisprudence, though their opponents, the realists, also felt obliged explicitly to condemn Machiavellianism. The realist jurists recognized that some degree of deceit is a necessary element of modern political prudence. They maintained that knowledge of the art of governing did not come directly from God but was derived from experience. Consequently, to understand what is required to rule effectively, jurists must distill the knowledge acquired from history.[35] The driving force behind Spanish reason of state literature 'was the need for a recognizable body of political advice which incorporated new techniques in order to respond to a situation of crisis'. But this advice, concludes Joan-Pau Rubiés, rejected any doctrines 'which had been defined as unchristian - those derived from almost all of Machiavelli, some ideas in Bodin and certain readings of Tacitus'.[36]

A pattern emerges from the Spanish experience. By the end of the sixteenth century Machiavellianism had become a term denoting the evil techniques of tyrannical rulers, invoked only to be condemned. In this form it was central to the debate between realists promoting modern techniques of political prudence associated with the revival of Tacitism[37] and conservatives who, recognizing changes afoot, wanted to redirect reason of state towards orthodox Christian purposes.[38]

---

[32] Ibid.   [33] Ibid. 358.
[34] Ibid. 361–2. See further R Bireley, *The Counter-Reformation Prince: Anti-Machiavellism or Catholic Statecraft in early modern Europe* (Chapel Hill, NC: University of North Carolina Press, 1990).
[35] Fernández-Santamaria, above n.31, 366.
[36] J-P Rubiés 'Reason of State and Constitutional Thought in the Crown of Aragon, 1580-1640' (1995) 38 *Historical J.*1–28, at 19.
[37] As the traditional regimes of Europe were being undermined by civil and religious war in the late sixteenth century, there was a remarkable revival of interest among scholars in the works of the Roman historian, Cornelius Tacitus. Writing about the disintegration of Rome after the fall of the Republic, Tacitus adopted a realist method that aimed to expose the underlying causes and the power interests at play. See Tacitus, *The Annals of Imperial Rome*, M Grant trans. (London: Penguin, 1996).
[38] The debate is in certain respects transcended by Richelieu, who dominates French policy in the second quarter of the seventeenth century. In his *Political Testament*, Richelieu justifies the occasional use of questionable means which necessity requires, but he remained confident that his policies remained

Reason of state first flourished in Italy and Spain but soon acquired Europe-wide currency.[39] It was then advanced under the banner of the 'new humanism', with northern European states, especially France, the Netherlands, and England, in the vanguard.[40] Here, the pace of social and economic change and the more systematic attention given to the expanding interests of states proved less fertile ground for conservatives and more favourable to Tacitism.[41] Jurists recognized that theology could no longer provide guidance on new modes of governing. But there was a significant body of historical knowledge that provided a valuable written record of political experience. Could this be distilled into rules that could be learned and applied?

For an answer to the question of how to establish a *doctrine* of reason of state, we turn to the most influential work on reason of state of the late-sixteenth century. Justus Lipsius' *Politica* was printed more than fifty times in the period between 1589 and 1760 and was the subject of twenty-four translations.[42] Shaped by a Neostoicism that accentuates discipline and the importance of practical action,[43] *Politica* is most directly concerned with the teachings of Tacitus and Machiavelli.[44] Its central focus is the 'resolute, prudent and realistically moral use of power', a strategy which might require the 'manipulative use of power' and whose thrust leads to the conclusion that 'reason of state-monarchy is the best form of government'.[45]

in compliance with Christian principles and served to uphold the Christian purpose of the state. *The Political Testament of Cardinal Richelieu*, HB Hill trans. and ed. (Madison: University of Wisconsin Press, 2005); WF Church, *Richelieu and Reason of State* (Princeton: Princeton University Press, 1972); JH Elliott, *Richelieu and Olivares* (Cambridge: Cambridge University Press, 1984), Ch.5.

[39] It also extended its influence to England's American colonies, albeit in Christian form, see: GL Mosse, 'Puritanism and Reason of State in Old and New England' (1952) 9 *William & Mary Quarterly* 67–80; id., *The Holy Pretence: A Study in Christianity and Reason of State from William Perkins to John Winthrop* (Oxford: Blackwell, 1957).

[40] R Tuck, *Philosophy and Government, 1572–1651* (Cambridge: Cambridge University Press, 1993), esp. 31–64. Cf M Stolleis, 'Arcana Imperii und Ratio Status: Bermerkungen zur politischen Theorie des frühen 17, Jahrhunderts' in his *Staat und Staatsräson*, above n. 28, 37–72, arguing that German-speaking lands were the last to assimilate reason of state, not least because they had no easy translation of the term. See further, H Dreitzel, 'Reason of state and the crisis of political Aristotelianism: an essay on the development of 17th century political philosophy' (2002) 28 *History of European Ideas* 163–87, at 166: 'The reception of the concept of reason of state was relatively late in Germany'. See also A Vagts, 'Intelligentsia versus Reason of State' (1969) 84 *Political Science Quarterly* 80–105, at 84: 'According to the accusations of their [17th century German] authors, French *ratio status* had upset all hitherto valid concepts of law in Europe; it had given rise to the closely related, equally dreadful concept of *raison de guerre*—the excuse for the frightful scorched earth burnings in the Palatinate including Heidelberg—both undermining justice, God, conscience, humaneness, honesty.' On the English experience of the period see F Raab, *The English Face of Machiavelli: A Changing Interpretation, 1500–1700* (London: Routledge & Kegan Paul, 1964); DS Berkowitz, 'Reason of State in England and the Petition of Right, 1603–1629' in Schnur (ed.), above n.29, 165–212.

[41] P Burke, 'Tacitism, scepticism and reason of state' in JH Burns (ed.), *The Cambridge History of Political Thought, 1450–1700* (Cambridge: Cambridge University Press, 1991), 479–98.

[42] J Lipsius, *Politica: Six Books of Politics or Political Instruction*, J Waszink trans. and ed. (Assen: Royal Van Gorcum, 2004), 3.

[43] G Oestreich, *Neostoicism and the early modern state*, D McLintock trans. (Cambridge: Cambridge University Press, 1982).

[44] As Harro Höpfl notes, Lipsius' fame 'rested in large part upon his revision of the canon, with Seneca and Tacitus now outranking Cicero and Livy': H Höpfl, 'History and Exemplarity in the Work of Lipsius' in E De Bom et al (eds), *(Un)masking the Realities of Power: Justus Lipsius and the Dynamics of Political Writing in Early Modern Europe* (Leiden: Brill, 2011), 43–72, at 48.

[45] Waszink, Introduction to *Politica*, above n.42, at 12, 78.

This message comes through strongly even in the way the work is organized. The first three books uphold a Christian-Ciceronian morality while the last three, promoting prudence and the use of deceit for the common good, overthrows that morality to establish a '*morally sound* Reason of State'.[46] However, notwithstanding his systematic treatment of prudence, Lipsius fails to reduce it to rules. He stresses that prudence is acquired through experience and that it is 'in reality unstable and changeable in every respect'. This is because all human affairs are 'veiled in deep darkness', and because the causes of things often remain unknown.[47] He concludes that it is simply not possible to formulate comprehensive rules of prudence.

Despite Lipsius' scepticism, there was a growing conviction during the seventeenth century that reason of state was not, as it was for Machiavelli, merely an expression of the art of governing. As the state emerged as 'an omnipotent yet impersonal power',[48] reason of state shifted its orientation away from the actions of the ruler towards a systematic body of knowledge for maintaining the authority of a way of organizing power relations. The doctrine developed as a body of scientific knowledge about how the state could preserve and enhance its authority. This development is most clearly signalled in Gabriel Naudé's *Considérations politiques sur les coups d'État*.[49]

Naudé's work of 1639 effects a subtle shift in the meaning of 'public good'. The public good, the orthodox justification of reason of state, is interpreted by Naudé to mean 'the good of the state'. Although it contains 'neither a theory of the prince, nor a doctrine of the foundations of politics',[50] certain passages read like a thoroughly modern account of the conduct of power politics and, to that extent, they provide a justification for the establishment of a *Machtstaat*.

Probably written to gain Richelieu's favour, *Considérations politiques* offers a 'fascinating example of Richelieu's doctrines being echoed by a contemporary scholar, and substantiated by a display of objective theorising'.[51] Naudé makes a clear distinction between science and morality in accounting for the pursuit of 'refin'd politicks' and he presents his analysis of *coups d'état*, the 'master strokes of state', quite dispassionately.[52] His first objective is to define and categorize *coups d'état*. They fall into one of two categories of prudence: the ordinary, which conforms to existing law and custom, and the extraordinary, which are 'rigorous and severe'.[53] He then explains that the idea of a *coup d'état* prompted by 'ordinary' prudence is already

---

[46] Ibid. at 81, 90 (emphasis in original).   [47] Lipsius, above n.42, Bk 4, ch 1 (383–5).

[48] Q Skinner, *The Foundations of Modern Political Thought* (Cambridge: Cambridge University Press, 1978), vol.2, 358.

[49] G Naudé, *Considérations politiques sur les coups d'État* [1639] (Paris: Éditions de Paris, 1988); Eng trans. G Naudé, *Political considerations upon refin'd politicks, and the master-strokes of state, As practis'd by the Ancients and Moderns*, W King trans. (London, 1711) [page refs to the English translation].

[50] YS Zarka, 'Raison d'État, maximes d'État et coups d'État chez Gabriel Naudé' in Zarka (ed.), above n.3, Ch.6, 151–69, at 160: 'On ne trouve dans *les Considérations politiques sur les coups d'État* ni une théorie du prince, ni une doctrine des fondements de la politique'.

[51] JV Rice, *Galbriel Naudé, 1603–1653* (Baltimore, Md: Johns Hopkins Press, 1939), 107. On Richelieu see above n.38.

[52] In this respect Naudé follows in the footsteps of Pierre Charron's *De la sagesse* (1601): see C Lazzeri, 'Le gouvernement de la raison d'État' in C Lazzeri and Reynié (eds), *Le pouvoir de la raison d'état* (Paris: Presses universitaires de France, 1992), 91–134, at 119–29; Sfez, above n.10, 50–8.

[53] Naudé, above n.49, 31.

well-established as 'the principal Rules and Maxims for the well-governing of States and Empires' and, being 'practis'd without any Suspicion of Injustice', it does not deserve the appellation of 'Secrets of State'.[54] Naudé's interest lies mainly with the extraordinary.

The practices of extraordinary prudence, he explains, 'cannot be appropriated to the Precepts and Maxims of a Science which is commonly understood and practised by every one'.[55] Knowledge of these practices is only for rulers, and the people ought simply 'to admire the happy effects of these master strokes of Policy, though wholly ignorant of those Causes from whence they result.'[56] Further, knowledge of these practices cannot be entirely absorbed into orthodox accounts of sovereignty since they entail 'Bold and extraordinary Actions, which Princes are constrain'd to execute when their Affairs are difficult and almost to be despair'd of'. These practices are 'contrary to the common Right' and do not observe 'any Order or Form of Justice', and entail 'hazarding particular Interest for the good of the Publick'.[57] Extraordinary action must be carried out in secret and, if ever made public, revealed only after the fact.

Since these 'master strokes of state' are 'like a Sword' in that they 'may be manag'd well or ill',[58] Naudé specifies five criteria for their honourable usage. First, since the world is 'full of Artifice and Malice' and 'by Fraud and Treachery Kingdoms are subverted', it is not wrong to preserve the state using similar methods. The law will 'pardon such Faults as Force obliges us to commit'.[59] Secondly, he asserts that these master strokes are done through necessity, 'for the evident and important Good of the State or Prince'. When that condition is satisfied, *salus populi* absolves rulers 'from abundance of little Circumstances and Formalities to which Justice would oblige them'.[60] Thirdly, rulers must never take such action rashly; they must always proceed cautiously. Fourthly, when faced with a choice of means, rulers should adopt the less intrusive method, the 'most easie and gentle' way.[61] And finally, whenever rulers have to take extraordinary action they should try to diminish their blame by showing concern and regret for having been obliged so to act.

Naudé's work marks the apotheosis of the doctrine, but it also contains the seeds of its demise. Reason of state reaches its highpoint in *Considérations politiques* because, as David Bates notes, Naudé clearly saw that the sovereign was not 'the agent of a cosmic order' but 'the founder of contingent order in a situation of cosmic disorder'.[62] Following the logic of this premise, Naudé maintains that since force institutes order and law is the product of this original force, a *coup*—a further exercise of force for the purpose of maintaining order—does not violate the laws of the realm. Naudé's account of the workings of these master strokes of state blurs the distinction between law and force, and between norm and exception. Indeed, he reinterprets the exception as 'the expression of the foundational power of law'.[63]

---

[54] Ibid. 33.   [55] Ibid. 35.   [56] Ibid. 37.   [57] Ibid. 60 (italics removed).
[58] Ibid. 68.   [59] Ibid. 69 (invoking Aristotle and Lipsius).   [60] Ibid. 70.
[61] Ibid. 71.
[62] DW Bates, *States of War: Enlightenment Origins of the Political* (New York: Columbia University Press, 2012), 49.
[63] Ibid. See also J Freund, 'La situation exceptionelle comme justification de la raison d'État chez Gabriel Naudé' in Schnur (ed.), above n.29, 141–64.

IV. State of Reason

Seeking to distance themselves from the evil of Machiavellianism, most seventeenth century proponents presented reason of state as a distillation of the arts of governing and a guide to prudence in modern political conduct. Reason of state was packaged as a doctrine that crystallized ways of bolstering the autonomy of the political. It stood for the scientific understanding of the means of founding a state and then of maintaining and augmenting ruling authority. It sought specifically to justify the circumstances in which rulers might conduct their business in secret and legitimately act contrary to established laws or conventional ethical standards. It also aimed to provide answers to political questions about the justification for exceptional action, about when action for the common good could excuse interference with private rights, and about the externally-orientated measures a state could take to protect its own standing or the interests of its citizens.[64] For most of its advocates, reason of state was not an amoral discourse about the will to power. It comprised not just the logic of effective state action but also the right and rationale of the state.[65]

Naudé's work shows how reason of state indicated certain profound changes in political behaviour.[66] The doctrine provided knowledge of ways of strengthening a ruler's authority but it was promoted just as the activity of ruling was being depersonalized and differentiated. This knowledge expressed a shift in the basis of authority away from a theological foundation towards a secular power sustained by political experience. But these modernizing changes were also diminishing the value of past practice. Reason of state was caught in the cleft between formalizing ancient prudence and promoting modern science, between enhancing princely power and consolidating institutional authority, and between asserting might and upholding right. When it reached its highpoint in the work of Naudé it advocated techniques that could only lead to the erosion of the authority of the modern state. Although reason of state aimed to present the foundational logic of political rule, in the face of modernization it actually exposed deficiencies in its own foundations. Facing the future,

---

[64] A clear illustration of foreign policy use is Richelieu's decision to pursue an independent foreign policy for France against the Habsburgs, by which it was encircled: Butterfield, above n.5, 14: '[M]any leading Catholics, in sixteenth and seventeenth-century France wanted foreign policy itself to be based on confessional considerations—in other words wanted France to be allied for religious reasons with the Habsburg dynasty in Spain—this at a time when the Habsburgs seemed on the point of acquiring universal dominion. In other words, there was doubt whether France could hope to keep her independence in the future unless she could be induced to follow a foreign policy based, rather, on reason of state.'

[65] Hexter, above n.18, 168, argues that the aspects of 'right' are often overlooked in the English terminology: 'The English phrase "reason of state" and the German phrase *Staatsräson* are unfortunate, or at least inadequate, translations of the Italian *ragione di stato* and the French *raison d'état*. They are unfortunate because they obscure the fact, clear in both Italian and French, that reason of state is in some measure concerned with the right of the state.'

[66] Sfez, above n.10, 132: 'Avec le deploiement de la raison d'État, de ses mystérieux pouvoirs et de ses machinations secretes, nait une certaine disposition d'esprit ou attitude individuelle et sociale, une nouvelle sensibilité, qui représente un changement profond des moeurs de la civilité'. (With the deployment of reason of state, due to its mysterious powers and its secret machinations, a certain frame of mind or individual and social attitude is established, a new sensitivity which represents a profound change of civil manners.)

reason of state had to be extended into a claim about the rational justification for the state.

These tensions were exhibited in the relationship between reason of state and related changes in natural law.[67] Throughout the seventeenth century, natural lawyers grappled with the task of providing a legitimate foundation for the modern state. Recognizing that it could not be founded on force, they sought a rational justification. Scholars such as Grotius, Hobbes, Pufendorf, and Locke continued to work within a natural law framework and 'did not on the face of it use the language of *raison d'état* and scepticism'.[68] But they did incorporate aspects of reason of state doctrine and, in doing so, transformed the basis of natural law, converting it into political jurisprudence.[69]

By removing the divine, the modern school of natural law rejected the idea that government was an expression of some form of natural or moral order. It embraced a more pessimistic philosophical anthropology which maintained that, far from being guided by reason, humans are mainly driven by potentially destructive passions. Government was required to establish order and provide individual security. But since those entrusted with ruling power were also creatures of passion, there was a need for institutional checks and constraints. As jurists worked through these requirements, they moved beyond scholasticism and political Aristotelianism and began to conceptualize the activity of governing as an autonomous field sustained by its own politico-legal norms and practices.[70]

From this perspective, reason of state and social contract theory do not operate in different universes, with one presenting the art of governing and the other concerned with issues of political obligation.[71] The driving force behind both innovations in thought was the need for new disciplinary structures to replace the eroded authority of medieval constitutionalism. Reason of state was its initial expression, but that doctrine was in turn overtaken by modern theories of natural law, that is, by political jurisprudence. The concern over collective self-preservation behind reason of state thinking was deepened and restated more systematically in modern natural law. It is in the work of Hobbes, Richard Tuck notes, that we find 'the most convincing transformation of *raison d'état* into natural jurisprudence'.[72] Hobbes' political jurisprudence, explains Noel Malcolm 'can be seen as solving problems which the reason of state literature had raised'.[73]

In seeking to bolster authority in the face of modernizing trends, reason of state discourse had to extend the categories of public good. But analysing its conceptual

---

[67] R Tuck, 'The "Modern" School of Natural Law' in A Pagden (ed.), *The Languages of Political Theory in Early-Modern Europe* (Cambridge: Cambridge University Press, 1987), 99–122. See Loughlin, FPL 73–83.

[68] R Tuck, *Philosophy and Government, 1572–1651* (Cambridge: Cambridge University Press, 1993), xiv.

[69] See Ch.1,II and, for the case of Hobbes, see Ch.2 above.   [70] See Dreitzel, above n.40.

[71] See KR Minogue, 'Remarks in the Relation between Social Contract and Reason of State in Machiavelli and Hobbes' in Schnur (ed.), above n.29, 267–74, at 272–4.

[72] Tuck, above n.67, xvii.

[73] N Malcolm, *Reason of State, Propaganda and the Thirty Years' War* (Oxford: Clarendon Press, 2007), 119 (and 114–23 on similarities between Hobbes and reason of state thinking).

language—safety, necessity, emergency and prudence, prerogative, higher law—exposed basic constitutional questions and these could not be answered by more precise articulation of the doctrine. A more radical account was required, not to find political reasons for promoting the ruling authority's policies but to establish the reason for the existence of the state. What was needed 'was not a prudence but a science – a system of certain knowledge'.[74] Reason *of* state was overcome by theories that presented the reason *for* the state.

Modern natural law sought to justify the state as an order tying rulers and people together in a bond of protection and allegiance by imposing a set of reciprocal duties and rights. The key to the constitutional order of the modern state was found in the concept of representation.[75] In constitutional regimes, rulers do not claim to rule the people but only to represent them. So we find Hobbes in his opening words to *Leviathan* explaining that he intends to speak 'not of the men, but (in the Abstract) of the Seat of Power' and to show how 'by Art is created that great *Leviathan* called a *Common-wealth*, or *State*'.[76] Hobbes' sovereign is all-powerful but this power is in no sense personal: it belongs entirely to the status of 'the office of the sovaraign representative' and whether the office is a monarchy or an assembly it exists for one purpose, 'namely the procuration of *the safety of the people*'.[77]

Hobbes resolved the problems arising from competing conceptions of the public good in reason of state doctrine with an absolute sovereign authority founded on consent. Once a sovereign state was established in order to maintain peace, the way was open to conceive the political as an autonomous realm operating by political-legal reason and sustaining itself through its constitutional order. This is how the modern school of natural law became the vehicle by which reason of state was transformed into generic political-legal reason, the reason of an autonomous conception of the political. Initially conceived as anti-constitutional, reason of state survived only by being subsumed into a type of constitutional reason.

This trajectory is clouded by two modern claims, Treitschke's *Machtstaat* thesis and Friedrich's 'constitutional reason of state'. Before addressing 'the reason of the constitutional state' these two themes should be briefly addressed.

V. The *Machtstaat* as Modern Reason of State

Reason of state lived on in the modern era mainly as an expression of international relations between European nation-states. It was invoked to justify the maintenance of a regional balance of power, although even in this context its influence had been eroded by the emerging *jus publicum Europaeum*.[78] But it 'was minted afresh after

---

[74] Ibid. 119.   [75] Loughlin, IPL, Ch.4.

[76] T Hobbes, *Leviathan* [1651], R Tuck ed. (Cambridge: Cambridge University Press, 1996), 3, 9.

[77] Ibid. 231. See also S Pufendorf, *On the Duty of Man and Citizen According to Natural Law* [1673], M Silverthorne trans., J Tully ed. (Cambridge: Cambridge University Press, 1991), i.2.8: 'The fundamental law is that every man ought to do as much as he can to cultivate and preserve sociality.'

[78] See C Schmitt, *The Nomos of the Earth in the International Law of the Jus Publicum Europaeum* [1950], GL Ulmen trans. (New York: Telos Press Publishing, 2003).

the beginning of the nineteenth century' in Germany.[79] In its most potent form, presented by Heinrich von Treitschke, it was converted from a means almost into an end in itself. Treitschke took his inspiration directly from Machiavelli and, inspired by the latter's goal of promoting Italian national liberation, he yoked the doctrine of reason of state to the Prussian cause of building a unified German national state.

Treitschke presented his *Machtstaat* thesis in contrast to the idea of the *Rechtsstaat* which had evolved in early nineteenth-century German liberal thought.[80] It marks a highpoint in the attempt to sustain the basic elements of early-modern reason of state discourse in the modern era. Treitschke erected his thesis on the foundation of Ludwig von Rochau's *Realpolitik* of 1853. Motivated by the failure of the 1848 revolutionary movement to establish a modern liberal constitution, Rochau maintained that liberals could succeed in their goals only when they openly acknowledged the material realities of national politics. Presented as aphorism, Rochau's message was: *Der Staat ist Macht.*[81] And power, he explained, could not be controlled by law; power could only be controlled by power.

The message was clear. A modern constitution could not be attained simply because of the nobility of the ideals it embodied but only when it was the product of a political power that had harnessed and structured material forces in society. It was a message that Treitschke enthusiastically embraced: 'Neither a principle, nor an idea, nor even a contract', he wrote, 'will suffice to unite the divided forces in Germany, but only some superior force that swallows up the others'.[82]

Treitschke thought in imperatives. Meinecke observed that 'his statements are like decrees' and his demonstrations thereby 'acquire a certain violence and explosiveness'.[83] But he was no mere caricature. By *Macht* he means something more than brute force; it connotes the joining together of a people in communion with the State's highest ideals. Yet he certainly assumes that the people are subservient to the State and by the State (here necessarily capitalized) he means the centralized authority that maintains political unity. Without the State's protection and guidance, he believes, the people could never cultivate a moral life.

For Treitschke, the State's function 'is merely protective and administrative'.[84] Its fundamental duties are to ensure the efficient administration of the law, to maintain an army, and to uphold the preparedness for war. He recognizes that with the progress of civilization wars were likely to be fewer and shorter, but claims they 'cannot and should not cease'. There would be wars 'so long as the State is sovereign and confronts other sovereign States'.[85]

---

[79] Meinecke, above n.22, 392.   [80] See Loughlin, FPL, Ch.11, 317–21.

[81] AL von Rochau, *Grundzüge der Realpolitik* (Stuttgart: Karl Göpel, 1853). See J Bew, *Realpolitik: A History* (Oxford: Oxford University Press, 2016), Ch.2. Bew notes that Rochau combined 'broadly liberal political principles with a conservative understanding of historical development' in a manner that 'resembled a German version of the Anglo-Irish writer Edmund Burke' (at 38).

[82] Treitschke, *Essays*: cited in Meinecke, above n.22, 396.   [83] Ibid. 397.

[84] H von Treitschke, *Politik*, i. 62; reproduced in HWC Davies, *The Political Thought of Heinrich von Treitschke* (London: Constable, 1914), 131. *Politik* is a compilation from fragmentary notes of his lectures and the notebooks of his pupils: *Politik: Vorlesungen gehalten an der Universität zu Berlin*, M Cornicelius ed. (Leipzig: Hirzel, 1899).

[85] *Selections from Treitschke's Lectures on Politics*, AL Gowans trans. and ed. (London: Gowans & Gray, 1914), i.2. 'The Aim of the State' (at 26).

Treitschke's account of the means needed to maintain the State's authority demonstrates the degree to which he remained steeped in the early-modern discourse of reason of state. He argues that seventeenth century political thought was suffused with Machiavellism, 'with a statesmanship which tramples the moral laws underfoot as a matter of principle'.[86] It was a discourse on reason of state which only addressed issues of expediency, becoming so discredited 'that we can no longer form an idea of nowadays'.[87] Consequently, he asserts that we must now 'distinguish between public and private morality' and acknowledge that a 'power that treads all right underfoot must in the end itself perish'.[88] So far, so liberal. But he continues that this 'should not stop us jubilantly stating that the ingenious Florentine, with his immense consistency of thought, was the first to place at the heart of his politics the great idea that the State is power'.[89] He follows this with a series of assertions that exemplify his own Machiavellianism: that the State's 'highest commandment' is that it must maintain itself and that this imperative 'is absolutely moral for it';[90] that 'brutality may be met with brutality and fraud countered with fraud';[91] and, as stated in correspondence, that 'positive law when injurious to the common good must be swept away'.[92]

Treitschke's reason of state thinking reaches new heights when he tackles international relations: 'All great nations of history, when they had become strong, have felt the craving to impress the seal of their nature on barbaric lands';[93] 'the supposition of the original [*ursprünglichen*] inequality of all human beings forms the foundation of all political reasoning' since 'only in this way can we explain the fact that some groups are found in subordination to other groups';[94] and that there can be 'no such thing... as international law' since the 'only law that binds them [States] is the law of their own interest'.[95] These bold declarations come as close to promoting Machiavellianism in the modern world as is conceivable.

Treitschke maintained that political science 'is the science of the state pure and simple', its task being threefold: to discover the fundamental basis of the State; to inquire into its aims, activities, and achievements; and to discover the historical laws and moral imperatives by which it operates.[96] Since there can be no such thing as a 'universal moral law' or an 'ideally best constitution', this science is guided not by a priori reasoning but by experience.[97] None of this is controversial. What does make for controversy is that, unlike political jurists from Hobbes to Hegel, Treitschke does

[86] Ibid. i.3, 'The Relation of the State to the Moral Law' (at 29).

[87] Ibid. i.3.   [88] Ibid. 32.

[89] Treitschke, *Politik*, above n.84, 90–1: '*Das soll uns nicht hindern freudig auszusprechen, dass der genial Florentiner mit der ganzen ungeheuren Consequenz seines Denkens zuerst in der Mitte aller Politik den grossen Gedanken gestellt hat: der Staat ist Macht.*'

[90] Treitschke, above n. 85 (Gowans ed.), i.3 (at 32).

[91] Treitschke, above n.84 (Davis ed.), i.100 (at 167).

[92] Treitschke, Letter, 22 May 1865: cited in Davis (ed.), above n.84, 26: 'In this matter [Schleswig-Holstein] positive law is irreconcilable with the vital interests of our country. We must set aside positive law and compensate those who may be injured in consequence.... positive law when injurious to the common good must be swept away.'

[93] Treitschke, above n.85 (Gowans ed.), i.4 (at 40),

[94] Treitschke, above n.84 (Davis ed.), i.18–19 (at 128) [translation modified].

[95] Treitschke above n.84 (Davis ed.), ii. 403 (at 162).

[96] Treitschke, above n.84 (Davis ed.), i.3 (at 121).   [97] Davis, above n.84, 124.

not view the state as a work of artifice or a regulatory idea: he treats it as an elemental force, a 'superior type of natural necessity'.[98] His work invoked reason of state mostly in the context of Prussian-led German state-building in the 1860/70s. Nevertheless his approach persisted in German thought as the will to power of this elemental State[99] with disastrous consequences for twentieth century European history.

VI. The Constitutional Reason of State

When in 1924 Meinecke published *Die Idee der Staatsräson*, he believed he was writing the history of an idea from early-modern thought which, *pace* Treitschke, could not survive into the modern era. The state had become a regulatory idea rather than an elemental force. The combination of an extensive role for government alongside the emergence of an active civil society made the notion of the state as the highest good simply anachronistic. *Raison d'état* had lost its *raison d'etre*. The doctrine seemed to be of only historical interest—that is until Carl Friedrich raised an issue that Meinecke had apparently overlooked.

Meinecke had examined reason of state as a doctrine used to justify political conduct in contravention to conventional morality in order to further a 'higher morality'. That higher morality was the maintenance or augmentation of the authority of the state. But in 1957 Friedrich suggested that there was another dimension of reason of state to be considered. When the modern state is established and has expressed its authoritative decision-making arrangements through the adoption of a formal constitution, can it ever be justified for governments to act contrary to those constitutional rules? This is the question of what Friedrich calls 'constitutional reason of state', which he sees as 'reason of state in its application to the government of law'.[100]

The modern question is not, says Friedrich, whether political action is contrary to morality, but whether political action is contrary to constitutional law. Can government legitimately act in violation of constitutional norms to protect the values of that constitutional order? Early-modern reason of state thinking maintained that if maintenance of political order was essential for human freedom, measures contrary to moral norms were justified to ensure the survival of that order. The modern, constitutional version of reason of state maintains that 'unconstitutional' governmental action might be justified to protect the basic conditions of equality and freedom that modern constitutions establish. This is sometimes called protecting

---

[98] Meinecke, above n.22, 404.

[99] Treitschke's thought provides the framework that enabled jurists like Schmitt not only to establish friend-enemy as the basic criterion of the political but also to perpetuate reason of state logic in his claim that sovereign is 'he who decides on the exception': see Ch.7 above. Schmitt's reason of state logic is most comprehensively articulated in his *Dictatorship: From the Origins of the Modern Concept of Sovereignty to Proletarian Class Struggle* [1921], M Hoelzl and G Ward trans. (Cambridge: Polity Press, 2014). But it might be noted that after Schmitt joined the Nazi Party in 1933 and made a pitch to become its Crown Jurist, he published a paper seeking to justify the political assassinations in July 1934 ('the night of the long knives') executed to consolidate Hitler's absolute hold on power: C Schmitt, 'Der Führer schützt das Recht', 39 *Deutsche Juristen-Zeitung* 945–50 (1 August 1934). In these six columns, Schmitt presents the defence in terms that directly follow Naudé justifications for *coups d'état*.

[100] CJ Friedrich, *Constitutional Reason of State* (Providence, RI: Brown University Press 1957), vii.

'the national interest' through the exercise of 'prerogative power' or by declaring a 'state of siege' or 'state of emergency'. But Friedrich suggests that reason of state is a more direct expression of the issues at stake.

Constitutional scholars, Friedrich asserted, were conscious that emergencies could arise in which strict compliance with the law might not be conducive to protection of the interests of the state. Emergencies arise in many sorts of unforeseen circumstances, including natural disasters, epidemics, financial crises, terrorist incidents, and insurgent movements. For the protection of the public, government agencies may need to deploy a range of extraordinary powers. But is reason of state really the appropriate term for addressing this issue?

The problem with Friedrich's advocacy of 'constitutional reason of state' derives from his usage of the terms 'state' and 'constitution'. He seems not to appreciate that in the modern world the term 'interests of the state' is ambiguous: does it mean the interests of the State as connoted by the Germanic distinction between State (*Staatsgewalt*) and Society or does it refer more abstractly to the interests of 'we the people'? These interests might coincide but, as his own example of McCarthyism in the USA in the 1950s illustrates, it cannot be assumed.[101] Friedrich also fails to take on board significant changes in the nature and status of a constitution. His argument is considerably weakened because his analysis mainly relies on studies written before the establishment of modern constitutional regimes.[102]

Friedrich thus invokes John Locke to exemplify constitutional reason of state. This is because Locke justifies a broad executive prerogative power, 'a power to act according to discretion, for the public good, without the prescription of the Law, and sometimes even against it'.[103] But Locke's argument has limited relevance to the modern world of governing. He was still working within a worldview in which the government acquired its authority from above, an authority only partially qualified at this stage by institutionalization.[104] Further, by 'the Law' Locke meant the 'promulgated standing Laws' enacted by the legislature,[105] a type of positive law that remained subservient to classical natural law.[106] The difficulty with Friedrich's references to Locke arises because Locke was still drawing on medieval practices of constitutionalism whose authority was being eroded by modern change, and to

---

[101] D Caute, *The Great Fear: The Anti-Communist Purge Under Truman and Eisenhower* (New York: Simon & Schuster, 1978).

[102] Apart from the Introduction and Conclusion, Friedrich's five chapters examine respectively: Machiavelli; Harrington, Spinoza, and Montesquieu; Calvin and Althusius; Milton, Locke, and Kant; and Hegel. This practice is followed by scholars who claim a continuity in the operation of reason of state/power of exception through to contemporary times: see, e.g., C Fatovic, *Outside the Law: Emergency and Executive Power* (Baltimore: Johns Hopkins University Press, 2009) (chs on Machiavelli, Locke, Hume, Blackstone, and then the American founding debates); Poole, above n.3 (chs on Hobbes, Harrington, Hume, Smith/Burke, then discussion of Mill, Hayek, Schmitt, and Oakeshott).

[103] J Locke, *Two Treatises of Government* [1680], P Laslett ed. (Cambridge: Cambridge University Press, 1988), ii. § 160.

[104] There was a time when 'the Government was almost all Prerogative'. Ibid. ii. § 162.

[105] Ibid. ii. § 136.

[106] Locke (ibid. ii. § 134) argues that 'the first and fundamental *positive* Law of all Commonwealths, is the establishing of the Legislative Power' and 'the first and fundamental *natural* Law, which is to govern even the Legislature itself, is the preservation of Society, and (as far as will consist with the public good) of every person in it' (emphasis supplied).

which the doctrine of reason of state was actually a response. Given Locke's assumptions, therefore, his acceptance of a residual prerogative power to act *extra et contra legem* is not at all surprising.[107]

Modern modifications of the meaning of state and constitution further undermine the cogency of Friedrich's thesis. The meaning of the word 'state' has been transformed. It is no longer conceived merely as an expression of the centralized ruling power. It can be defined as 'the autonomous organization and activation of social cooperation within a territory' incorporating the constituent elements of territory, people and institutional arrangement,[108] but its juristic meaning does not inhere in any one of those constituent parts. Due to the principle of representation, the juristic idea of the state provides a comprehensive way of seeing, understanding, and acting in the world.[109] The meaning of the idea of the state is expressed through its constitutional form.[110] The issues of order and security that concerned Friedrich remain. Defence of the constitutional values of the state may require measures that appear to run counter to the values enumerated in its constitution. But if Friedrich's 'constitutional reason of state' suggests that today government is able to take justifiable action that is contrary to law then it is anachronistic because the processes by which such action is now taken are recognized by, and justified according to, the state's constitution. The modern issue does not concern 'constitutional reason of state' but 'the reason of the constitutional state'.

VII. Reason of the Constitutional State

Locke does in fact raise a new aspect of reason of state, but not one Friedrich recognized. Proposing a governmental framework based on a division between legislative and executive, he holds that ultimately there can be no institutional solution to tensions that might arise between these two powers.[111] The people must simply place their trust in the prudence of those holding governmental power. Locke then explains that if the constituted authorities act contrary to the public good, 'the Power devolve[s] into the hands of those that gave it, who may place it anew where they shall think best for their safety and security'.[112] He here asserts the *right* of the people to rebel and overthrow the established government to promote the public good. Locke advocates a right of rebellion justified by reason of state. This is a potent and rather unruly right. He tries to soften its force by assuming that the people will not rebel 'upon every little mismanagement in public affairs',[113] yet it is the assertion of this right that led to the great revolutionary movements of the late-eighteenth century. And it was the changes effected by these revolutions that brought about the new age of the constitutional state.

---

[107] See further Loughlin, FPL, Ch.13.
[108] H Heller, *Staatslehre* [1934] in his *Gesammelte Schriften* (Leiden: A.W. Sijthoff, 1971), vol.3, 79–395, at 310.
[109] See further, Loughlin, FPL, Ch.7   [110] See further, Loughlin, FPL, Ch.8.
[111] Locke, above n.103, ii.§ 168.   [112] Ibid. ii.§§ 149, 240.
[113] Ibid. ii.§ 225. See further Loughlin, IPL, Ch.6.

In 1787, the Americans established the world's first modern political constitution. Although the French experienced great difficulty in converting their revolutionary ideals into a stable constitutional form,[114] they had established the constitution as the locus of 'public utility' and ushered in what Guéry calls a 'political secularization' of the idea of the common good.[115] These Enlightenment-inspired revolutionary upheavals strengthened the idea that a political unity of the people precedes the establishment of its constitution and that 'the people' is 'the state'. They also signal the opening of a new era that consolidates the shift from a world of empires to one of nation-states.[116] The critical moment of rupture in which a new nation-state is established becomes the occasion for drafting a constitution which, written in the name of the people, has the potential to be the medium for the people's collective political identity.

The effects of modernizing forces on conceptions of the constitution of political authority are profound. The destruction of the old world, in which harmony and proportion were a function of hierarchy, becomes the pre-condition for innovation in the new world. Instead of shaping the social order, nature becomes a resource to be harnessed and exploited by new social forces. These forces displace the centrality of the political but, because they need to be regulated, they also generate new political responsibilities. In modernity, state and society no longer operate in distinct realms; the state is as extensive as society and is seen as the way in which society assumes a political form. The state becomes the expression of a way of thinking in which 'we the people' of a defined territory establish a set of governing institutions through which a collective political identity is acquired.

The process of modernization is simultaneously one of democratization, though, as Alexis de Tocqueville shows, democracy is as much a social as a political phenomenon.[117] Democracy has a profound impact not just on political but also on social relations; it effects a revolution in sensibility as much as in government. Consequently, democracy is not merely the name for a system of government by the people; it is 'an account of the complex nature of the immaterial power that conditioned' that system.[118] With the emergence of this new type of social power the early-modern doctrine of reason of state is overcome. Social power subverts the hierarchical image of the sovereign's ruling authority, replacing it with a diversity of expressive forms. Orientated towards the future, the value of distilling the art of governing from past experience is diminished. Social power replaces the cult of secrecy surrounding reason of state with the need for transparency. And it expresses an abstract reason which, taking its cue from advances in scientific knowledge, constructs a new version of the political.

The idea of the constitution is one of the most distinctive products of modernity. The social power unleashed in revolutionary breaks with the past needs to be chan-

---

[114] See Ch.5,V–VII above.   [115] See Guéry, above n.13, at 34.

[116] S Subrahmanyam and D Armitage (eds), *The Age of Revolutions in Global Context, c.1760–1840* (New York: Palgrave Macmillan 2010).

[117] A de Tocqueville, *Democracy in America*, H. Reeve trans., DJ Boorstin intro. (New York: Vintage Books, 1990), 2 vols.

[118] SS Wolin, *Tocqueville Between Two Worlds: The Making of a Political and Theoretical Life* (Princeton, NJ: Princeton University Press, 2001), 251.

nelled and organized. This is the key task of modern constitutions: there can be no successful revolution without constitution. Modern constitutions are simultaneously enabling and constraining. They empower citizens in relation to their governments and establish techniques by which governors control and discipline their subjects. Constitutions express high ideals, but in practice they commonly strengthen the authority of central government,[119] subjugate aboriginal populations,[120] and bolster the hegemony of the dominant power.[121] Constitutions transform 'the people' from a collective subject that establishes its own governing framework into an object to be managed and governed. They do this projecting a particular account of the political, inscribing a narrative which makes it 'normal'. The constitution enables and facilitates a particular worldview and by classifying and setting boundaries it 'normalizes' and constrains.[122] Reason of state is absorbed into constitutional reason.

This sketches a general trajectory, but the developments in particular regimes are obviously more complicated, ambiguous, and uncertain. For much of the modern era, constitutions have not been able to deliver on aspiration. Initially, they were vehicles of 'negative constitutionalism', constraining government, policing the public-private division, and normalizing the existing power distribution.[123] This is evident not only from practice in the early USA,[124] but also from the nineteenth-century export of this constitutional model to the newly-independent countries of Latin America. In these countries, lacking traditions of liberalism, republicanism, and limited government, constitutions, although *ex facie* liberal, were obliged to give the executive broad powers to suspend constitutional protections and establish regimes of exception for the purpose of upholding public order.[125]

---

[119] See, e.g., in the case of the US: MM Edling, *A revolution in favor of government: origins of the US Constitution and the making of the American state* (Oxford: Oxford University Press, 2003).

[120] See, e.g., in the case of colonial powers: J Tully, *Strange Multiplicity: Constitutionalism in an Age of Diversity* (Cambridge: Cambridge University Press, 1995); Tully, 'The Imperialism of Modern Constitutional Democracy' in M Loughlin and N Walker (eds), *The Paradox of Constitutionalism: Constituent Power and Constitutional Form* (Oxford: Oxford University Press, 2007), 315–38.

[121] See, e.g., in the case of the Napoleonic Europe: SJ Woolf, *Napoleon's Integration of Europe* (London: Routledge, 1991), esp. 124–32. See also RM Johnston (ed.), *The Corsican: A Diary of Napoleon's Life in His Own Words* (Boston: Houghton Mifflin Co, 1910), 182: '15 May 1804: It is not as a general that I rule, but because the nation believes I have the civilian qualifications for governing. My system is quite simple. It has seemed to me that under the circumstances the thing to do was to centralize power and increase the authority of the Government, so as to constitute the Nation. I am the constituent power.'

[122] P Wagner, *A Sociology of Modernity: Liberty and Discipline* (London: Routledge, 1994), 27.

[123] M Loughlin, 'The Constitutional Imagination' (2015) 78 *Modern Law Review* 1–25, esp. at 7–8, 17.

[124] See JB Thayer, 'The Origin and Scope of the American Doctrine of Constitutional Law' (1893) 7 *Harvard Law Rev* 129–56. But Locke provides a founding influence. He inveighs against the 'political slavery' that absolute monarchy entails, while performing a critical role in institutionalizing chattel slavery in the Carolinas. Locke, *Two Treatises*, i.Ch.1: 'Slavery is so vile and miserable an Estate of Man, and so directly opposite to the generous Temper of Courage of our Nation; that tis hardly to be conceived that an Englishman, much less a Gentleman, should plead for't.' Cf. J Locke, *Political Writings*, D Wootton ed. (London: Penguin, 1993), 230: 'Every freeman of Carolina shall have absolute power and authority over his Negro slaves'.

[125] Of the 103 Latin American constitutions established between 1811 and 1900, more than eighty also made provision for a constitutional role for the military: B Loveman, *The Constitution of Tyranny: Regimes of Exception in Spanish America* (Pittsburgh: University of Pittsburgh Press, 1993), 370, at 398–402. See further R Gargarella, *The Legal Foundations of Inequality: Constitutionalism in the Americas, 1776–1860* (Cambridge: Cambridge University Press, 2010).

In light of this history, social reformers and political radicals regarded the constitution as a barrier to, rather than as a means of, achieving their goals. They placed greater faith in reform through legislative action, evident in the extensive growth of governmental programmes to regulate social and economic life and to meet social welfare requirements. Despite instances of constitutional conflict,[126] these manifestations of social power eventually eroded the basis of negative constitutionalism. They loosened constraints on government by conferring broad discretionary powers which modified property distribution and blurred the public-private distinction. Negative constitutionalism was gradually displaced, though more speedily since the last decade of the twentieth century, by positive constitutionalism, in which the constitution is seen as a medium for the state's aspirations of achieving equal liberty in conditions of solidarity.[127]

These developments illustrate the way that reason of state thinking is now inscribed within, or condoned by, modern constitutions, whether in the conferral of constitutional power to declare a state of emergency[128] or by constitutional acceptance that administrative power is necessary to protect the economy and promote the public welfare.[129] But this type of argument underplays the way in which the doctrine has been thoroughly transformed by modern constitutional developments.

Reason of state authorizes action *extra et contra legem* in circumstances where the ruler deems it necessary for some higher end. This proposition has only to be stated to realize the degree of change effected in contemporary practice. Who for this purpose is the ruler? And does that ruler have unfettered power to determine necessity? It is invariably for the head of state to initiate action but this is not unilateral. A ruler cannot exercise unfettered prerogative power[130] since the conditions for triggering the suspension of norms are now commonly prescribed in the constitution, as are the procedures to be adopted before the declaration, and even then the decision is susceptible to judicial review.[131] The exercise of these powers continues to provoke

---

[126] See notoriously in the USA, *Lochner v New York* 198 US 45 (1905).

[127] Loughlin, 'Constitutional Imagination' above n.123, esp. at 8–9, 18–22. See further Ch.5 above.

[128] C Schmitt, *Political Theology: Four Chapters on the Concept of Sovereignty*, G Schwab trans. (Chicago: University of Chicago Press, 2005), 5: 'Sovereign is he who decides on the exception'.

[129] M Weber, *Economy and Society*, G Roth and C Wittich eds (Berkeley: University of California Press, 1978), 979: 'The rule and the rational pursuit of "objective" purposes, as well as devotion to these, would always constitute the norm of conduct. Precisely those views which most strongly glorify the "creative" discretion of the official accept, as the ultimate and highest lodestar for his behaviour in public administration, the specifically modern and strictly "objective" idea of raison d'état.' See further SS Wolin, 'Democracy and the Welfare State: The Political and Theoretical Connections between Staatsräson and Wohlfahrtsstaatsräson' (1987) 15 *Political Theory* 467–500, at 480: 'The welfare state, I want to suggest, is *Staatsräson*, or Reason of State, in the age of the economic polity'.

[130] See Loughlin, FPL, Ch.13 for an account of prerogative powers and how in the modern era they have been transformed and sublated.

[131] See, e.g., French Constitution, art. 16: 'When the institutions of the Republic, the independence of the nation, the integrity of its territory, or the fulfillment of its international commitments are under grave and immediate threat and when the proper functioning of the constitutional governmental authorities is interrupted, the President of the Republic shall take the measures demanded by these circumstances after official consultation with the Prime Minister, the presidents of the Assemblies, and the Constitutional Council.' After thirty days, the Constitutional Council can be asked to determine whether the conditions continue to exist. See also European Convention on Human Rights, art.15.

controversy,[132] but the point is that this is no longer a matter of conscience for the ruler; the decision is now institutionalized to an extent inconceivable in the seventeenth century.

The question today is whether emergency action authorized through these procedures is contrary to law. When Locke justified action taken 'without the prescription of the Law', he was appealing to natural law. The 'reason of the constitutional state', by contrast, makes a distinction between written rules and the principles of legality inscribed in the constitution, that is, between law and legality.[133] In the constitutional state, governments do not claim authority to act unlawfully, even when acting for what Friedrich calls 'constitutional reasons of state'. They either invoke formal constitutional procedures, such as the declaration of a state of emergency, or they exercise broad discretionary powers conferred on them by legislation. In either case, governments make no claim to possess the innate power to act by virtue of necessity, emergency, or higher good; they claim only to invoke an already existing lawfully-conferred power on those grounds. This is a fundamental change,[134] or it is once such executive declarations are subject to the institutional checks that are central elements of the constitutional state.[135] In the constitutional state, the exception has been normalized. In the state of reason, reason of state is converted into constitutional legality.

Constitutional legality is a relatively new phenomenon but during the fifty or so years of its existence its influence has been growing exponentially. This is of considerable significance for political jurisprudence. Constitutional legality (otherwise, superlegality) expresses a new type of power: de-personal, abstract, and ahistorical. It has emerged from a combination of legal and social conditions. First, the constitution acquires the status of 'higher law' and the judiciary is accepted as the authority on its meaning. Secondly, the constitution is accepted not only as the authoritative framework of government but also as the expression of society's political principles.[136]

Constitutional legality is depersonal. All public authority emanates from and is conditioned by the constitutional state; there is no sovereign beyond the constitution. The constitution is abstract because it is not merely a set of rules; it provides a set of general principles that express the basic values of political order. And it is ahistorical because the constitution is no longer seen as a text adopted at a moment

---

[132] See O Beaud and C Guérin-Bargues, *L'état d'urgence: Une étude constitutionelle, historique et critique* (Paris: LGDJ, 2016); C Rossiter, *Constitutional Dictatorship: Crisis Government in the Modern Democracies* (Princeton, NJ: Princeton University Press, 1948).

[133] Note also the refinement made in the Introduction, above pp.4–5, between law, legality, and superlegality.

[134] In his Conclusion, Friedrich notes that constitutional states use four main mechanisms to address the threat of subversion: to outlaw by legislation a party or organization seeking to undermine constitutional order; to achieve the same by judicial action; to place a ban on the employment of potential subversives from official positions; and to ban specific practices such as assemblies. Friedrich, above n.100, 115–18. But he does seem to register the fact that each of these are mechanisms are authorized by the constitution.

[135] This point has added force owing to the fact that there has been a remarkable expansion in the constitutional jurisdiction of courts since 1957, when Friedrich published his thesis.

[136] EW Böckenförde, 'The Concept and Problems of the Constitutional State' in his *Constitutional and Political Theory: Selected Writings*, M Künkler and T Stein eds (Oxford: Oxford University Press, 2017), Ch.5 (141–51).

in history but as an evolving value order explicated by a judiciary that gives meaning to its principles according to contemporary social conditions. [137]

To say that constitutional law is 'higher law' does not adequately express the point that it is a new type of law. The modern idea of law as a set of rules enacted by the legislature (that is, of the type Locke envisaged) is still an essential regulatory instrument that covers all aspects of social life, but it is overladen by a new type of law—constitutional legality—that expresses the ordering principles of the state. Ordinary law is a product of will (*voluntas*) but this type of superlegality is formed as a result of an elaboration of reason (*ratio*). Today, so many disputes in law, politics, and society are caused by competing understandings of the relative meaning and status of these different types of law. What emerges in the constitutional state is that there is no political issue on which the constitution is entirely silent, and the answers are provided by reference to the principles of superlegality. All governmental action is subject to the principle of objective justification. Tests devised across jurisdictions may differ but are all variants on a common theme: can the measures in question be justified as necessary and proportionate in the constitutional state?[138]

This may look like a progressive evolution, but for political jurists it is a development of considerable ambivalence. This was clearly revealed from the outset by the authors of the *Federalist Papers*, the essays drafted in 1787 to convince American citizens to embrace the federal constitution. Reflecting on the powers of the President in Article II of the US Constitution, Publius argues that these general powers must be given a generous interpretation. Since government is entrusted with the safety and well-being of the state and the factors that endanger this are infinite, he argues that 'no constitutional shackle can wisely be imposed on the power to which the care of it is committed'.[139] Failure to confer 'a degree of power commensurate to the end', he elaborates, 'would be to violate the most obvious rules of prudence and propriety, and improvidently to trust the great interests of the nation to hands which are disabled from managing them with vigour and success'.[140] Arguing from the principles that 'the means ought to be proportioned to the end'[141] and that 'no precise bounds could be set to the national exigencies',[142] he maintains that 'a power equal to every possible exigency must exist somewhere in the government' and that, if not otherwise specified, it rests with the President.[143]

Publius will not countenance a governmental power that acts contrary to law or to constitutional norms in response to emergency. Instead he interprets the constitution as conferring broad executive discretionary powers to act proportionately to perceived threats. The question of whether extraordinary executive powers are constitutional or extra-constitutional has provoked intense debate ever since,[144]

---

[137] H-G Gadamer, *Truth and Method* [1960], J Weinsheimer and DG Marshall trans. (London: Sheen & Ward, 2nd rev. edn. 1989), xxxii: 'people read the sources differently [over time] because they were moved by different questions, prejudices, and interests'.

[138] See A Barak, *Proportionality: Constitutional Rights and their Limitations* (Cambridge: Cambridge University Press, 2012).

[139] J Madison, A Hamilton, and J Jay, *The Federalist Papers* [1787], I Kramnick ed. (London: Penguin, 1987), no.23, at 185.

[140] Ibid. 186.   [141] Ibid. 185.   [142] Ibid. no.26.   [143] Ibid.

[144] See C Fatovic and BA Kleinerman (eds), *Extra-Legal Power and Legitimacy: Perspectives on the Prerogative* (Oxford: Oxford University Press, 2013), chs 5 (G Thomas, 'The Limits of Constitutional

but in the constitutional state there can be no doubt that these powers have been constitutionalized.[145] Reason of state has been institutionalized and the exception normalized.

The constitutional state is a regime of government according to law. But the emergence of the principle of constitutional legality makes this an uncertain precept. Government is unable to act in direct contravention to law, simply because the institutional safeguards of the constitutional state will not permit this.[146] But modern legislatures have in practice delegated broad statutory powers to executives not only to deal with emergencies but also to act in a general regulatory capacity.[147] Further, the principle of 'proportionate empowering' gives governments wide latitude under general constitutional authorizations to take the necessary executive action.[148] And both innovations are strengthened by an expansive legal interpretation of these powers by government lawyers.[149] Reason of state is institutionalized, normalized, and transformed into the reason of the constitutional state.[150]

Government: Alexander Hamilton on Extraordinary Power and Executive Discretion') and 6 (JD Bailey, 'The Jeffersonian Executive: More Energetic, More Responsible, Less Stable'); EW Böckenförde, 'The Repressed State of Emergency: The Exercise of State Authority in Extraordinary Circumstances' in Böckenförde, above n.136, Ch.4; O Gross and F Ní Aoláin, *Law in Times of Crisis: Emergency Powers in Theory and Practice* (Cambridge: Cambridge University Press, 2006); D Dyzenhaus, *The Constitution of Law: Legality in a Time of Emergency* (Cambridge: Cambridge University Press, 2006).

[145] President Lincoln's action during the American civil war (blockading ports, suspending habeas corpus, establishing military commissions, emancipating slaves, all without congressional or explicit constitutional authorization) is the strongest counter-illustration: on which see Rossiter, above n.132, Ch.15; MK Curtis, 'Lincoln and Executive Power during the Civil War: A Case Study' in Fatovic and Kleinerman (eds), above n.144, Ch.7; DA Farber, *Lincoln's Constitution* (Chicago: University of Chicago Press, 2003). But this action, in the extreme case of civil war, long predates the idea of the constitutional state. Consider, by contrast, the fact that after the 11 September 2001 attacks, President Bush immediately sought legislative powers to respond. Based on the Bush precedent, Jack Goldsmith makes the cogent argument that reason of state ('executive action in open defiance of law or legal authority') 'is no longer part of a president's justificatory toolkit' because the political and legal costs are too high. Any reason of state argument 'has been rendered practically non-operative by legal, political, and social change': J Goldsmith, 'The Irrelevance of Prerogative Power, and the Evils of Secret Legal Interpretation' in Fatovic and Kleinerman (eds), above n.144, Ch.10, at 214–15.

[146] See Goldsmith, ibid. at 217: 'They [White House lawyers] will not act in defiance of law even if the president orders them to do so. The Central Intelligence Agency (CIA) detention and interrogation program, for example, would never have gotten off the ground without the written imprimatur of OLC [Office of Legal Counsel] and the CIA General Counsel that the program was authorized by and compliant with relevant law.'

[147] On emergency powers see J Lobel, 'Emergency Power and the Decline of Liberalism' (1989) 98 *Yale LJ* 1385. For critique of the legal basis of discretionary administrative programmes see: P Hamburger, *Is Administrative Law Unlawful?* (Chicago: University of Chicago Press, 2014); EA Posner and A Vermeule, *The Executive Unbound: After the Madisonian Republic* (New York: Oxford University Press, 2010); A Vermeule, *Law's Abnegation: From Law's Empire to the Administrative State* (Cambridge, MA: Harvard University Press, 2016)

[148] Alexander Somek calls this 'the iron law of an ever more expansive executive branch': A Somek, *The Cosmopolitan Constitution* (Oxford: Oxford University Press, 2014), 216.

[149] Goldsmith, above n.145; id., *The Terror Presidency: Law and Judgment in the Bush Administration* (New York: WW Norton, 2009); id., *Power and Constraint: The Accountable Presidency after 9/11* (New York: WW Norton, 2012); J Steyn, 'Guantanamo Bay: The Legal Black Hole' (2004) 53 ICLQ 1–15.

[150] This is the main point of the rise of *potentia* analyzed in Loughlin, FPL, chs 14 and 15. There it is argued that 'although the origins of *potentia* can be traced to the exercise of the king's prerogatives, its significance in the modern era has been altered out of all recognition' (407). This shift is attributed to the disciplinary revolution that follows from the technological revolution, establishing the state, and the

VIII. Conclusion

The discourse of reason of state emerged as an attempt to specify the main character-istics of modern political reason. It was an expression not only of the autonomy but also the primacy of the political. The claim to primacy had ethical and legal aspects. The ethical aspect is its claim to action in pursuit of a higher end, asserting the pri-macy of what Max Weber termed the priority of a public ethics of responsibility (or consequences) over a private morality of conscience.[151] Reason of state also main-tained that, under certain conditions for the ruler to determine, political reason might justify action taken contrary to existing legal rules. The doctrine did not mark the triumph of might over right, but of political right over legal and moral right.

Expressed as an articulation of political right (*droit politique*), the transformation of reason of state in the modern era is clear. Locke's *Second Treatise of Government* presents two aspects of reason of state in the language of right: the right of the sovereign ruler to act contrary to the law in the cause of the higher good and the right of the sovereign people to overthrow the regime. But once this latter right is executed and the constitutional state established, both rights are extinguished or, more accurately, transcended. This is because within the constitutional state governmental authority is institutionalized. The rights of the sovereign ruler are now differentiated and insti-tutionalized. Any right to act contrary to written law is replaced with a requirement that government comply with general principles of constitutional legality. The sov-ereign people's right of rebellion is similarly institutionalized and replaced with the right to pursue a claim that government is acting unconstitutionally before the state's constitutional court. Reason of state is transcended when political right melds into a new type of political-legal right, that of constitutional legality.

This institutionalization of political reason leads in turn to the politicization of legal reason. Government according to law no longer means governing in accord-ance with the enacted rules; it means governing in accordance with certain abstract principles of legality whose explication is as much a consequence of political as legal reason. This is because these abstract principles acquire meaning only when infused with values. But there is no rational means of choosing among the competing values that claim to be the best iteration of the principle. 'Freedom, equality, justice, security, self-realization, solidarity, protection of life', explains Ernst-Wolfgang Böckenförde, 'today these are all placed side by side as "values" contained in the constitution, without any explanation of why they are "values", and how they—and the practical legal demands that are supposed to arise from them—relate to one another within a hierarchical system'.[152] Constitutional legality absorbs reason of state. With the extension of constitutional jurisdiction, the legal issues at stake are less about

---

bourgeois revolution, establishing modern constitutions, and whose main aim is to place the 'well-or-dered commonwealth' at the heart of public law.

[151] M Weber, 'The Profession and Vocation of Politics' in his *Political Writings*, P Lassman and R Spiers eds (Cambridge: Cambridge University Press, 1994), 309–69.

[152] E-W Böckenförde, 'The Historical Evolution and Changes in the Meaning of the Constitution' in Böckenförde, above n.136, 152–68, at 168.

whether the rules have been complied with and more about reconciliation between liberal principles of political right (liberty, equality) and the reason of state claims of necessity, security, secrecy, and means-end analysis. The meaning of constitutionalism changes: rather than connoting limitation on government, it is a power-generating discourse. With no fixed meaning, adherence to the constitution changes through time in accordance with social, economic, and political circumstances.[153]

The constitutional state may be more an idea than an actuality but there can be little doubt about the trajectory of change. It is said that Aristotle's Lyceum could specify 158 different types of political constitution but, as Sheldon Wolin notes, de Tocqueville 'was convinced that the political world, insofar as it was becoming modernized, was being reduced to one'.[154]

Over the last fifty years, the triumph of this single type—constitutional democracy—has been remarkable. It is evident not only in the adoption of new constitutions across the world,[155] but also in the increasing significance of constitutions in the regulation of political life. There has been a dramatic expansion in the constitutional role of courts, an erosion of the doctrinal restrictions on jurisdiction (ripeness, mootness, justiciability, etc.), a growing trade in jurisprudence between national constitutional courts, and the increased influence of international courts.[156] In the words of Israel's former Chief Justice, 'nothing [now] falls beyond the purview of judicial review; the world is filled with law; anything and everything is justiciable'.[157] Yet, constitutional legality is an ambivalent achievement. Its abstract character and de-historicized meaning creates a new type of political-legal reason which institutionalizes—that is, structures rather than entirely eliminates—reason of state thinking. A new era is opening, the significance of which is as yet undetermined.

---

[153] This is a further reason why Locke's right of rebellion is extinguished: see Tocqueville, above n.117, vol.2, Ch.21, 'Why great revolutions will become rare'.

[154] Wolin, above n.118, 97.

[155] See Z Elkins, T Ginsburg, and J Melton, *The Endurance of National Constitutions* (Cambridge: Cambridge University Press, 2009), Ch.2.

[156] R Hirschl, 'The Judicialization of Mega-Politics and the Rise of Political Courts' (2008) 11 *Annual Review of Political Science* 93–118; D Grimm, *Constitutionalism: Past, Present, and Future* (Oxford: Oxford University Press, 2016), esp. Ch.15: 'The Constitution in the Process of De-nationalization'.

[157] Aharon Barak, cited in Hirschl, ibid., at 95.

Bibliography

Abensour, M *Democracy Against the State: Marx and the Machiavellian Moment*, M Blechman and M Breaugh trans. (Cambridge: Polity, 2011).

Agamben, G *The Kingdom and the Glory: For a Theological Genealogy of Economy and Government*, L Chiesa trans. (Stanford: Stanford University Press 2011).

Allan, TRS *Law, Liberty, and Justice: The Legal Foundations of British Constitutionalism* (Oxford: Clarendon Press, 1993).

Allan, TRS 'Constitutional Dialogue and the Justification of Judicial Review' (2003) 23 OJLS 563–84.

Allan, TRS *The Sovereignty of Law* (Oxford: Oxford University Press, 2013).

Althusser, L *On the Reproduction of Capitalism: Ideology and Ideological State Apparatuses*, GM Goshgarian trans. (London: Verso, 2014).

Arendt, H *Eichmann in Jerusalem: A Report on the Banality of Evil* (New York: Penguin Books, rev. edn. 1965).

Arendt, H *On Revolution* (Harmondsworth: Penguin, 1973).

Armitage, D 'Edmund Burke and Reason of State' (2000) 61 *J. of the History of Ideas* 617–34.

Austin, J *The Province of Jurisprudence Determined*, WE Rumble ed. (Cambridge: Cambridge University Press, 1995).

Badiou, A *Metapolitics*, J Barker trans. (London: Verso, 2005).

Bagehot, W *The English Constitution* (Oxford: Oxford University Press, 2001).

Bailey, JD 'The Jeffersonian Executive: More Energetic, More Responsible, Less Stable' in C Fatovic and BA Kleinerman (eds), ch.6.

Balibar, É '"Rights of Man" and "Rights of the Citizen": The Modern Dialectic of Equality and Freedom' in his *Masses, Classes, Ideas: Studies in Politics and Philosophy before and after Marx* (London: Routledge, 1993), ch.2.

Balibar, É *Spinoza and Politics*, P Snowden trans. (London: Verso, 1998).

Balibar, É *Politics and the Other Scene* (London: Verso, 2002).

Balibar, É *Citizenship*, T Scott-Railton trans. (Cambridge: Polity, 2015).

Barak, A *Proportionality: Constitutional Rights and their Limitations* (Cambridge: Cambridge University Press, 2012).

Barker, E 'Blackstone on the British Constitution' in his *Essays on Government* (Oxford: Clarendon Press, 1945), 121–54.

Barthélemy, J *Le role du pouvoir exécutif dans les républiques modernes* (Paris: Giard & Brière, 1906).

Bates, DW 'Political Unity and the Spirit of the Laws: Juridical Concepts of the State in the Late Third Republic' (2005) 28 *French Historical Studies* 69–101.

Bates, DW *States of War: Enlightenment Origins of the Political* (New York: Columbia University Press, 2012).

Beaud, O 'Hauriou et le droit naturelle' (1989) 8 *Revue d'histoire des facultes de droit* 123–38.

Beaud, O *La Puissance de l'État* (Paris: Presses universitaires de France, 1994).

Beaud, O *Théorie de la Fédération* (Paris: Presses universitaires de France: 2007).

Beaud, O and C Guérin-Bargues, *L'état d'urgence: Une étude constitutionelle, historique et critique* (Paris: LGDJ, 2016).

Beer, SH *To Make a Nation: The Rediscovery of American Federalism* (Cambridge MA: Harvard University Press, 1993).

Beiser, FC *The German Historicist Tradition* (Oxford: Oxford University Press, 2011).

Berkowitz, DS 'Reason of State in England and the Petition of Right, 1603–1629' in Schnur (ed.), 165–212.

Bew, J *Realpolitik: A History* (Oxford: Oxford University Press, 2016).

Bireley, R *The Counter-Reformation Prince: Anti-Machiavellism or Catholic Statecraft in early modern Europe* (Chapel Hill, NC: University of North Carolina Press, 1990).

Blackstone, W *Commentaries on the Laws of England* (Oxford: Clarendon Press, 1765), 4 vols.

Blum, C *Rousseau and the Republic of Virtue: The Language of Politics in the French Revolution* (Ithaca: Cornell University Press, 1986).

Bobbio, N *Thomas Hobbes and the Natural Law Tradition*, D Gobetti trans. (Chicago: University of Chicago Press, 1993).

Böckenförde, EW *Constitutional and Political Theory: Selected Writings*, M Künkler and T Stein eds (Oxford: Oxford University Press, 2017).

Bodin, J *Method for the Easy Comprehension of History*, B Reynolds trans. (New York: Columbia University Press, 1945).

Bodin, J *The Six Bookes of a Commonweale*, R Knolles trans., KD McRae ed. (Cambridge, MA: Harvard University Press, 1962).

Bogdandy, A von 'Deutsche Rechtswissenschaft im europäische Rechtsraum' (2011) 66 *Juristen Zeitung* 1–6.

Bogdandy, A von et al (eds) *Handbuch des Öffentlichen Rechts in Europa: Ius Publicum Europaeum*, (Heidelberg: CF Müller Verlag, 6 vols, 2007–16).

Bogdandy A von and J Bast (eds) *Principles of European Constitutional Law* (Oxford: Hart/ Beck, 2nd edn. 2009).

Bolingbroke, Viscount *Political Writings*, D Armitage ed. (Cambridge: Cambridge University Press, 1998).

Bolsinger, E *The Autonomy of the Political: Carl Schmitt's and Lenin's Political Realism* (Westport, CT: Greenwood Press, 2001).

Botero, G *The Reason of State*, PJ and DP Waley trans. (London: Routlege & Kegan Paul, 1956).

Botwinick, A 'Same/Other versus Friend/Enemy: Levinas contra Schmitt' in J Meierhenrich and O Simons (eds), *The Oxford Handbook of Carl Schmitt* (Oxford: Oxford University Press, 2016), ch 12.

Bourdieu, P 'From the King's House to the Reason of State: A Model of the Genesis of the Bureaucratic Field' (2004) 11 *Constellations* 16–36.

Bradstock, A (ed.) *Winstanley and the Diggers, 1649–1999* (London: Frank Cass, 2000).

Brailsford, HN *The Levellers and the English Revolution*, C Hill ed. (London: The Cresset Press, 1961).

Bredin, J-D *Sieyès: Le clé de la revolution française* (Paris: Éditions de Fallois, 1988).

Brewer, J *The Sinews of Power: War, Money and the English State, 1688–1783* (New York: Knopf, 1989).

Burdeau, G *L'État* (Paris: Éditions du Seuil, 1970).

Burgess, G *Absolute Monarchy and the Stuart Constitution* (New Haven: Yale University Press, 1996).

Bourke, R *Empire and Revolution: The Political Life of Edmund Burke* (Princeton: Princeton University Press, 2015).

Burke, E *An Appeal from the New to the Old Whigs*, JM Robson ed. (Indianapolis: Bobbs-Merrill, 1962).

Burke, E *Reflections on the Revolution in France*, CC O'Brien ed. (London: Penguin, 1968).

Burke, E 'Speech to the Electors of Bristol, 1774' in Burke, *Speeches and Lectures on American Affairs* (London: Dent, 1908), 68–75.

Burke, E 'Thoughts on the Cause of the Present Discontents' in *The Writings and Speeches of Edmund Burke, vol. II: Party, Parliament and the American Crisis, 1776–1774*, P Langford ed. (Oxford: Clarendon Press, 1981), 241–323.

Burke, E 'Speech on American Taxation, 19 April 1774' in *The Writings and Speeches of Edmund Burke, vol. II: Party, Parliament and the American Crisis, 1776–1774*, P Langford ed. (Oxford: Oxford University Press, 1981), 406–501.

Burke, E 'Speech on Conciliation with America, 22 March 1775' in *The Writings and Speeches of Edmund Burke, vol. III: Party, Parliament, and the American War 1774–1780*, WM Elofson and JA Woods eds (Oxford: Clarendon Press, 1996), 106–69.

Burke, E 'Speech on Fox's India Bill, 1 December 1783' in *The Writings and Speeches of Edmund Burke, vol. V: India: Madras and Bengal 1774–1785*, PJ Marshall ed. (Oxford: Oxford University Press, 1981), 378–451.

Burke, E 'Speech on the Opening of Impeachment, 15–19 February, 1788' in *The Writings and Speeches of Edmund Burke, vol. VI: India*, PJ Marshall ed. (Oxford: Clarendon Press, 1991), 264–471.

Burke, E 'Heads for Consideration on the Present State of Affairs, November 1792' in *The Writings and Speeches of Edmund Burke, vol. VIII: The French Revolution 1790–1794*, LG Mitchell ed. (Oxford: Oxford University Press, 1998), 386–402.

Burke, E 'Letter to Richard Burke, post 19 February 1792' in *The Writings and Speeches of Edmund Burke, vol. IX: The Revolutionary War 1794–1797 and Ireland*, RB McDowell ed. (Oxford: Clarendon Press, 1991), 640–58.

Burke, E 'Third Letter on a Regicide Peace' in *Selected Works of Edmund Burke: vol.3, Letters on a Regicide Peace* (Indianapolis: Liberty Fund, 1999), 191–306.

Burke, P 'Tacitism, scepticism and reason of state' in JH Burns (ed.), 479–98.

Burns, JH (ed.) *The Cambridge History of Political Thought, 1450–1700* (Cambridge: Cambridge University Press, 1991).

Butterfield, H 'Raison d'État: The Relations between Morality and Government' (Martin Wight Memorial Lecture, University of Sussex, 23 April 1975).

Cairns, JW 'The Origins of the Edinburgh Law School: the Union of 1707 and the Regius Chair' (2007) 11 *Edinburgh Law Review* 300–48.

Cannadine, D 'The Context, Performance and Meaning of a Ritual: The British Monarchy and the "Invention of Tradition", c.1820–1977' in E Hobsbawm and T Ranger (eds), *The Invention of Tradition* (Cambridge: Cambridge University Press, 1983), 101–64.

Cannon, J *Parliamentary Reform, 1640–1832* (Cambridge: Cambridge University Press, 1973).

Carré de Malberg, R *Contribution à la théorie générale de l'Etat, spécialement d'après les données fournies par le droit constitutionnel français* (Paris: Sirey, 1920), 2 vols.

Carrithers, DW et al (eds) *Montesquieu's Science of Politics* (Lanham: Rowman & Littlefield, 2001).

Cassirer, E *The Philosophy of Enlightenment*, FCA Koelln and JP Pettegrove trans. (Princeton: Princeton University Press, 1951).

Cassirer, E *The Question of Jean-Jacques Rousseau*, P Gay trans. (New Haven: Yale University Press, 1963).

Castoriadis, C *Philosophy, Politics and Autonomy*, DA Curtis ed. (New York: Oxford University Press, 1991).

Caute, D *The Great Fear: The Anti-Communist Purge Under Truman and Eisenhower* (New York: Simon & Schuster, 1978).

Church, WF *Constitutional Thought in Sixteenth-Century France: A Study in the Evolution of Ideas* (Cambridge, MA: Harvard University Press, 1941).

Church, WF *Richelieu and Reason of State* (Princeton: Princeton University Press, 1972).

Church, WF 'The Decline of the French Jurists as Political Theorists, 1660–1789' (1967) 5 *French Historical Studies* 1–40.

Cicero, MT *De Respublica*, CW Keyes trans. (London: Heinnemann, 1928).

Clark, JCD 'A general theory of party, opposition and government, 1688–1832' (1980) 23 *Historical Journal* 295–325.

Clark, JCD *The Language of Liberty 1660–1832* (Cambridge: Cambridge University Press, 1994).

Coke, E Twelfth Reports, *Prohibitions del Roy* (1607) 12 Co.Rep. 63.

Colley, L *Britons: Forging the Nation, 1707–1837* (London: Pimlico, 1992).

Collins, JR *The Allegiance of Thomas Hobbes* (Oxford: Oxford University Press, 2005).

Comte, A *Cours de philosophie positive* (Paris: Ballière, 2nd edn. 1864).

Comte, A *Auguste Comte and Positivism: The Essential Writings*, G Lenzer ed. (New York: Harper, 1975).

Conniff, J 'Edmund Burke's Reflections on the Coming Revolution in Ireland' (1986) 47 *J. of the History of Ideas* 37–59.

Constant, B *Principles of Politics Applicable to all Governments* [1810], D O'Keeffe trans., E Hoffman ed. (Indianapolis: Liberty Fund, 2003).

Constant, B 'Principles of Politics applied to all Representative Governments' [1815] in his *Political Writings*, B. Fontana trans. (Cambridge: Cambridge University Press, 1988), 169–305.

Constant, B 'The Spirit of Conquest and Usurpation and their Relation to European Civilization' in his *Political Writings*, 43–167.

Constant, B 'The Freedom of the Ancients Compared with that of the Moderns' in his *Political Writings*, 307–28.

Constant, B *Fragments d'un ouvrage abandonné sur la possibilité d'une constitution républicaine dans un grand pays*, H Grange ed. (Paris: Aubier, 1991).

Cover, RM 'Foreword: *Nomos* and Narrative' (1983–4) 97 *Harvard Law Rev.* 4–68.

Cover, RM 'Violence and the Word' (1985–6) 95 *Yale Law J.* 1601–29.

Coyle, S 'Thomas Hobbes and the Intellectual Origins of Legal Positivism' (2003) 16 *Canadian J. of Law & Jurisprudence* 243–70.

Craig, P 'The Common Law, Shared Power and Judicial Review' (2004) 24 OJLS 237–57.

Craiutu, A *Liberalism under Siege: The Political Thought of the French Doctrinaires* (Lanham, Md: Rowman & Littlefield, 2003).

Creveld, M van *The Rise and Decline of the State* (Cambridge: Cambridge University Press, 1999).

Croce M and A Salvatore *The Legal Theory of Carl Schmitt* (Abingdon: Routledge, 2013).

Cromartie, A *The Constitutionalist Revolution: An Essay on the History of England, 1450–1642* (Cambridge: Cambridge University Press, 2006).

Curtis, MK 'In Pursuit of Liberty: The Levellers and the American Bill of Rights' (1991) 8 *Constitutional Commentary* 359–93.

Curtis, MK 'Lincoln and Executive Power During the Civil War: A Case Study' in Fatovic and Kleinerman (eds), ch.7.

Davis, JC 'The Levellers and Democracy' (1965) 40 *Past & Present* 174–80.

Delos, JT 'La théorie de l'institution: la solution réaliste du problème de la personnalité morale et le droit à fondement objectif' (1931) 1 *Archives de philosophie du droit et de sociologie juridique* 97–153.

Dicey, AV *Introduction to the Study of the Law of the Constitution* (London: Macmillan, 8th edn. 1915).

Dilthey, W *Introduction to the Human Sciences: An Attempt to Lay a Foundation for the Study of Society and History*, RJ Batanzos trans. (London: Harvester Wheatscheaf, 1988).

Doyle, W *The Oxford History of the French Revolution* (Oxford: Oxford University Press, 2nd edn. 2002).

Dreitzel, H 'Reason of state and the crisis of political Aristotelianism: an essay on the development of 17th century political philosophy' (2002) 28 *History of European Ideas* 163–87.

Dreitzel, H 'The reception of Hobbes in the political philosophy of the early German Enlightenment' (2003) 29 *History of European Ideas* 255–89.

Duguit, L 'The Law and the State' (1917) 31 *Harvard Law Review* 1–185.

Duguit, L *Law in the Modern State*, F and H Laski trans. (London: Allen & Unwin, 1921).

Durkheim, É *Montesquieu and Rousseau as Forerunners of Sociology*, R Mannheim trans. (Ann Arbor: Michigan University Press, 1960).

Durkheim, É *The Elementary Forms of Religious Life*, C Cosman trans. (Oxford: Oxford University Press, 2001).

Dworkin, R *Freedom's Law: The Moral Reading of the American Constitution* (Oxford: Oxford University Press, 1996).

Dworkin, R 'In Praise of Theory' in his *Justice in Robes* (Cambridge, MA: Belknap Press: 2006), ch.2.

Dyzenhaus, D 'Hobbes and the Legitimacy of Law' (2001) 20 *Law & Philosophy* 461–98.

Dyzenhaus, D *The Constitution of Law: Legality in a Time of Emergency* (Cambridge: Cambridge University Press, 2006).

Edelstein, D *The Terror of Natural Right: Republicanism, the Cult of Nature and the French Revolution* (Chicago: University of Chicago Press, 2009).

Edling, MM *A revolution in favor of government: origins of the US Constitution and the making of the American state* (Oxford: Oxford University Press, 2003).

Eisenman, C 'L'Esprit des lois et la séparation des pouvoirs' (1984–5) 2 *Cahiers de philosophie politique* 3–34.

Elkins, Z, T Ginsburg, and J Melton *The Endurance of National Constitutions* (Cambridge: Cambridge University Press, 2009).

Elliott, JH *Richelieu and Olivares* (Cambridge: Cambridge University Press, 1984).

Eleftheriades, P 'Law and Sovereignty' (2010) 29 *Law and Philosophy* 535–69.

Ertman, T *Birth of the Leviathan: Building States and Regimes in Medieval and Early Modern Europe* (Cambridge: Cambridge University Press, 1997).

Esmein, A *Eléments de droit constitutionnel français et comparé* (Paris: Sirey, 1921).

Farber, DA *Lincoln's Constitution* (Chicago: University of Chicago Press, 2003).

Fatovic, C *Outside the Law: Emergency and Executive Power* (Baltimore: Johns Hopkins University Press, 2009).

Fatovic, C and BA Kleinerman (eds) *Extra-Legal Power and Legitimacy: Perspectives on the Prerogative* (Oxford: Oxford University Press, 2013).

Ferrari, J *Histoire de la raison d'état* (Paris: Michel Lévy Frères, 1860).

Franklin, JH *Jean Bodin and the Rise of Absolutist Theory* (Cambridge: Cambridge University Press, 1973).

Friedrich, CJ *Constitutional Reason of State* (Providence, RI: Brown University Press 1957).

Feldman, D (ed.) *English Public Law* (Oxford: Oxford University Press, 2004).

Fernández-Santamaria, JA 'Reason of State and Statecraft in Spain (1595-1640)' (1980) 41 *J. of the History of Ideas* 355–79.

Finer, SE *The History of Government, vol. 3: Empires, Monarchies and the Modern State* (Oxford: Oxford University Press, 1997–9).

Foord, AS *His Majesty's Opposition, 1714–1830* (Oxford: Oxford University Press, 1964).

Forsyth, C (ed.) *Judicial Review and the Constitution* (Oxford: Hart, 2000).

Forsyth, M *Reason and Revolution: The Political Thought of the Abbé Sieyes* (Leicester: Leicester University Press, 1987).

Foucault, M *Power/Knowledge* (Brighton: Harvester, 1980).

Foucault, M 'Governmentality' in *Essential Works of Foucault 1954–1984, vol. 3. Power* (London: Penguin, 2000), 201–22.

Foucault, M *Society must be defended: Lectures at the Collège de France, 1975–76*, D Macey trans. (London: Penguin, 2003).

Frank, J *The Levellers: A History of the Writings of Three Seventeenth-Century Social Democrats: John Lilburne, Richard Overton, William Walwyn* (Cambridge, MA: Harvard University Press, 1955).

Fraenkel, E *The Dual State: A Contribution to the Theory of Dictatorship*, EA Shils trans. (New York: Oxford University Press, 1941).

Freund, J 'La situation exceptionelle comme justification de la raison d'État chez Gabriel Naudé' in Schnur (ed.), 141–64.

Fuller, LL *The Morality of Law* (New Haven: Yale University Press, 2nd edn. 1969).

Furet, F *Interpreting the French Revolution* (Cambridge: Cambridge University Press, 1981).

Furet, F *The French Revolution, 1770–1814*, A. Nevill trans. (Oxford: Blackwell, 1992).

Gadamer, HG *Truth and* Method, J Weinsheimer and DG Marshall trans. (London: Sheen & Ward, 2nd rev. edn. 1989).

Gargarella, R *The Legal Foundations of Inequality: Constitutionalism in the Americas, 1776–1860* (Cambridge: Cambridge University Press, 2010).

Gauchet, M *La Démocratie contre elle-même* (Paris: Gallimard, 2002).

Gauchet, M 'Liberalism's Lucid Illusion' in Rosenblatt (ed.), 23–46.

Gay, P *The Enlightenment: An Interpretation* (New York: Knopf, 1966).

Geertz, C *Negara: The Theatre State in Nineteenth-Century Bali* (Princeton: Princeton University Press, 1980).

Gentles, I 'The *Agreements of the people* and the political contexts, 1647–1649' in Mendle (ed.), 148–74.

Gerber, CF von *Grundzüge eines Systems des deutschen Staatsrechts* (Leipzig: Tauchnitz, 1865).

Gibb, MA *John Lilburne, The Leveller: A Christian Democrat* (London: Lindsay Drummond Ltd, 1947).

Glover, SD 'The Putney Debates: Popular versus Elitist Republicanism' (1999) 164 *Past & Present* 47–80.

Goldsmith, J *The Terror Presidency: Law and Judgment in the Bush Administration* (New York: WW Norton, 2009).

Goldsmith, J *Power and Constraint: The Accountable Presidency after 9/11* (New York: WW Norton, 2012).

Goldsmith, J 'The Irrelevance of Prerogative Power, and the Evils of Secret Legal Interpretation' in Fatovic and Kleinerman (eds), ch.10.

Goldsmith, MM 'Hobbes on Law' in T Sorell (ed.), *The Cambridge Companion to Hobbes* (Cambridge: Cambridge University Press, 1996), ch.12.

Gorski, PS *The Disciplinary Revolution: Calvinism and the Rise of the State in Early Modern Europe* (Chicago: University of Chicago Press 2003).

Gough, JW *Fundamental Law in English Constitutional History* (Oxford: Clarendon Press, 1955).

Gray, CB *The Methodology of Maurice Hauriou* (Amsterdam: Rodopi, 2010).

Gregg, P *Free-Born John: The Biography of John Lilburne* (London: Phoenix Press, 2000).

Greenleaf, WH 'Burke and State Necessity: The Case of Warren Hastings' in R Schnur (ed.), 549–67.

Griffith, JAG 'The Political Constitution' (1979) 42 MLR 1–21.

Gross O and F Ní Aoláin *Law in Times of Crisis: Emergency Powers in Theory and Practice* (Cambridge: Cambridge University Press, 2006).

Grimm, D *Constitutionalism: Past, Present, and Future* (Oxford: Oxford University Press, 2016).

Guéry, A 'The State: The Tool of the Common Good' in P Nora (ed.), *Rethinking France: Les Lieux de Mémoire, Vol. 1*, M Trouille trans. (Chicago: University of Chicago Press, 2001), 1–52.

Gusy, C 'Considérations sur le "droit politique"' (2009) 1 *Jus Politicum*.

Haakonssen, K *Natural Law and Moral Philosophy: From Grotius to the Scottish Enlightenment* (Cambridge: Cambridge University Press, 1996).

Habermas, J *Between Facts and Norms: Contributions to a Discourse Theory of Law and Democracy*, W Rehg trans. (Cambridge: Polity Press, 1996).

Halifax, Marquess of 'The Character of a Trimmer' in his *Complete Works*, JP Kenyon ed. (Harmondsworth: Penguin, 1969), 49–102.

Haller, W (ed.) *Tracts on Liberty in the Puritan Revolution* (New York: Columbia University Press, 1934).

Haller, W and G Davies *The Leveller Tracts, 1647–1653* (New York: Columbia University Press, 1944).

Hamburger, P *Is Administrative Law Unlawful?* (Chicago: University of Chicago Press, 2014).

Hampshire, S *Innocence and Experience* (Cambridge, MA: Harvard University Press, 1989).

Hampson, N *Will and Circumstance: Montesquieu, Rousseau and the French Revolution* (London: Duckworth, 1983).

Hampton, J *Hobbes and the Social Contract Tradition* (Cambridge: Cambridge University Press, 1986).

Harrington, J *The Commonwealth of Oceana*, JGA Pocock ed. (Cambridge: Cambridge University Press, 1992).

Hart, HLA *The Concept of Law*, L Green, J Raz, and PA Bulloch eds (Oxford: Oxford University Press, 3rd edn. 2012).

Hauriou, M *Précis de droit administratif* (Paris: Larose et Forcel, 1892).

Hauriou, M *La science sociale traditionelle* (Paris: Larose, 1896).

Hauriou, M *Précis de droit administratif et de droit public* (Paris: Larose et Tenin, 6th edn. 1907).

Hauriou, M *Principes de droit publique* (Paris: Larose et Tenin, 1910).

Hauriou, M 'Les idées de M. Duguit' (1911) 7 *Recueil de legislation de Toulouse* 1–40.

Hauriou, M 'Le fondement de l'autorité publique' (1916) 33 *Revue de droit publique* 20–25.

Hauriou, M *Précis de droit constitutionnel* (Paris: Sirey, 1923).

Hauriou, M 'The Theory of the Institution and the Foundation: A Study in Social Vitalism' in A. Broderick (ed.), *The French Institutionalists: Maurice Hauriou, Georges Renard, Joseph T. Delos* (Cambridge, MA: Harvard University Press, 1970), 93–124.

Hauriou, M 'The Two Realisms' in Broderick (ed.), *The French Institutionalists: Maurice Hauriou, Georges Renard, Joseph T. Delos* (Cambridge, MA: Harvard University Press, 1970), 45–51.

Hawthorn, G *Enlightenment and Despair: A History of Social Theory* (Cambridge: Cambridge University Press, 2nd edn. 1987).

Hayek, FA *Law, Legislation and Liberty: Vol.1 Rules and Orders* (London: Routledge & Kegan Paul, 1973).

Hazareesingh, S *How the French Think: An Affectionate Portrait of an Intellectual People* (London: Allen Lane, 2015).

Hegel, GWF *Lectures on the History of Philosophy* (London: Bell, 1894).

Hegel, GWF *Philosophy of Right*, TM Knox trans. (Oxford: Clarendon Press, 1952).

Heller, H *Staatslehre* in his *Gesammelte Schriften* (Leiden: A.W. Sijthoff, 1971), vol.3, 79–395.

Herzog, D 'Puzzling through Burke' (1991) 19 *Political Theory* 336–63.

Hexter, JH *The Vision of Politics on the Eve of the Reformation: More, Machiavelli, and Seyssel* (London: Allen Lane, 1973).

Hill, C 'The Norman Yoke' in his *Puritanism and Revolution* (London: Secker & Warburg, 1958), 50–122.

Hill, C *Intellectual Origins of the English Revolution* (Oxford: Clarendon Press, 1965).

Hill, C *The World Turned Upside Down: Radical Ideas during the English Revolution* (London: Temple Smith, 1972).

Hill, C *Milton and the English Revolution* (London: Faber, 1977).

Hintze, O *Staat und Verfassung: Gesammelte Abhandlungen zur Allgemeinen Verfassungsgeschichte*, G Oestreich ed. (Göttingen: Vandenhoeck & Ruprecht, 3rd edn. 1970).

Hintze, O *The Historical Essays of Otto Hintze*, F Gilbert ed. (New York: Oxford University Press, 1975).

Hirschl, R 'The Judicialization of Mega-Politics and the Rise of Political Courts' (2008) 11 *Annual Review of Political Science* 93–118.

Hobbes, T *The English Works of Thomas Hobbes of Malmesbury*, W Molesworth ed. (London: J. Bohn, 1839).

Hobbes, T *A Dialogue between a Philosopher and a Student of the Common Laws of England*, J Cropsey ed. (Chicago: University of Chicago Press, 1971).

Hobbes, T *Behemoth or the Long Parliament*, S Holmes ed. (Chicago: University of Chicago Press, 1990).

Hobbes, T *The Elements of Law Natural and Politic (Human Nature and De Corpore Politico)*, JCA Gaskin intro. (Oxford: Oxford University Press, 1994).

Hobbes, T *Leviathan*, R Tuck ed. (Cambridge: Cambridge University Press, 1996).

Hobbes, T *On the Citizen*, R Tuck and M Silverthorne eds (Cambridge: Cambridge University Press, 1998).

Holmes, Jr, OW *The Common Law* (London: Macmillan, 1887).

Holmes, S *Benjamin Constant and the Making of Modern Liberalism* (New Haven: Yale University Press, 1984).

Holmes, S *Passions & Constraint: On the Theory of Liberal Democracy* (Chicago: University of Chicago Press, 1995).

Holmes, S 'The Liberty to Denounce: Ancient and Modern' in Rosenblatt (ed.), 47–69.

Honneth, A *The Pathologies of Individual Freedom: Hegel's Social Theory* (Princeton: Princeton University Press, 2010).

Höpfl, H 'Orthodoxy and Reason of State' (2002) 23 *History of Political Thought* 211–37.

Höpfl, H 'History and Exemplarity in the Work of Lipsius' in E De Bom et al (eds), *(Un)masking the Realities of Power: Justus Lipsius and the Dynamics of Political Writing in Early Modern Europe* (Leiden: Brill, 2011), 43–72.

Hume, D 'That politics may be reduced to a science' in his *Political Essays*, K Haakonssen ed. (Cambridge: Cambridge University Press, 1994), 4–15.

Hunter, I *Rival Enlightenments: Civil and Metaphysical Philosophy in Early Modern Germany* (Cambridge: Cambridge University Press 2001).

Hutchins, RM 'The Theory of the State: Edmund Burke' (1943) 5 *Review of Politics* 139–55.

James, W *Pragmatism and Other Essays* (New York: Washington Square Press, 1963).

Jellinek, G *The Declaration of the Rights of Man and of the Citizen: A Contribution to Modern Constitutional History*, M Farrand trans. (New York: Holt, 1901).

Jellinek, G *Allgemeine Staatslehre* (Berlin: Springer, 3rd edn. 1921).

Jennings, J *Revolution and Republic: A History of Political Thought in France since the Eighteenth Century* (Oxford: Oxford University Press, 2011).

Jennings, WI 'The Institutional Theory' in WI Jennings (ed.), *Modern Theories of Law* (London: Oxford University Press, 1933), 68–85.

John of Salisbury *Policraticus*, C Nederman ed. (Cambridge: Cambridge University Press, 1990).

Johnston, RM (ed.) *The Corsican: A Diary of Napoleon's Life in His Own Words* (Boston: Houghton Mifflin Co, 1910).

Jones, HS *The French State in Question: Public law and political argument in the Third Republic* (Cambridge: Cambridge University Press, 1993).

Judson, MA 'Henry Parker and the Theory of Parliamentary Sovereignty' in *Essays in History and Political Theory in Honor of Charles Howard McIlwain* (Cambridge, MA: Harvard University Press, 1936), ch.5.

Judson, MA *The Crisis of the Constitution: An Essay in Constitutional and Political Thought, 1603–1645* (New York: Octagon Books, 1971).

Kahn, P *Political Theology: Four New Chapters on the Concept of Sovereignty* (New York: Columbia University Press, 2011).

Kant, I 'An Answer to the Question: "What is Enlightenment?"' in his *Political Writings*, HB Nisbet trans., H Reiss ed. (Cambridge: Cambridge University Press, 2nd edn. 1991), 54–60.

Kantorowicz, H 'Savigny and the Historical School of Law' (1937) 53 *Law Quarterly Rev.* 326–43.

Kavka, GS *Hobbesian Moral and Political Theory* (Princeton: Princeton University Press, 1986).

Kelley, DR *Foundations of Modern Historical Scholarship: Language, Law, and History in the French Renaissance* (New York: Columbia University Press, 1970).

Kelsen, H *Introduction to the Problems of Legal Theory*, BL Paulson and SL Paulson trans. of first edn. [1934] of *Reine Rechtslehre* (Oxford: Clarendon Press, 1992).

Kempshall, MS *The Common Good in Late Medieval Political Thought* (Oxford: Oxford University Press, 1999).

Kersten, J *Georg Jellinek und die klassische Staatslehre* (Tübingen: Mohr Siebeck 2000).

Kilcup, RW 'Burke's Historicism' (1977) 49 *J. of Modern History* 394–410.

Kingdon, RN 'Calvinism and Resistance Theory, 1550-1580' in Burns (ed.), 193–218.

Kidder, J 'Acknowledgement of Equals: Hobbes's Ninth Law of Nature' (1983) 33 *Philosophical Quarterly* 133–46.

Kishlansky, M 'The Army and the Levellers: The Roads to Putney' (1979) 22 *Hist. J.* 795–824.

Kishlansky, M 'What Happened at Ware?' (1982) 25 *Hist. J.* 827–39.

Kishlansky, M *A Monarchy Transformed: Britain 1603–1714* (London: Penguin, 1996).

Kloppenberg, JT *Uncertain Victory: Social Democracy and Progressivism in European and American Thought, 1870–1920* (New York: Oxford University Press, 1986).

Koselleck, R *Critique and Crisis: Enlightenment and the Pathogenesis of Modern Society* (Cambridge, MA: MIT Press, 1988).

Koselleck, R *Futures Past: On the Semantics of Historical Time*, K Tribe trans. (New York: Columbia University Press, 2004).

Kumm, M 'The Cosmopolitan Turn in Constitutionalism: On the Relationship between Constitutionalism in and beyond the State' in JL Dunoff and JP Trachtman (eds), *Ruling the World? Constitutionalism, International Law and Global Governance* (Cambridge: Cambridge University Press, 2009), 258–324.

Laband, P *Das Staatsrecht des deutschen Reiches* (Tübingen: Laupp, 4 vols, 1876–2).

Lacoue-Labarthe, P and J-L Nancy *Retreating the Political*, S Sparks ed. (London: Routledge, 1997).

Lake, P *Anglicans and Puritans? Presbyterianism and English Conformist Thought from Whitgift to Hooker* (London: Unwin Hyman, 1988).

Lamont, WM 'The Puritan Revolution: A Historiographical Essay' in JGA Pocock (ed.), *The Varieties of British Political Thought, 1500–1800* (Cambridge: Cambridge University Press, 1993), 119–45.

Larrère, C *Actualité de Montesquieu* (Paris: Presses de Sciences Po, 1999).

Laski, HJ *Studies in the Problem of Sovereignty* (New Haven: Yale University Press, 1917).

Laski, HJ *Authority in the Modern State* (New Haven: Yale University Press, 1919).

Laski, HJ *The Foundations of Sovereignty and other essays* (New York: Harcourt Brace, 1921).

Laski, HJ *The State in Theory and Practice* (London: George Allen and Unwin, 1935).

Laski, HJ *Law and Justice in Soviet Russia* (London: Hogarth Press, 1935).

Lassalle, F 'Über Verfassungswesen' in his *Gesamtwerke*, E Blum ed. (Leipzig: Pfau, 1901), vol.1, 40–69.

La Torre, M *Law as Institution* (Dordrecht: Springer, 2010).

Lazzeri, C 'Le gouvernement de la raison d'État' in C Lazzeri and Reynié (eds), *Le pouvoir de la raison d'état* (Paris: Presses universitaires de France, 1992), 91–134.

Lefort, C *L'invention démocratique: Les limits de la domination totalitaire* (Paris: Fayard, 1981).

Lefort, C *The Political Forms of Modern Society* (Boston, MA: MIT Press, 1986).

Lefort, C *Democracy and Political Theory*, D Macey trans. (Cambridge: Polity Press, 1988).

Lenzer, G (ed.) *Auguste Comte and Positivism: The Essential Writings* (New York: Harper, 1975).

Lestition, S 'The Teaching and Practice of Jurisprudence in Eighteenth Century East Prussia: Konigsberg's First Chancellor, RF von Sahme (1682–1753)' (1989) 16 *Ius Commune* 27–80.

Levy, LW *Origins of the Fifth Amendment: The Right Against Self-Incrimination* (New York: Oxford University Press, 1968).

Lipsius, J *Politica: Six Books of Politics or Political Instruction*, J Waszink trans. and ed. (Assen: Royal Van Gorcum, 2004).

Lloyd, SA *Morality in the Philosophy of Thomas Hobbes: Cases in the Law of Nature* (Cambridge: Cambridge University Press, 2009).

Lobel, J 'Emergency Power and the Decline of Liberalism' (1989) 98 *Yale LJ* 1385.

Locke, J *Two Treatises of Government*, P Laslett ed. (Cambridge: Cambridge University Press, 1988).

Locke, J *Political Writings*, D Wootton ed. (London: Penguin, 1993).

Loughlin, M *Public Law and Political Theory* (Oxford: Clarendon Press, 1992).

Loughlin, M *The Idea of Public Law* (Oxford: Oxford University Press, 2003) [IPL].

Loughlin, M 'Constituent Power Subverted: From English Constitutional Argument to British Constitutional Practice' in Loughlin and Walker (eds), 2007, 27–48.

Loughlin, M 'Constitutional Theory: A 25th Anniversary Essay' (2005) 25 *Oxford J. of Legal Studies* 183–202.

Loughlin, M *Foundations of Public Law* (Oxford: Oxford University Press, 2010) [FPL].

Loughlin, M 'The Concept of Constituent Power' (2014) 13 *European J. of Political Theory* 218–37.

Loughlin, M 'Constitutional Pluralism: An Oxymoron?' (2014) 3 *Global Constitutionalism* 9–30.

Loughlin, M 'Nomos' in D Dyzenhaus and T Poole (eds), *Law, Liberty and State: Oakeshott, Hayek and Schmitt on the Rule of Law* (Cambridge: Cambridge University Press, 2015), ch.4.

Loughlin, M 'The Constitutional Imagination' (2015) 78 *Modern Law Review* 1–25.

Loughlin, M 'Political Jurisprudence' (2016) 16 *Jus Politicum: Revue de droit politique* 15–32.

Loughlin, M 'The Silences of Constitutions' (2018) 16 *International J. of Constitutional Law* forthcoming.

Loughlin M and N Walker (eds) *The Paradox of Constitutionalism: Constituent Power and Constitutional Form* (Oxford: Oxford University Press, 2007).

Loveman, B *The Constitution of Tyranny: Regimes of Exception in Spanish America* (Pittsburgh: University of Pittsburgh Press, 1993).

Löwith, K 'The Occasional Decisionism of Carl Schmitt' in his *Martin Heidegger and European Nihilism*, R Wolin ed. (New York: Columbia University Press, 1995), 137–59.

Luca, S de 'Benjamin Constant and the Terror' in H Rosenblatt (ed.), 92–114.

Lucas, P 'On Edmund Burke's Doctrine of Prescription'; Or, an Appeal from the New to the Old Lawyers' (1968) 11 *Historical J.* 35–63.

MacCormick, DN *Questioning Sovereignty: Law, State and Nation in the European Commonwealth* (Oxford: Oxford University Press, 1999).

MacCormick, DN *Institutions of Law: An Essay in Legal Theory* (Oxford: Oxford University Press, 2007).

Macintyre, A *After Virtue. A Study in Moral Theory* (London: Duckworth, 2nd edn. 1985).

Machiavelli, N *The Discourses*, LJ Walker trans., B Crick ed. (Harmondsworth: Penguin, 1983).

Macpherson, CB *The Political Theory of Possessive Individualism: Hobbes to Locke* (Oxford: Oxford University Press, 1962).

Macpherson, CB *Democratic Theory: Essays in Retrieval* (Oxford: Oxford University Press, 1973), ch.12.

Madison, J, A Hamilton, and J Jay *The Federalist Papers*, I Kramnick ed. (London: Penguin, 1987).

Maine, HS *Ancient Law: Its Connection with the Early History of Society and its Relation to Modern Ideas* (London: Murray, 10th edn.1919).

Maistre, J de 'Considerations on France' in J Lively (ed.), *The Works of Joseph de Maistre* (London: Allen & Unwin, 1965), 47–91.

Malcolm, N *Aspects of Hobbes* (Oxford: Oxford University Press, 2002).

Malcolm, N *Reason of State, Propaganda, and the Thirty Years' War: An Unknown Translation by Thomas Hobbes* (Oxford: Oxford University Press, 2007).

Mann, M *The Sources of Social Power*, 3 vols (Cambridge: Cambridge University Press, 1986, 1993, 2012).

Meek, RL *Social Science and the Ignoble Savage* (Cambridge: Cambridge University Press, 1976).

Meinecke, F *Machiavellism: The Doctrine of Raison d'État and Its Place in Modern History*, D Scott trans. (New Haven: Yale University Press, 1957).

Mendle, M (ed.) *The Putney Debates of 1647: The Army, the Levellers and the English State* (Cambridge: Cambridge University Press, 2001).

Michoud, L *La théorie de la personnalité morale et son application au droit français* (Paris: Librairie Générale de Droit et de Jurisprudence, 1906).

Miliband, R *Parliamentary Socialism: A Study in the Politics of Labour* (London: Merlin Press, 2nd edn. 1972).

Minogue, KR 'Remarks in the Relation between Social Contract and Reason of State in Machiavelli and Hobbes' in Schnur (ed), 267–74.

Mirkine-Guetzévitch, B 'Le gouvernement parlementaire sous la Convention' in J Barthélemy and B Mirkine-Guetzévitch (eds), *Le droit public de la Révolution* Cahiers de la Révolution 6 (Paris: Sirey, 1937), 45–91.

Montesquieu, CL *The Spirit of the Laws*, A Cohler, B Miller, and H Stone trans. and eds (Cambridge: Cambridge University Press, 1989).

Morgan, ES *Inventing the People: The Rise of Popular Sovereignty in England and America* (New York: Norton, 1989).

Morgenthau, HJ *The Concept of the Political*, M. Vidal trans. (New York: Palgrave Macmillan, 2012).

Morley, J *Edmund Burke: A Historical Study* (London: Macmillan, 1879).

Mortati, C *La Costituzione in Senso Materiale* (Milan: Guiffrè, 1940).

Mosse, GL 'Puritanism and Reason of State in Old and New England' (1952) 9 *William & Mary Quarterly* 67–80.

Mosse, GL *The Holy Pretence: A Study in Christianity and Reason of State from William Perkins to John Winthrop* (Oxford: Blackwell, 1957).

Müller, J 'Carl Schmitt's Method: Between Ideology, Demonology and Myth' (1999) 4 *J. of Political Ideologies* 61–85.

Murphy, L 'Was Hobbes a Legal Positivist?' (1995) 105 *Ethics* 846–73.

Naudé, G *Considérations politiques sur les coups d'État* (Paris: Éditions de Paris, 1988); Eng trans. G Naudé, *Political considerations upon refin'd politicks, and the master-strokes of state, As practis'd by the Ancients and Moderns*, W King trans. (London, 1711).

Oakeshott, M 'On the Character of a Modern European State' in his *On Human Conduct* (Oxford: Clarendon Press, 1975), 185–326.

Oakeshott, M 'Introduction to Leviathan' in Oakeshott, *Hobbes on Civil Association* (Indianapolis: Liberty Fund, 2000), 1–79.

Oestreich, G *Neostoicism and the early modern state*, D McLintock trans. (Cambridge: Cambridge University Press, 1982).

Osiander, A *Before the State: Systemic Political Change in the West from the Greeks to the French Revolution* (Oxford: Oxford University Press, 2007).

Paine, T *Rights of Man, Common Sense and other Political Writings*, M Philp ed. (Oxford: Oxford University Press, 1995).

Pascal, B *Pensées and other writings*, H Levi trans. (Oxford: Oxford University Press, 1995).

Passerin d'Entrèves, A *The Notion of the State: An Introduction to Political Theory* (Oxford: Clarendon Press, 1967).

Peacey, JT 'John Lilburne and the Long Parliament' (2000) 43 *Hist.J.* 625–45.

Pettit, P *Made with Words: Hobbes on Language, Mind, and Politics* (Princeton: Princeton University Press, 2008).

Pocock, JGA *The Ancient Constitution and the Feudal Law* (Cambridge: Cambridge University Press, rev. edn 1987).

Pocock, J GA *Barbarism and Religion: Vol.2 Narratives of Government* (Cambridge: Cambridge University Press, 1999).

Poole, T *Reason of State: Law, Prerogative and Empire* (Cambridge: Cambridge University Press, 2015).

Posner, EA and A Vermeule *The Executive Unbound: After the Madisonian Republic* (New York: Oxford University Press, 2010).

Post, G 'Ratio Publicae Utilitatis, Ratio Status and "Reason of State", 1100-1300' in his *Studies in Medieval Legal Thought: Public Law and the State, 1100–1322* (Princeton, NJ: Princeton University Press, 1964), ch.5.

Post, R 'Theories of Constitutional Interpretation' (1990) 30 *Representations* 13–41.

Prest, W *Albion Ascendant: English History, 1660–1815* (Oxford: Oxford University Press, 1998).

Pufendorf, S *On the Duty of Man and Citizen According to Natural Law*, M Silverthorne trans., J Tully ed. (Cambridge: Cambridge University Press, 1991).

Quaritsch, H 'Staatsraison in Bodins *République*' in Schnur (ed.), 43–63.

Raab, F *The English Face of Machiavelli: A Changing Interpretation, 1500–1700* (London: Routledge & Kegan Paul, 1964).

Raeff, M *The Well-Ordered Police State: Social and Institutional Change through Law in the Germanies and Russia, 1600–1800* (New Haven: Yale University Press, 1983).

Rancière, J *Aux bords du politique* (Paris: La Fabrique, 1998).

Rancière, J *Disagreement: Politics and Philosophy*, J Rose trans. (Minneapolis: University of Minnesota Press, 1999).

Rancière, J 'Who is the Subject of the Rights of Man?' in his *Dissensus: On Politics and Aesthetics*, S Corcoran trans. (London: Continuum, 2010) 62–75.

Rauh, Jr, JL 'The Privilege against Self-Incrimination from John Lilburne to Ollie North' (1988) 5 *Constitutional Commentary* 405–10.

Reill, PH *The German Enlightenment and Rise of Historicism* (Berkeley: University of California Press, 1975).

Renard, G *La théorie de l'institution: essai de l'ontologie juridique* (Paris: Sirey, 1930).

Rice, JV *Galbriel Naudé, 1603–1653* (Baltimore, Md: Johns Hopkins Press, 1939).

Richelieu, AJ *The Political Testament of Cardinal Richelieu*, HB Hill trans. and ed. (Madison: University of Wisconsin Press, 2005).

Roberts, C *The Growth of Responsible Government in Stuart England* (Cambridge: Cambridge University Press, 1966).

Rochau, AL von *Grundzüge der Realpolitik* (Stuttgart: Karl Göpel, 1853).

Rohan, H, duc de *De l'Interest des Princes et Estats de la Chrestienté* (Paris, 1639).

Romano, S *Principi di diritto amministrativo italiano* (Milan: Società editrice libraria, 1901).

Romano, S *L'ordinamento giuridico* (Pisa: Mariotti, 1918); Eng. trans. *The Legal Order*, M Croce trans. (London: Routledge 2017).

Romano, S 'Lo stato moderno e la sua crisi'(1910) *Rivisita di diritto pubblico* 87; French trans. 'L'État moderne et sa crise' (2014)14 *Jus Politicum* 1–15.

Rosa, H *Social Acceleration: A New Theory of Modernity*, J Trejo-Mathys trans. (New York: Columbia University Press, 2013).

Rosanvallon, P *Le Peuple introuvable: Histoire de la représentation démocratique en France* (Paris: Gallimard 1998).

Rosanvallon, P *Pour une histoire conceptuelle du politique* (Paris: Éditions du Seuil, 2003).

Rosanvallon, P *Le Modèle politique français: La Société civile contre le jacobinisme de 1789 à nos jours* (Paris: Éditions du Seuil, 2004).

Rosanvallon, P *Counter-Democracy: Politics in an Age of Distrust*, A Goldhammer trans. (Cambridge: Cambridge University Press, 2008).

Rosanvallon, P *Democratic Legitimacy: Impartiality, Reflexivity, Proximity*, A Goldhammer trans. (Princeton: Princeton University Press, 2011).

Rosanvallon, P *The Society of Equals*, A Goldhammer trans. (Cambridge, MA: Harvard University Press, 2013).

Rosenblatt, H 'Why Constant? A Critical Overview of the Constant Revival' (2004) 1 *Modern Intellectual History* 439–53.

Rosenblatt, H (ed.) *The Cambridge Companion to Constant* (Cambridge: Cambridge University Press, 2009).

Rousseau, J-J *The Discourses and other early political writing*, V Gourevitch ed. (Cambridge: Cambridge University Press, 1997).

Rousseau, J-J *The Social Contract and other later political writings*, V Gourevitch ed. (Cambridge: Cambridge University Press, 1997).

Rousseau, J-J *Emile, or Education*, B Foxley trans. (Indianapolis: Liberty Fund, 2010).

Rubiés, J-P 'Reason of State and Constitutional Thought in the Crown of Aragon, 1580-1640' (1995) 38 *Hist. J.* 1–28.

Russell, C *The Causes of the English Civil War* (Oxford: Clarendon Press, 1990).

Sabine, GH *A History of Political Theory* (London: Harrap, 3rd edn. 1963).

Saint-Just, L-A de *Oeuvres complètes*, A Kupiec ed. (Paris: Gallimard, 2004).

Salmon, JHM 'Rohan and Interest of State' in R Schnur (ed.), 121–40.

Saunders, D and I Hunter 'Bringing the State to England: Andrew Tooke's translation of Samuel Pufendorf's *De officio hominis et civis* (2003) 24 *History of Political Thought* 218–34.

Savigny, FC von *Vorlesungen über juristische Methodologie, 1802–1842*, A Mazzacone ed. (Frankfurt: Klostermann, 2004).

Savigny, FC von *System des heutigen römischen Rechts* (Berlin: Veit, 8 vols 1840–1849).

Schapiro, FR and M Pearse 'The Most-Cited Law Review Articles of All Time' (2012) 110 *Michigan Law Rev.* 1483–520.

Scheuerman, WE *Liberal Democracy and the Social Acceleration of Time* (Baltimore: Johns Hopkins University Press, 2004).

Schmitt, C *Hugo Preuss: Sein Staatsbegriff und seine Stellung in der deutschen Staatslehre* (Tübingen: Mohr, 1930); Eng. trans.: 'Hugo Preuss: His Concept of the State and his Position in German State Theory' (2017) 38 *History of Political Thought* 345–70.

Schmitt, C *Der Hüter der Verfassung* (Tübingen: Mohr, 1931).

Schmitt, C 'Der Führer schützt das Recht', 39 *Deutsche Juristen-Zeitung* 945–50 (1 August 1934).

Schmitt, C *Ex Captivitate Salus: Erfahrungen der Zeit 1945–47* (Cologne: Greven, 1950).

Schmitt, C *Verfassungsrechtliche Aufsätze aus den Jahren 1924–1954* (Berlin: Duncker & Humblot, 1958).

Schmitt, C 'The Legal World Revolution' [1987] 72 *Telos* 72–89.

Schmitt, C *Positionen und Begriffe im Kampf mit Weimar-Genf-Versailles, 1923–1939* (Berlin: Duncker & Humblot 1988).

Schmitt, C *Glossarium: Aufzeichnungen der Jahre 1947–1951* (Berlin: Duncker & Humblot, 1991).

Schmitt, C *Roman Catholicism and Political Form*, GL Ulmen trans. (Westport, CT: Greenwood, 1996).

Schmitt, C *State, Movement, People: The Triadic Structure of Political Unity*, S Draghici trans. (Corvallis, Oregon: Plutarch Press, 2001).

Schmitt, C *Legality and Legitimacy*, J Seitzer trans. (Durham, NC: Duke University Press, 2004).

Schmitt, C *On the Three Types of Juristic Thought*, JW Bendersky trans. (Westport, CT: Praeger, 2004).

Schmitt, C *Political Theology: Four Chapters on the Concept of Sovereignty*, G Schwab trans. (Chicago: University of Chicago Press, 2005).

Schmitt, C *The* Nomos *of the Earth in the International Law of the* Jus Publicum Europaeum, GL Ulmen trans. (New York: Telos Press, 2006).

Schmitt, C *The Concept of the Political*, G Schwab trans. (Chicago: University of Chicago Press, 2007).

Schmitt, C *The Leviathan in the State Theory of Thomas Hobbes: Meaning and Failure of a Political Symbol*, G Schwab trans. (Chicago: University of Chicago Press 2008).

Schmitt, C *Constitutional Theory*, J Seitzer trans. (Durham, NC: Duke University Press 2008).

Schmitt, C *Dictatorship: From the Origins of the Modern Concept of Sovereignty to Proletarian Class Struggle*, M Hoelzl and G Ward trans. (Cambridge: Polity Press, 2014).

Schnur, R (ed.) *Staatsräson: Studien zur Geschichte eines politischen Begriff* (Berlin: Duncker & Humblot, 1975).

Scott, J *England's Troubles: Seventeenth- century English political instability in a European context* (Cambridge: Cambridge University Press, 2000).

Scott, J *Commonwealth Principles: Republican Writing of the English Revolution* (Cambridge: Cambridge University Press, 2004).

Scott, JW *Parité: Sexual Equality and the Crisis of French Universalism* (Chicago: University of Chicago Press, 2005).

Seaborg, RB 'The Norman Conquest and the Common Law: The Levellers and the Argument from Continuity' (1981) 24 *The Historical J.* 791–806.

Searle, JR 'What is an Institution?' (2005) 1 *J. of Institutional Economics* 1–22.

Senellart, M *Machiavélisme et raison d'état, XIIe–XVIIIe siècle* (Paris: Presses universitaires de France, 1989).

Sewell, Jr, WH *A Rhetoric of Bourgeois Revolution: The Abbé Sieyes and What is the Third Estate?* (Durham: Duke University Press, 1994).

Sfez, G *Les doctrines de la raison d'état* (Paris: Armand Colin 2000).

Sharp, A (ed.) *The English Levellers* (Cambridge: Cambridge University Press, 1998).

Sieyès, E-J 'What is the Third Estate?' in his *Political Writings*, M Sonenscher trans. (Indianapolis: Hackett, 2003), 92–162.

Skinner, Q *The Foundations of Modern Political Thought* (Cambridge: Cambridge University Press, 1978), 2 vols.

Skinner, Q 'The State' in T Ball, J Farr, and RL Hanson (eds), *Political Innovation and Conceptual Change* (Cambridge: Cambridge University Press, 1989), 90–131.

Skinner, Q *Reason and Rhetoric in the Philosophy of Hobbes* (Cambridge: Cambridge University Press, 1996).

Skinner, Q 'Retrospect: Studying Rhetoric and Conceptual Change' in his *Visions of Politics. Vol.1: Regarding Method* (Cambridge: Cambridge University Press, 2002), 175–87.

Skinner, Q 'Hobbes's changing conception of civil science' in his *Visions of Politics: vol.3 Hobbes and Civil Science* (Cambridge: Cambridge University Press, 2002), 66–86.

Smith, A *Lectures on Jurisprudence*, RL Meek, DD Raphael, and PG Stein eds (Oxford: Oxford University Press, 1978).

Somek, A *The Cosmopolitan Constitution* (Oxford: Oxford University Press, 2014).

Sommerville, JP *Royalists and Patriots Politics and Ideology in England, 1603–1640* (London: Longman, 2nd edn. 1999).

Sonenscher, M *Before the Deluge: Public Debt, Inequality, and the Intellectual Origins of the French Revolution* (Princeton: Princeton University Press, 2007).

Sonenscher, M *Sans-Culottes: An Eighteenth-Century Emblem in the French Revolution* (Princeton: Princeton University Press, 2008).

Sorell, T 'Hobbes's persuasive civil science' (1990) 40 *Philosophical Quarterly* 342–51.

Spinoza, B de *Tractatus Theologico-Politicus*, RHM Elwes trans. (London: Routledge, 1951).

Sreedhar, S *Hobbes on Resistance: Defying the Leviathan* (Cambridge: Cambridge University Press, 2010).

Stedman Jones, G *Languages of Class: Studies in English Working Class History 1832–1982* (Cambridge: Cambridge University Press, 1983).

Steyn, J 'Guantanamo Bay: The Legal Black Hole' (2004) 53 ICLQ 1–15.

Stone, J *Social Dimensions of Law and Justice* (London: Stevens, 1966).

Stolleis, M *Staat und Staatsräson in der frühen Neuzeit* (Frankfurt aM: Suhrkamp, 1990).

Stolleis, M *Public Law in Germany, 1800–1914* (New York: Berghahn Books, 2001).

Stolleis, M *A History of Public Law in Germany, 1914–1945* (Oxford: Oxford University Press, 2004).

Stone, L *The Causes of the English Revolution, 1529–1642* (London: Routledge & Kegan Paul, 1972).

Strauss, L *Natural Right and History* (Chicago: University of Chicago Press 1953).

Strauss, L 'Notes on *The Concept of the Political*' in Schmitt, *The Concept of the Political* 2007, 97–122.

Subrahmanyam, S and D Armitage (eds) *The Age of Revolutions in Global Context, c.1760–1840* (New York: Palgrave Macmillan 2010).

Tacitus, C *The Annals of Imperial Rome*, M Grant trans. (London: Penguin, 1996).

Taylor, BJ 'Reflections on the Revolution in England: Edmund Burke's Uses of 1688' (2014) 35 *History of Political Thought* 91–120.

Thayer, JB 'The Origin and Scope of the American Doctrine of Constitutional Law' (1893) 7 *Harvard Law Rev.* 129–56.

Thomas, G 'The Limits of Constitutional Government: Alexander Hamilton on Extraordinary Power and Executive Discretion' in C Fatovic and BA Kleinerman (eds), ch 5.

Thomas, K 'The Levellers and the Franchise' in GE Aylmer (ed.), *The Interregnum: The Quest for Settlement, 1646–1660* (London: Macmillan, 1972), 57–78.

Thompson, EP *Whigs and Hunters: The Origins of the Black Act* (Harmondsworth: Penguin, 1977).

Tocqueville, A de *The Ancien Régime*, J Bonner trans. (London: Dent, 1988).

Tocqueville, A de *Democracy in America*, H Reeve trans., D J Boorstin intro. (New York: Vintage Books, 1990), 2 vols.

Todorov, T *A Passion for Democracy: Benjamin Constant* (London: Algora, 1999).

Tracy, JD (ed.) *The Rise of Merchant Empires: Long-Distance Trade in the Early Modern World 1350–1750* (Cambridge; Cambridge University Press, 1993).

Treitschke, H von *Politik: Vorlesungen gehalten an der Universität zu Berlin*, M Cornicelius ed. (Leipzig: Hirzel, 1899); sections reproduced in HWC Davies, *The Political Thought of Heinrich von Treitschke* (London: Constable, 1914); and *Selections from Treitschke's Lectures on Politics*, AL Gowans trans. and ed. (London: Gowans & Gray, 1914).

Tribe, K 'Cameralism and the sciences of the state' in M Goldie and R Wokler (eds), *The Cambridge History of Eighteenth-Century Political Thought* (Cambridge: Cambridge University Press, 2006), 525–46.

Troper, M *La Séparation des pouvoirs et l'histoire constitutionelle français* (Paris: Librairie générale de droit et jurisprudence, 1980).

Tuck, R *Natural Rights Theories: Their Origin and Development* (Cambridge: Cambridge University Press, 1979).

Tuck, R 'The "Modern" School of Natural Law' in A Pagden (ed.), *The Languages of Political Theory in Early-Modern Europe* (Cambridge: Cambridge University Press, 1987), 99–122.

Tuck, R *Philosophy and Government, 1572–1651* (Cambridge: Cambridge University Press, 1993).

Tully, J *Strange Multiplicity: Constitutionalism in an Age of Diversity* (Cambridge: Cambridge University Press, 1995).

Tully, J 'The Imperialism of Modern Constitutional Democracy' in M Loughlin and N Walker (eds), 315–38.

Ullmann, W *Principles of Government and Politics in the Middle Ages* (London: Methuen, 1961).

Underdown, D *Pride's Purge: Politics in the Puritan Revolution* (Oxford: Clarendon Press, 1971).

Vagts, A 'Intelligentsia versus Reason of State' (1969) 84 *Political Science Quarterly* 80–105.

Vasoli, C 'Machiavel inventeur de la raison d'Etat?' in Zarka (ed.), ch 2.

Veall, D *The Popular Movement for Law Reform, 1640–1660* (Oxford: Clarendon Press, 1970).

Vermeule, A *Law's Abnegation: From Law's Empire to the Administrative State* (Cambridge, MA: Harvard University Press, 2016).

Vile, MJC *Constitutionalism and the Separation of Powers* (Oxford: Clarendon Press, 1967).

Vinx, L (ed.) *The Guardian of the Constitution: Hans Kelsen and Carl Schmitt on the Limits of Constitutional Law* (Cambridge: Cambridge University Press, 2015).

Viroli, M *From politics to reason of state: the acquisition and transformation of a language of politics, 1250–1650* (Cambridge: Cambridge University Press, 1993).

Wagner, P *A Sociology of Modernity: Liberty and Discipline* (London: Routledge, 1994).

Walwyn, W *The Writings of William Walwyn*, JR McMichael and B Taft eds (Athens: University of Georgia Press, 1989).

Walzer, M *The Revolution of the Saints: A Study of the Origins of Radical Politics* (London: Weidenfeld & Nicolson, 1966).

Walzer, M (ed.) *Regicide and Revolution: Speeches at the trial of Louis XVI* (Cambridge: Cambridge University Press, 1974).

Warrender, H *The Political Philosophy of Hobbes* (Oxford: Oxford University Press, 1957).

Watkins, JWN *Hobbes's System of Ideas* (London: Hutchinson, 1973).

Weber, M *Economy and Society*, G Roth and C Wittich eds (Berkeley: University of California Press, 1978).

Weber, M *Political Writings*, P Lassman and R Spiers eds (Cambridge: Cambridge University Press, 1994).

Weinacht, PL 'Fünf Thesen zum Begriff der Staatsräson. Die Entdeckung der Staatsräson für die deutsche politische Theorie (1604)' in R Schnur (ed.), 65–71

Weinberger, O *Law, Institution and Legal Politics: Fundamental Problems of Legal Theory and Social Philosophy* (Dordrecht: Kluwer, 1991).

Weinberger, O and N MacCormick *An Institutional Theory of Law: New Approaches to Legal Positivism* (Dordrecht: Reidel, 1986).

Williams, D *Condorcet and Modernity* (Cambridge: Cambridge University Press, 2007).

Wokler, R 'The Enlightenment Science of Politics' in C Fox, R Porter, and R Wokler (eds), *Inventing Human Science: Eighteenth Century Domains* (Berkeley: University of California Press, 1995), 323–45.

Wolfe, DM (ed.) *Leveller Manifestoes of the Puritan Revolution* (New York: Humanities Press, 1967).

Wolfram, HW 'John Lilburne: Democracy's Pillar of Fire' (1952) 3 *Syracuse Law Rev.* 213–58.

Wolin, SS 'Democracy and the Welfare State: The Political and Theoretical Connections between Staatsräson and Wohlfahrtsstaatsräson' (1987) 15 *Political Theory* 467–500.

Wolin, SS *Tocqueville Between Two Worlds: The Making of a Political and Theoretical Life* (Princeton, NJ: Princeton University Press, 2001).

Wolin, SS *Politics and Vision: Continuity and Innovation in Western Political Thought* (Princeton: Princeton University Press, exp. edn. 2008).

Woolf, H 'Droit Public – English Style' 1995 PL 57–72.

Woolf, SJ *Napoleon's Integration of Europe* (London: Routledge, 1991).

Wootton, D 'Leveller Democracy and the Puritan Revolution' in JH Burns (ed.), *The Cambridge History of Political Thought, 1450–1700* (Cambridge: Cambridge University Press, 1991), 412–42.

Wootton, D 'The Levellers' in J Dunn (ed.), *Democracy: The Unfinished Journey, 508BC to AD 1993* (Oxford: Oxford University Press, 1993), 71–89.

Woolrych, A *Britain in Revolution, 1625–1660* (Oxford: Oxford University Press, 2002).

Worden, B 'The Levellers in history and memory, c.1660–1960' in Mendle (ed.), 256–82.

Wormuth, FD *The Origins of Modern Constitutionalism* (New York: Harper, 1949).

WB Yeats, 'The Second Coming' in P Larkin (ed.), *The Oxford Book of Twentieth-Century English Verse* (Oxford: Oxford University Press, 1972), 79.

Zagorin, P *Hobbes and the Law of Nature* (Princeton: Princeton University Press, 2009).

Zarka, YC 'Raison d'État, maxims d'État et coups d'État chez Gabriel Naudé' in Zarka (ed.), ch.6.

Zarka, YC (ed.) *Raison et Déraison d'État: Théoriciens et théories de la raison d'État aux XVI et XVII siècles* (Paris: Presses Universitaires de France, 1994).

Index